Developing the Gull-Winged F4U Corsair
– And Taking It To Sea

Developing the Gull-Winged F4U Corsair
– And Taking It To Sea

Ralph Harvey

Published in the United States of America

Developing the Gull-Winged F4U Corsair – And Taking It To Sea
by Ralph Harvey

Copyright © 2012 by Ralph Harvey

All rights reserved. No part of this book may be reproduced in any manner without written permission from the author, except for brief excerpts used in critical reviews and articles.

ISBN-10: 1469991225
ISBN-13: 9781469991221

Subject headings:
Aircraft history / military history / technology.

Published in the United States of America

Table of Contents

Dedication .... *vii*
A Note To Readers .... *ix*
Acknowledgements .... *xi*
Prologue *1*
Chapter One *15*
Uncharted Territory – A 400 m.p.h. Fighter

Chapter Two *37*
Ugly Duckling or Revolutionary Design?

Chapter Three *55*
At the Factory – Winning Through Mass Production

Chapter Four *97*
The F4U Corsair Goes To War

Chapter Five *119*
Fleet Air Arm Methods – Taming the Ill- Mannered Beast

Chapter Six *137*
F4U Corsairs of the U.S. Navy and Marine Corps

Chapter Seven...*179*
Corsairs of the Fleet Air Arm and the
Royal New Zealand Air Force

Chapter Eight..*201*
Moving To Texas, Then Deploying To Korea

Epilogue *221*

Glossary *233*

Appendix *257*

Selected Bibliography *269*

Notes on Image Sources and Credits *271*

Dedication

This book is dedicated to all those who contributed to the Vought F4U Corsair and its legacy. This includes all those who were involved in the design, development, production, testing, technical support and all related activities. Those who served in the U.S. Navy Bureau of Aeronautics, and those employed by what was then called United Aircraft Corporation, its divisions, and those subcontractors who went above and beyond to bring this aircraft to fruition, are included. In particular, all those who served in the armed forces of the U.S. Navy, U.S. Marine Corps, Royal Navy Fleet Air Arm and the Royal New Zealand Air Force, and especially those pilots and test pilots who repeatedly went in harms way, have the utmost respect and gratitude of this author. Their efforts and sacrifices will never be forgotten.

A Note To Readers

The story of the Vought F4U Corsair is an important part of aviation history, and it is a pleasure to share this perspective with you. Born at the end of the biplane era, the F4U was a radical design, an aerial hot-rod that pushed the performance envelope of naval fighters past 400 m.p.h. airspeeds and operational ceilings to well over thirty-thousand feet. The Corsair played a critically important role in the Pacific theater after the Battle of Midway, but along with many great successes it had significant shortcomings as a shipboard fighter. How those deficiencies were overcome are as important to the history of the F4U as its 11:1 kill ratio in aerial combat.

Unlike other books about World War Two fighter aircraft, this is not a first-person narrative of wartime experience. Rather, it is a look back at the development of this fine aircraft, and how it eventually became one of the leading American naval fighters of World War Two. This includes information about the period in which the Corsair was developed; how it compared to other important fighters; how America was able to produce these fighters in large numbers, plus some often overlooked information about the contributions of the Fleet Air Arm of Britain's Royal Navy. And that's important, because it was the Royal Navy's Fleet Air Arm, and not the U.S. Navy, that first used the Corsair as a shipboard fighter during the war.

As the reader, your interests and historical perspectives are important. In fact, this book is very much about you. Since many of you will not have had any personal experience with the F4U Corsair or its development, the author attempts to take you back in time to an era where military aviation, and world events, were very different. Thanks to advances in book publishing, the Internet and the ability to download books onto your laptop or reader, you and other readers around the world can easily partake of this amazing story. So wherever you are, and whatever your age or life experience, I hope you enjoy it.

Ralph Harvey
Stratford, CT. USA
January 2012

Acknowledgements

Only the educated are free.

– Epictetus

Many individuals and organizations were helpful in the author's effort to research, organize and interpret data, and otherwise prepare this book for publication. Since this book is the culmination of decades of discussions with individuals who had some connection with the F4U Corsair, it is impossible to name everyone who contributed useful information. This general thank you, while not adequate, will at least recognize the importance of these countless but unnamed contributors.

Trying to ferret out new additional information about the development of the F4U Corsair was challenging but rewarding. The radical nature of the airplane design and demands of wartime production required major changes in the factory complex in Stratford, Connecticut. Much of this author's recent research utilized conventional methods, such as examining old documents, and discovering what records even exist. In addition, this author had some unanswered questions about how the necessary techniques to use this warplane aboard aircraft carriers were developed. So let me make some introductions.

Dan Libertino, president of the Igor I. Sikorsky Memorial Archives, Inc. was of tremendous help in assisting me in searching for historical records and images. He and his cadre of archivists and volunteers were extremely supportive of all of my requests, and made this lengthy project much easier. In addition, Dan – a Sikorsky Aircraft veteran and retiree – provided some important details for establishing a timeline of the Chance Vought and Vought-Sikorsky history. He also was extremely helpful in locating important documents, such as Charles A. Lindbergh's archived letters to Vought-Sikorsky and United Aircraft Corporation (now United Technologies). These archives are a treasure trove of important documents and photographs, and the volunteers who maintain the records perform a critical link to our industrial past. This book would not have been possible without their help.

Andrew "Drew" King, Executive Director of the Connecticut Air and Space Center, also in Stratford, Connecticut, was also extremely helpful and generous with his time. Along with his cadre of CASC volunteers, Drew was able to locate many historic images of the plant during the major expansion of 1939-44. In addition, Drew spent considerable time explaining some of the often overlooked details of the plant design and construction, reviewing historic photos and explaining the plant building by building. He did this while providing me with many insights into the finer points of restoring a Corsair, which is one of the projects that his group is undertaking. Drew also read and critiqued the manuscript, catching some errors that would have otherwise gone unnoticed. My thank you here is not sufficient.

Sue French, daughter of Chance Vought test pilot John R. French, was gracious and helpful in providing access to her father's pilot logbooks, which provided a wealth of information about the life of an F4U production test pilot during World War Two. Sue also knew, or knew about, other Vought test pilots, especially Connie Grasso, Charlie Sharp and Bill Horan. In fact, her records provided a good deal of information about how Vought managed to hire very good pilots during the very hectic war years, when qualified civilian pilots were hard to find. Sue's considerable efforts were a big help to this author.

Richard "Dick" Steele of the Stratford Historical Society and the Connecticut Air and Space Center was also very helpful. Dick is a retired Marine Corps officer and pilot; he flew the F4U at MCAS Cherry Point and NAS Jacksonville until the U.S. Navy "repossessed" the F4Us for shipboard duty. He went on to fly combat missions in Helldivers at Ulithi Atoll in the Pacific, and then flew jet fighters during the 1950s. Dick's input as a Marine Corps F4U pilot in World War Two was extremely useful. So thanks Dick for your help, and your many years of Marine Corps service. Thanks also to the other members of the Stratford Historical Society, who have contributed much in the effort to preserve the local history of the F4U Corsair.

Acknowledgements

George "Doc" Gunther, retired state senator from Stratford, was instrumental in creating and supporting the Connecticut Air and Space Center. His decades long interest in Connecticut history, especially in his native Stratford, helped preserve countless records of the F4U and the old Chance Vought factory complex that might otherwise have been lost. And State Senator George Gunther was the leader who helped designate the F4U Corsair as Connecticut's official state airplane. Connecticut residents, this author, and all those with an interest in the history of the F4U Corsair, have and will benefit from Doc Gunther's indefatigable efforts.

The Society of Manufacturing Engineers (SME), based in Dearborn, Michigan, evolved from the American Society of Tool Engineers (ASTE). This fine organization offers a plethora of services to its members and chapters, including student chapters. SME also provides considerable information on lean manufacturing and lean process design, including the hardcover book *A Hitchhiker's Guide To Lean* by Jamie Flinchbaugh and Andy Carlino. This author has for years benefited from knowledge that has been disseminated by SME, which was very useful as this book was researched, and for which he is most appreciative.

Connecticut Corsair, LLC is in the process of restoring an F4U-4 aircraft. Craig McBurney is the founder of is group's founder, and their website is another source of useful information about the Corsair, and what it takes to return a Corsair to airworthy status.

Donald V. Richardson provided extremely important insights into Vought-Sikorsky's F4U project for this author. Don distinguished himself in tandem careers. He spent many years as an engineer for United Technologies Corporation divisions, and then served as an assistant professor of electrical engineering technology (now an emeritus professor). Don was hired by Vought-Sikorsky as a mechanical engineer on the F4U project right after he graduated from the University of New Hampshire. He worked on flight-test instrumentation and structural engineering assignments on the XF4U-1 and F4U-1. Igor Sikorsky then arranged for his transfer to the VS-300/R-4 helicopter project; many patents and other significant contributions to what was then called United Aircraft Corporation followed. Don's recollections and insights about Vought-Sikorsky's wartime engineering efforts were unique, and provided answers that would not have otherwise been available. He also read the manuscript, and offered constructive suggestions for this book. My humble thank you here is not enough.

Another person who was extremely helpful was retired Royal Navy Captain Eric M. "Winkle" Brown, CBE, DSC, AFC, who corresponded with this author from his home in England. A Fleet Air Arm pilot with 2.5 "kills" while flying the Grumman F4F, Brown spent much of the war as a test pilot with the Royal Aircraft Establishment (RAE). He flight tested every major Allied fighter of World War Two, and almost all German and Japanese fighters of note. In particular, Capt. Brown was instrumental in evaluating the use of the naval version of the famous Supermarine Spitfire aboard aircraft carriers, and also test flew the Vought F4U Corsair. His contributions to the war effort and naval aviation were enormous, and give him a unique perspective of key topics in this book. I am humble and honored that Capt. Brown took the time to provide detailed answers to questions that no one else could provide.

Some individuals who are mentioned in this book were known to the author during his years as a pilot. These quiet heroes worked and served in Vought's flight test department, and were a big impetus for writing this book. After the war production test pilot Connie Grasso became the manager of the nearby Monroe Airport, where he promoted general aviation for decades. Connie was the instructor who checked out this author in the J-3 Piper Cub in 1970. After the war, experimental test pilot Bill Horan went on to a successful career in corporate aviation, spending years flying DC-3s and the Convair 580. But that career almost didn't happen. In 1946, Bill bailed out of an F4U after an inflight engine fire occurred during a test flight over Long Island Sound. It was a close call. Before that, he performed some rather risky inverted spin tests on the Corsair; the data gathered from those tests was important to the Navy. It was a pleasure to have known Bill while he was the chief pilot for Great Lakes Carbon Corporation. Like many others, he deserves more recognition than he ever received for his service as an F4U test pilot. Perhaps this book will help make that right. And this author also had the pleasure of having some acquaintance with James "Jim" Malarky, the Vought director of flight operations during the war years. Jim later became the manager of the Bridgeport Airport, and ran the Tweed New Haven Airport after that. He had a reputation as being a great flight operations manager, and was a wonderful guy.

Acknowledgements

Susan Todd Brook, Subsidiary Rights Manager for the Naval Institute Press in Annapolis, Maryland, was kind enough to quickly grant permission to quote an excerpt from Capt. Brown's excellent book *Wings of the Navy: Flying Allied Carrier Aircraft of World War Two* (Second Edition). Capt. Brown's books are highly recommended for those with an interest in the F4U or military aircraft in general.

Gill Richardson, director of sales and editorial services at Crécy Publishing in Manchester, England, also responded quickly. Mr. Richardson granted permission to quote from Jeffrey Quill's wonderful biography *Spitfire: A Test Pilot's Story*. In addition to being the Spitfire's longtime experimental test pilot, Quill test flew the F4U Corsair. Of particular interest to this author is the fact that it was Quill who developed the doctrines that were exemplified in the curved approach to aircraft carriers. This technique enabled pilots of the F4U to keep the Landing Signal Officer (known as Deck Landing Control Officers in the Fleet Air Arm) in view during the approach. As with Capt. Eric Brown, Jeffrey Quill was both a giant in the flight test world and a gifted writer.

One highly experienced pilot who is very knowledgeable about local aviation history is Morgan Kaolian. Morgan was the superintendant of operations, and then airport manager, of what came to be called Sikorsky Memorial Airport. He has been very supportive of historical preservation efforts, and provided useful information about Bridgeport Airport during the 1940s.

As you will no doubt understand, any study of the F4U as a complete weapon system requires some understanding of the underlying technologies. One of the technologies that emerged as the F4U broke the 400 m.p.h. speed barrier was radar. Since the F4U-2 was one of America's first night fighters, radar is an important topic. There are several good histories about the development of radar. The one that this author finds most useful is the late Dr. Louis Brown's unequalled *A Radar History of World War II: Technical and Military Imperatives*. Brown, a Fellow of the American Physical Society, provides an excellent, not-too-technical overview of the development of radar, and how it made its way into each combat theater. This author is grateful for the breadth of Dr. Brown's work, and highly recommends his book for those with an interest in this technology.

Curt Lawson at the Emil Buehler Naval Aviation Library at the National Naval Air Museum in Pensacola, Florida was kind enough to promptly grant my permissions request for the use of images in their collection. The staff at the library and museum does a tremendous job of preserving and making available our nation's naval aviation history. My thanks go out to all the staff for the fine work that they do.

The Fleet Air Arm Museum, located at RNAS Ilchester in Somerset, England, does a superb job in preserving historic aircraft and service records of Fleet Air Arm personnel. Those records can be useful to any FAA researcher, and this author is grateful for their resources and assistance.

Bruce Williams, a director of Captain's Cove Seaport and the founder of the Dundon House maritime museum in Bridgeport, Connecticut, was kind enough to read and critique this manuscript prior to publication. Bruce caught some historical references that needed clarification, and has been my go-to guy for questions about shipyards and naval vessel construction. Having a maritime historian with Bruce's knowledge to consult with was a real blessing.

Thanks also to the entire staff at the Stratford Library and Stratford Library Association for their efforts to promote reading, preserve local history and bring as much information as possible to the public.

During the research and writing of this book, many officials and employees of the Town of Stratford were most helpful. Mayor John A. Harkins is always available to help local citizens, including authors. Assessor Melinda Fonda and her staff went above and beyond the call of duty, locating some long forgotten property and records for the old Vought-Sikorsky factory (now known as the Strafford Army Engine Plant). So thanks also to Diane Romano, Sarah Scacco, Rosalyn Dupuis and Carol Mordowanec in the Assessor's Office. Town Clerk Susan M. Pawluk and her fine staff were very helpful in locating old land titles and property transfers. That includes Assistant Town Clerk Sandra M. Maleski and Assistant Registrars of Vital statistics Deborah Brunson and Jessica Johnson. The author sends a "well-done" and special thanks to all.

Then there is the author's end game. Making this book available to readers like you is the culmination of the research, writing, editorial review and gathering of permissions that precede publication. That is a team effort, and publishing consultant Ginnie Gale and the CreateSpace team in South Carolina did a fine job of guiding this author through the necessary steps to turn his manuscript and images into a real book, and make it happen expeditiously.

Acknowledgements

Of course, this book is an acknowledgement of the efforts of all individuals who contributed to making the Vought F4U Corsair a reality, and to those who flew and supported it in the military. With this acknowledgement comes an explanation. The engineers, production workers, officials of the U.S. Navy's Bureau of Aeronautics and other government agencies, along with test pilots and members of the armed forces, all gave us much more that a spectacular naval fighter. They did far more than push aeronautical technology far ahead of where it was in 1940. All of those dedicated men and women created a superior warplane that would help bring a just end to the deadliest global war in history, and do so as quickly s possible.

When the XF4U-1 first flew in 1940, Chancellor Adolph Hitler's Nazi apparatus controlled Germany. The Fuhrer and his Third Reich were bringing war to the United Kingdom, Europe, Russia, and large portions of the globe. The Third Reich also created death camps: i.e., Auschwitz-Birkenau, Cheimno, Belzec, Majdanek, Sobibor and Treblinka. These camps were in addition to large numbers of concentration camps, and enabled the Nazis to begin the systematic extermination of Jews, gypsies and other unfavored groups that came within their deadly grasp. Italy, under Prime Minister Benito Mussolini, had become a fascist war state. From its perch in the Mediterranean, Mussolini's Italy joined with Hitler to attack unaligned nations, including Greece and areas of the old Ottoman Empire. In Japan, a more belligerent government was formed. Emperor Hirohito remained the titular head, but Prince Fumumaro Konoye became the militant new prime minister. Japan continued its war with China, and expanded the conflict into Indo-China and throughout the Pacific Rim. The unprovoked attack on the United States at Pearl Harbor would soon follow.

The global war that ensued caused more than fifty million deaths by the time it ended in 1945. Not well understood is how perilously close the America and its Allies came to losing that war. In 1940 Britain was being starved by the German U-boats, and bombed by the Luftwaffe during the Battle of Britain. It survived – but just barely. By the time the United States entered the war on 8 December 1941, Japan controlled vast portions of the Pacific Ocean and the Far East; even the West Coast was fearful of a Japanese naval attack. America and its Allies were losing the war, and they knew it.

Among all of the weapons that enabled America and its Allies to reverse the course of the war and prevail, the F4U Corsair was prominent. Beginning with its combat debut at Guadalcanal, it was the F4U that took on and bested the vaunted Japanese Zero in aerial combat. In those dark days at Guadalcanal, that gull-winged hot-rod was our best fighter interceptor and our only true air superiority fighter. The Corsair was also America's first true fighter-bomber, a high-speed reconnaissance aircraft and, as mentioned above, a night fighter. In fact, the Corsair could not only outfight any Japanese fighter; it could carry a greater payload of bombs than most medium-bombers, and almost as much as the B-17 Flying Fortress. Marine Corps and Navy pilots repeatedly attacked vastly superior numbers of enemy aircraft with their Corsairs, fighting under adverse odds over enemy territory but confidant that they were flying the greatest naval fighter in the world. That the F4U helped shorten the war is a truth and, almost certainly, an understatement.

The events that followed the end of World War Two are telling. The once totalitarian nations were freed of their Nazi and fascist dictators; their citizens transitioned from war and deprivation to a climate of peace and freedom. In America, Britain and the Dominion nations, Germany, Italy and Japan, nations and peoples found new friends and alliances in the much better post-war world. In acknowledging our debt to those whose sacrifice brought that peace and freedom, we begin to appreciate what is often taken for granted.

Shortly after this book first goes into print and electronic format, a young generation of students will be completing their spring semester at school. In Stratford, Connecticut, where what was perhaps the greatest naval fighter of World War Two was born, students at Frank Scott Bunnell High School and Stratford High School will contemplate their future. Encouraged by Superintendant Irene Cornish and the Board of Education, they will read their textbooks, think about opportunities that lie ahead and study under now peaceful skies. Seniors will not be asked to drop out of school to enlist in the military, nor will they be forced to face death and destruction on a battlefield. Great warplanes will no longer zoom overhead.

In June 2012, and each year thereafter, the day will come when those seniors walk across their high school stage and receive their highly valued diploma. As they graduate under the quiet skies over Stratford,

Acknowledgements

will they remember the earlier generation that preserved the freedom that they now enjoy? Will they understand the enormity of that generation's sacrifices, and the role that the gull-winged F4U played in bringing peace to a world once engulfed in a global war? Let us hope that they will. And as they cross the stage and graduate before an audience of parents, relatives and teachers, let us hope they have an appreciation of their history, a love of life, and the courage of an earlier generation that was determined to stay free.

Ralph Harvey
January 2012

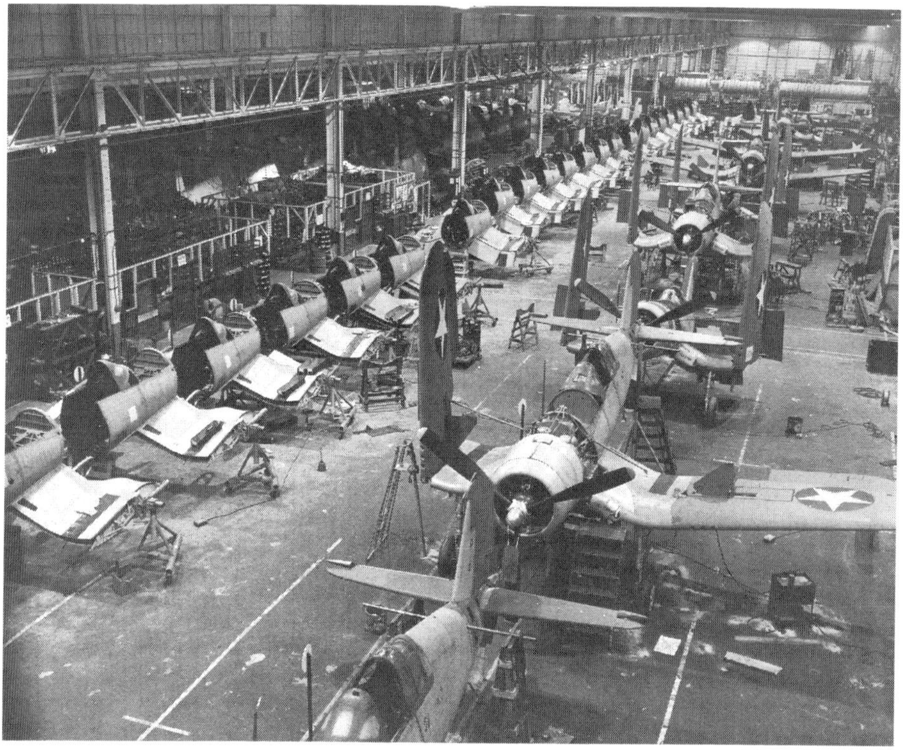

Prologue

> *For myself and my four American-born sons, I am happy and proud to be a citizen of this great, powerful, free country, that has no reason to envy or fear any other country in the world.*
>
> – Igor I. Sikorsky, founder of Sikorsky Aircraft, in his response to a Associated Press request pertaining to their 'I Am An American Day' Program. Sent on 20 April 1941, as Vought-Sikorsky was completing a production contract for the F4U Corsair with the U.S. Navy. Source: Igor I. Sikorsky Historical Archives, Inc.

Rising above the nearby marshland and just west of the Housatonic River, an imposing masonry building stood out in quiet, pre-war Lordship. Distinct from its surroundings, the building was part of an expanding factory complex that for nearly six decades would facilitate the manufacture of engines for aircraft, army tanks and – most importantly – commercial and military aircraft. At first a solitary facility, the expanding plant was at the southernmost part of the town's manufacturing footprint, a hodge-podge of industrial properties that were interspersed with residential areas, a town center and the railroad. To the north and south of the factory the seaside community was known for its neat neighborhoods of single-family houses, shorefront homes and a picturesque lighthouse.

Lordship was a section of the Town of Stratford, which bordered Long Island Sound to the south and the Housatonic River to the east. The town was settled in 1939 by a group of Puritans headed by the Rev. Adam Blakeman, a commanding figure who led his church and presided over town affairs until his death in 1665. Arriving on a small boat, this contingent of Pilgrims landed in a lagoon on the western shore of the Housatonic, just a mile north of the modern brick edifice. The town was originally called Cupheag, but the name was later changed to Stratford in order to recognize a lineage with Stratford upon Avon, England. In future years, a replica of William Shakespeare's theater in Stratford upon Avon would be built next to the lagoon where the Puritans first landed.

To the west of Stratford is Bridgeport, a city that became an important manufacturing center before and during the first half of the twentieth century. Bridgeport had been a veritable arsenal during the First World War, with companies such as Bridgeport Brass, General Electric, Jenkins Valves, and Union Metallic Cartridge becoming major employers. Lake Torpedo Boat Company produced submarines for the U.S. Navy during the World War, and Locomobile – the producer of what was arguably the finest American automobile in the early years of the century – made the ubiquitous Riker trucks for the U.S. Army. In a city that designed, developed and manufactured products as diverse as Frisbee pies, automobiles and machine guns, it was almost inevitable that there would be an involvement with aviation. That happened in 1937, when Bridgeport acquired an airport and its roughly eight hundred acres of land in the Lordship section of Stratford. Well liked by pilots because some runways had over water approaches, the airport was just north of the residential area where Lordship met the Sound.

Bridgeport Airport, as the airfield came to be known, was originally called Avon Field. The site of one of America's first civilian air shows (in 1911), it was later named Mollison Field after famed aviator Jim Mollison crash-landed there on a non-stop flight from Wales. During the Great Depression, funding from Works Progress Administration (WPA) programs contributed to the paving of the runways, while barnstorming pilots offered visitors "a million dollar thrill for a five-dollar bill." From the northern half of the airport one merely had to cross Main Street to get to the front of the large factory. In the coming years, these adjoining but separate properties would be inexorably linked in a historic effort to build America's fastest naval fighter aircraft.

Sitting on a thirty-six acre parcel that would in time more than double in size, the factory was constructed in 1929-30 to house what had been called the Sikorsky Manufacturing Corporation. Founded by a Russian immigrant named Igor I. Sikorsky, the firm began operations in March 1923 on a Long Island chicken farm owned by Victor Utgoff. It was an important step in a personal and professional odyssey. Sikorsky had fled his homeland after the 1917 Russian Revolution, arriving in New York in March 1919. With limited cash but unlimited enthusiasm, Sikorsky named his business Sikorsky Aero Engineering Corporation. A highly regarded aeronautical engineer, Sikorsky's prior work included the design of the world's first four-engine aircraft (the 1913 S-21 *Russky Vityaz*) and the world's first four-engine bomber (the S-22 derivative *Ilya Muromets*, also used as a transport). Utgoff was a classmate of Sikorsky at the Russian Naval Academy, and had served as a pilot in the Russian Imperial Navy. In 1917, Lt. Cdr. Utgoff and his family migrated to America because of the Russian Revolution; his farm thus became the birthplace of a major aerospace manufacturer.

It was at this humble base on Long Island that Sikorsky pursued his interest in the design and construction of multi-engine seaplanes. The first such aircraft was his fourteen-passenger S-29A (the 'A' stood for America), built outdoors at Utgoff's farm. But his friend's farm could not serve as an airport, so Sikorsky and his young company began to use nearby Roosevelt Field for its flight operations. Sikorsky's small business struggled and grew, and in late 1926 he moved to rented factory space in College Point, Long Island, very close to the future site of New York's LaGuardia Airport. By that time Sikorsky was building his twin-engine S-38 seaplane, and the College Point factory, while larger than the Roosevelt Field hangar, was still not adequate. So once again, Sikorsky was on the lookout for a new location to build and test his aircraft. And when the entrepreneurial engineer found property between the Housatonic River and the municipal airport in Stratford, he knew that he had the perfect location. Sikorsky Manufacturing purchased the property in 1928.

Acquiring the property was an important business move, but the new location did not provide additional capital for manufacturing. So in 1929 Sikorsky sold his firm to the United Aircraft and Transportation Corporation, after which the new corporate owner built the Stratford factory. Thereafter Sikorsky, in his position as the chief engineer, developed seaplanes such at the S-42 and experimented with helicopters. The somewhat protected mouth of the Housatonic

River afforded an excellent location for seaplane operations, while the nearby Bridgeport Airport provided suitable runways for land aircraft. Along the southern end of the plant, a street called Sniffens Lane ran from the river to Main Street, separating the building from an employee parking lot and some open areas. That land was adequate and convenient for low, tethered helicopter test flights. And it was there, on 14 September 1939, that Sikorsky – in his dual roles as the engineering manager and test pilot for the Vought-Sikorsky Aircraft division of United Aircraft Corporation – would make a tethered, maiden flight of his revolutionary VS-300 helicopter. Sikorsky's historic flight was the first of an American helicopter, and serves as an important benchmark in the development of practical, rotary-wing flight.

The name Vought-Sikorsky suggests that there were other players in this corporate history, and indeed there were. Chauncey (Chance) Vought was born in New York in 1890. A talented engineer, he learned to fly in 1910, and by 1916 had become the chief design engineer for the Wright Corporation. At this point the conflict that was then known as the World War had been waged for two years, but America was not yet a belligerent. That changed the following year, and as America entered the war against Germany, Vought saw opportunity. American armed forces would need aircraft – lots of them – so Chance Vought left the Wright Corporation and, with Birdseye Lewis, formed the Lewis-Vought Corporation.

Vought's new company found its first major success after hostilities ended. The customer was the U.S. Navy, and the product was the VE-7 – a biplane trainer that could operate from either a land base or a ship. The Navy liked the VE-7, so much so that it also used the plane as one of its early fighters. And in 1922, the Navy used a VE-7 to make the very first takeoff from America's first aircraft carrier, the *U.S.S. Langley*. Defense budgets were tight in this period, but the success of the VE-7 solidified Vought's position as a qualified manufacturer of naval aircraft. Other successful aircraft followed, including the O2U-1 Corsair, a scout bomber and the first U.S. Navy aircraft to bear the Corsair name.

Prologue

Sikorsky S-38 amphibian flying past the designer's rented factory space in the Queens section of New York City, circa 1928. The water below the aircraft is adjacent to the present day LaGuardia Airport, which did not exist until 1939. Image source/credit: Courtesy of the Igor I. Sikorsky Historical Archives, Inc.

Chance Vought died prematurely in 1930, and the Chance Vought Corporation (as it was known since 1922) ended up in East Hartford, Connecticut as part of the United Aircraft and Transportation (UATC) holding company. The Air Mail Act of 1934 forced the breakup of UATC and its interesting lineup of companies. Boeing and United Airlines became independent, while the newly formed United Aircraft Corporation retained Sikorsky Aircraft, Chance Vought Aircraft, Hamilton Standard Steel Propeller Corp. (manufacturer of propellers) and Pratt & Whitney Aircraft Company (an engine manufacturer). The East Harford location was convenient. Chance Vought's facility was adjacent to the big Pratt & Whitney plant, and (beginning in 1933) was at the perimeter of a military airport that became known as Rentschler Field. The East Hartford location was also close to United Aircraft's corporate headquarters. But the acquisition of Chance Vought and its move to East Hartford occurred during the Great Depression, a period in which both naval and civil aviation budgets grew increasingly tight.

In 1939, the decision-makers at United Aircraft decided to integrate Chance Vought, still an established U.S. Navy contractor, and Sikorsky Aircraft. The new combined division would be named Vought-Sikorsky, and the large factory complex in Stratford would thereafter become the sole site for aircraft manufacturing. The Vought product lineup would include naval reconnaissance aircraft, dive bombers and, most importantly, a new high-performance air superiority fighter for the U.S. Navy. The eventual production of Sikorsky's R-4 helicopters for the military, an aircraft that would evolve from the radical VS-300, was still beyond the planning horizon. Later on, when it was clear that the R-4 was going into wartime production, Vought and Sikorsky would re-emerge as separate companies, with helicopter production going to a new factory in Bridgeport. That separation would occur at the beginning of 1943. In the meantime, external events were about to change the company's future.

On 1 September 1939, Adolf Hitler unleashed his blitzkrieg (tank and infantry attack) into Poland; the Second World War had begun in Europe. Much has been written about that global conflict, but of interest here is how technological change – and in particular, the changes that led to one revolutionary naval fighter – contributed to the outcome of that war. Harnessing that technological change was imperative if America, the United Kingdom and its assorted Allies would overcome the technical and numerical deficiencies that hindered their ability to wage war. So too were America's manufacturing capabilities. In the United States, for example, every branch of the armed forces was severely undersized and poorly equipped. And unlike Great Britain, the United States even lacked an independent air force. As the clouds of war darkened its small Air Corps was still part of the U.S. Army and, while it would grow and evolve into the Army Air Force (with its own chief of staff, Gen. Henry H. "Hap" Arnold), it would not be until September 1947 – two years to the month after the Japanese surrender – that an independent U.S. Air Force would be born. In the United Kingdom, the Fleet Air Arm (FAA) was removed from the Royal Air Force and re-established as a part of the Royal Navy in May 1939, with operational control exclusively under the Admiralty. It was an adroit move that enabled the Admiralty to systematically expand that branch from just 232 aircraft at the beginning of the war to over 3,700 aircraft and 59 aircraft carriers at the war's end.

During the late-1930s, the U.S. Navy and the Marine Corps (both part of the Department of the Navy, but each with its own uniformed chain-of-command) were better prepared for war organizationally than was the U.S. Army, but they too faced tremendous hurdles. In the spring of 1938, as Hitler's Third Reich absorbed Austria and the Sudetenland portion of Czechoslovakia, naval aviation in the United States was still transitioning from obsolete biplanes to closed canopy, metal covered monoplanes. Aboard straight-decked aircraft carriers like the *U.S.S. Lexington*, bombing squadrons began to replace their Boeing F4B-4s (the naval version of the Army Air Corps P-12 biplane fighter) with the new Vought SB2U-1 dive-bomber. Vought's dive-bomber was a noticeable advance for the American fleet, but even it would be soon be surpassed by more modern aircraft. The Grumman F4F Wildcat, the Navy's first 300 m.p.h. fighter, was still in the development phase; it was originally conceived as a biplane and would have to be substantially re-designed. The Brewster F2A-1 Buffalo, the Navy's first monoplane fighter, would quickly reveal its dismal performance and maneuverability after its service introduction. By 1942, the Buffalo would have all but disappeared from the U.S. naval inventory. These were all changes in the making, but even by 1938 the Navy knew it would need a much faster – and much more capable – shipboard fighter.

The growing pains of U.S. naval aviation and the Army Air Corps derived in large measure from the American public's political apathy and general disinterest in military preparations. Indeed, a 1940 military preparedness bill that authorized a military draft passed the House of Representatives by just one vote. The September 1940 Destroyer for Base Deal and the May 1941 Lend-Lease Act would ensure that Britain could receive at least some of what it needed from America, but even these measures required considerable persuasion from President Franklin D. Roosevelt – even with members of his own party. Americans, tired from eleven years of economic depression, were ready to return to work but not ready for another world war.

Developing the Gull-Winged F4U Corsair - And Taking It To Sea

The Sikorsky plant in Stratford, Connecticut in 1929. The Housatonic River is at the top of the image, while the runways of the future Bridgeport Airport are out of view below the foreground. Sniffens Lane, at the right side of the plant, is where Igor I Sikorsky made the first flight of the VS-300 helicopter in September 1939. Image source/credit: Courtesy of the Igor I. Sikorsky Historical Archives, Inc.

Across the Atlantic Britain faced a similar set of problems, albeit far more severe. The cumulative effects of the global depression, including the burdens of maintaining its far-flung empire, currency issues that derived from the 1925 pegging of Sterling to a gold standard, and chronic material shortages all hindered military preparations. Meanwhile, Hitler's Reich secretly and not so secretly rebuilt its high seas fleet (Kriegsmarine), its air force (Luftwaffe) and its army panzer divisions. In 1938 Winston Churchill, then out of office but privy to military secrets, wrote his famous book *While England Slept*. Churchill's forceful arguments did not immediately sway the public, and they put him at odds with Prime Minister Neville Chamberlain, Foreign Secretary Lord Halifax and most members of all major parties. But if *While England Slept* failed to change the political dynamic in 1938, it placed in public discussion the argument for greater military preparations.

Prologue

That the public mood in England was not focused on the forces that would nearly defeat it was understandable. Unlike the United States, Britain had been fully involved in the First World War from its 1914 beginning until hostilities ended in November 1918. It was a conflict of unimaginable death and destruction, and the United Kingdom had sacrificed much. So even more than most Americans, the British wanted a respite from war, despite the ominous behavior of Hitler and his Third Reich, and regardless of the futility of appeasement. But not all Britons slept.

Around the English countryside, the then secret Chain Home series of early warning radar stations were taking shape. This resulted from an awareness of potential threats, a willingness to act, and the availability of a promising new technology. Even the primitive, long wavelength Chain Home radars would enable Royal Air Force fighter pilots to receive advance warning of Luftwaffe air attacks during the Battle of Britain. More than that, as enemy aircraft formations drew closer tactical air controllers could direct airborne RAF squadrons to proper intercept courses, a critical capability that would help overcome the enemy's numerical superiority. Technology itself cannot overcome a lack of will, but even while Prime Minister Neville Chamberlain sought peace with Hitler through appeasement, military preparations – however inadequate the pace – continued.

Britain's entry in the Second World War in September 1939 exposed how unprepared that nation was for war. Still, new tactical aircraft were moving into operational status with the Royal Air Force and the Fleet Air Arm of the Royal Navy. The first was the fabric-covered Hawker Hurricane, a low-wing monoplane fighter that was rugged, with good flight characteristics, and with sufficient speed and maneuverability for attacking enemy bombers. The even faster and more maneuverable Supermarine Spitfire, Britain's premiere fighter of the war, was entering production, albeit in smaller numbers. In the summer of 1940, during Britain's darkest hours, these magnificent machines and their courageous pilots would deny the Luftwaffe an expected victory in the Battle of Britain, and thereby degrade the risk of an invasion. Yet none of this could have been predicted, not even in 1939. And when the Luftwaffe threat and risk of a German invasion receded in late October 1940, the Fleet Air Arm's newest aircraft proved woefully inadequate.

The Blackburn Skua (plus the Roc, a version with an aft gun turret) and the Fairey Fulmar, were slow and hopelessly outclassed as fighters. These aircraft were designed under the mistaken belief within the Royal Navy that a fighter should be large enough to carry an observer. The naval version of the Hurricane was delayed until 1941, and the Seafire version of the Spitfire until 1943. So it would be America to which the Fleet Air Arm would rely on most heavily for modern fighters, and America responded – with Grumman's F4F Wildcat (which the British first called the Martlet), the Vought F4U Corsair, and later Grumman's F6F Hellcat.

The questions arise: How did Britain's wartime vulnerabilities intertwine with the history of the Vought F4U Corsair? Was not the Corsair an American-built fighter that primarily saw service in the Pacific theater of operations? But unlike other American naval fighters, the F4U was originally rejected for shipboard duty by the U.S. Navy. The Corsair's spectacular performance did not mitigate the aircraft's severe deficiencies in aircraft carrier landings, and it spent much of the Second World War as a shore-based naval fighter. A high percentage of Corsairs were assigned to Marine Corps squadrons, where this otherwise superb aircraft met with great success. But America's war in the Pacific was largely a naval war involving the U.S. Navy and Marine Corps, so the inability to operate from aircraft carriers was a severe limitation. The Fleet Air Arm helped to change that.

While F4Us were operating out of forward bases such as Guadalcanal, Espiritu Santo and New Georgia Island, plans were developed to equip Fleet Air Arm pilots with this powerful but troublesome weapon. On 1 June 1943 – one year after the crucial Battle of Midway – No. 1830 Squadron of the Fleet Air Arm began training on the F4U Corsair at the Quonset Point (Rhode Island) Naval Air Station. It would be the first of nineteen Fleet Air Arm squadrons to use the Corsair, enabling the FAA to achieve operational status aboard carriers nine critical months before the U.S. Navy did.

There are other aspects to the history of developing the F4U Corsair, and the protracted efforts to take it to sea. One of these is the plethora of technological hurdles that the F4U had to meet or surpass; these are covered in the various chapters that follow. Another aspect is the environment in which the F4U would be used. And for this, one needs to have some understanding of the surrounding events.

Prologue

For the United States, the F4U Corsair was largely (but not exclusively) used in the combat theaters of the Pacific Ocean. In the Pacific, the critical turning point in the war was the defeat of a superior Japanese naval force at the Battle of Midway in June 1942. But Midway was not just significant because it was strictly an aircraft carrier engagement. After the Battle of Midway, the aircraft carrier replaced the battleship as the most important surface combatant. Without negating the brilliance of Rear Admiral Raymond Spruance as a tactician, Midway showed that the force with the most capable aircraft in adequate numbers has the advantage. But despite its loss at Midway, the Imperial Japanese Navy (IJM) remained a formidable force until late 1944. So American naval forces had to achieve and maintain air superiority over vast areas of the Pacific Ocean; effectively intercept and destroy enemy air and naval forces; support Marine Corp and Army amphibious and ground operations, and always protect the American fleet. Yet the U.S. Navy did not receive its first production Corsairs until nearly two months after Midway ended, and it was really the beginning of 1943 before shore-based F4Us were operational. It would take until 16 May 1944 to get the F4U approved for aircraft carrier use by the U.S. Navy. By that time the war in Europe had less than a year left, and less than fifteen months until the first atomic bomb was dropped on Hiroshima. But though the Corsair was late in arriving onboard American carriers, it was there for the critical final phases of the war.

Across the Atlantic, the F4U was developed as the United Kingdom was fighting for its very survival. The greatest risk of invasion was felt during the Battle of Britain, the German aerial bombardment of England that began in July 1940 and lasted until late October. Had Britain not repulsed those air attacks, a German invasion was likely. But while the Royal Air Force fighters managed to defeat the Luftwaffe, it was a purely defensive operation that was won over its own soil – and by the barest of margins. Britain was determined to win the war, but it could not win it alone. Of course, the British purchasing commission had been buying aircraft before the Battle of Britain started. Fighter aircraft such as the Grumman F4F were just starting to flow in, with many thousands of aircraft to follow. But by the time Winston Churchill became prime minister in May 1940, there needed to be more cooperation in a variety of technological areas. By September, as the Battle of Britain was at its peak, President Roosevelt offered help. The 2 September 1940

Destroyer for Base Agreement provided the Royal Navy with fifty old destroyers in return for the right to use British bases in the Western Hemisphere. That deal would help with the U-boat menace, but Britain wanted more. And it had some secrets to bargain with.

To facilitate a mission to trade secrets for more cooperation and production, Prime Minister Churchill established a special delegation. Officially titled the British Technical and Scientific Mission and headed by Sir Henry Tizard, it came to be known informally as the Tizard Mission. Tizard, a brilliant chemist who developed what became known as octane numbers for fuel, had been the chairman of Britain's Aeronautical Research Committee and was an early proponent of radar. Included in his handpicked group were six others, including Edward "Taffy" Bowen, a leading radar expert and John Cockcroft, a physicist whose early proton accelerator would lead to significant advances in nuclear fission experiments. The group, well qualified to reveal both the underlying science and the emerging technologies, was Britain's best hope in an important gamble. Only by showing Americans the enormous advantages in exploiting Britain's technological advantages, and the enormous risks in not doing so, could high-resolution radar, jet engines and Asdic ever be produced in the huge quantities needed to defeat the Axis powers. Winning the war would mean not just out fighting, but out producing, the free world's totalitarian enemies.

The Tizard Mission, as critical as it was to the eventual Allied victory, was not without some unusual twists. Unknown to Britain's leading scientists and generals, their Chain Home radar was very similar to the CXAM radar that RCA was already delivering to the U.S. Navy; it was being installed on the aircraft carrier *U.S.S. Yorktown* as they met. The British were also surprised at the research that had been done on an advanced, 10-centimeter wavelength radar. But the British had the cavity magnetron, a solution that the Americans badly needed for the high power demands of such a small radar. Similar meetings were held on Britain's research and development in jet engine technology, nuclear research, gyroscopic gunsights, and self-sealing fuel tanks for aircraft. The greater cooperation that resulted from the Tizard Mission would greatly aid the Allied cause. Some technologies, such as the self-sealing fuel tanks, would save the lives of many fighter pilots. The F4U Corsair would be modified to incorporate that technology. And then there was the Corsair itself.

Prologue

In the large and busy factory in Stratford, the needs of the government and the imperative of time were well understood. Ever since February 1938, when the U.S. Navy's Bureau of Aeronautics (BuAer) sent out its specifications for a next generation fighter, the Vought-Sikorsky design teams had pondered over the stringent requirements for high maximum speed, a low 70 m.p.h. stalling (i.e., minimum flight) speed, and a 1,000 mile range. The Vought team submitted two proposals to the Navy, and by June 1938 the design with the larger engine was deemed worthy of a contract. The Navy designated the aircraft the XF4U-1.

Designing an airplane is a complicated process, and the creation of the F4U proceeded in a unique juxtaposition of time and events. For the Vought team, the process began at the end of the biplane era of naval aviation. As the design and development proceeded in Stratford, Connecticut, World War Two began and soon Britain was fighting for its survival. America, while officially neutral, was quietly preparing for war. At the Stratford factory, the design team, engineers, technicians and test pilots all knew that their fighter would push existing aeronautical technologies to the limit. But what were those limits? How would the production version of the XF4U-1 measure up against the deadly adversaries it was likely to face in the skies over the Atlantic and Pacific? And could the radical new fighter do all of the things that were expected of it while flying off a ship?

To the last question, an unexpected answer would come from Britain, the very ally that needed America the most. But for the U.S. Navy, another important question remained: how fast could its new propeller-driven fighter actually fly? With the disappointing performance of the Brewster Buffalo and with the winds of war approaching, the Navy's Bureau of Aeronautics (BuAer) could not afford another failure. Then, on 1 October 1940, the day before Sir Henry Tizard returned to Britain, the prototype of the XF4U-1 took off again from the Bridgeport Airport. Soaring into the skies over Stratford, Connecticut, test pilot Lyman Bullard, Jr. pointed the aircraft to the northeast, leveled off and set the power to test the XF4U-1's level flight speed capability. Before the flight Vought and BuAer officials were highly confident in the design and cautiously optimistic about the outcome. Several minutes later, those officials – and the naval aviation community – had their answer.

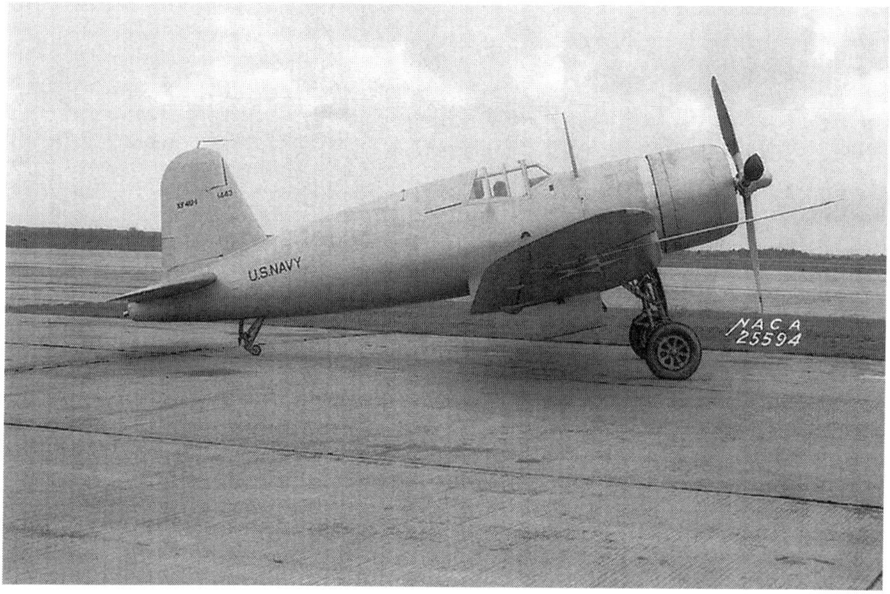
U.S.NAVY
NACA
25594

Chapter One

Uncharted Territory – A 400 m.p.h. Fighter

This is not a question of fighting for Danzig or fighting for Poland. We are fighting to save the whole world from the pestilence of Nazi tyranny and in defense of all that is most sacred to man.

- Winston Churchill, addressing Britain's House of Commons after Hitler's invasion of Poland on 1 September 1939 (the start of WW II in Europe).

Combat conditions have changed – rapidly in the air. With the amazing progress in the design of planes and engines, the airplane of a year ago is out of date now. It is too slow, it is improperly protected, it is too weak in gun power.

- President Franklin D. Roosevelt, in his 16 May 1940 speech entitled 'Ominous Days' less than two weeks before the first flight of the Vought-Sikorsky XF4U-1 in Stratford, Connecticut.

When Rex Beisel led the design team that created the Vought SBU-1, the expectations for aircraft speed and performance were limited. Beisel, the brilliant designer and then the assistant chief engineer for Vought Aircraft (originally Chance Vought), had already proven his abilities with the design and development of the experimental XF3U-1 biplane fighter. A follow up project, the XSBU-1 (later designated the SBU-1 and named the Corsair) would provide an important but evolutionary advance in capabilities. Like other naval aircraft, it would be a fixed-landing gear biplane. But despite its conventional design, Beisel knew that he could improve on the mid-1930s technology.

Unlike the previous fighter project, the SBU-1 would be a scout bomber for the U.S. Navy. As the extended eyes of the fleet, the new aircraft would be able to patrol, detect unobserved warships and, through the vertical maneuvers inherent to dive-bombing, attack enemy combatants. Yet the impetus for the Corsair did not originate from the U.S. Navy. Eugene Wilson, a former executive with Pratt & Whitney, was by 1932 the head of Vought Aircraft. Politically adroit and experienced with the economic risks in bidding for military contracts, Wilson was concerned about investing money in a fighter that would have two crewmen. Even in the mid-1930s fighters were evolving, and the trend was for single-seat aircraft with improved performance. In addition to changing trends in fighter aircraft, Vought was one of just seven companies competing for a possible Navy contract. In the midst of the Great Depression and with little public interest in military programs, Vought was in a high-risk business. To increase the likelihood of earning at least a modest profit, Smith suggested that Vought's XF3U-1 fighter could be modified into a scout bomber for the fleet. Smith was aware of a groundswell of interest for such an aircraft within the Navy's Bureau of Aeronautics, and had ensured that the XF3U-1 would be sturdy enough for modification into a dive bomber. It was a wise move, as the two-seat fighter never came to fruition; the dive bomber did.

The morphing of the XF3U-1 fighter into the XSBU-1 dive bomber illustrates how political factors and bureaucratic preferences can affect military procurement. But while the XSBU-1 design was evolutionary, the Navy expected that the new scout bomber would be highly capable. Therein came the problems associated with the adaptation of a very conventional design. The double-wing configuration of a biplane, while generating ample lift for takeoffs with full bomb loads, also produced considerable aerodynamic drag. The retention of the basic design was mandatory; the Navy had already completed preliminary tests on the aircraft's fighter version, the results of which paved the way for the bomber project. So Vought had to stay with the same basic design configuration, beefing up the airframe for the stresses of dive bombing while finding ways to improve the scout bomber's performance. Part of the solution was the increased power of the Pratt & Whitney R-1535 Wasp, Jr., the supercharged, 14-cylinder twin-row radial engine that was selected for the aircraft. But even with 700 horsepower the desired performance would not be met, and elimination of all unnecessary drag remained a top priority. Aware of the dilemma, Beisel and the Vought Aircraft engineers went to work.

One drag reducing innovation that appeared in the new aircraft was a controllable-pitch propeller, thanks to the engineers at Pratt & Whitney and Hamilton Standard (like Vought, both were United Aircraft divisions with Hamilton Standard the propeller manufacturer). Unlike fixed-pitch propellers, a controllable-pitch prop could be adjusted by the pilot so that in cruise flight the blade angle would be more streamlined. The streamlining of the prop blade angle would reduce aerodynamic drag, thereby producing a slightly higher cruise speed. Another incremental improvement was made in the design of the cowl flaps, incorporated into the NACA cowling that would surround the engine. Designed to streamline the aircraft and provide protection against the elements, the cowling had to permit sufficient airflow around the engine for cooling. At the rear of the cowling were gills that provided an opening for the mass airflow that passed between the outside of the engine and the inside of the cowling. After leveling off at the desired cruise altitude, the higher cruise speeds resulted in increased cooling airflow (air-cooled engines did not use radiators). So by designing adjustable cowl flaps that could also be streamlined, it was expected that a few more knots of additional speed could be realized. This was soon validated in flight tests, in which the experimental XSBU-1 was able to achieve a top speed of 178 knots, or 205 m.p.h. It was the first time that a light bomber was able to surpass the 200 m.p.h. airspeed mark in level flight. After co-authoring a paper entitled "Cowling and Cooling of Radial Air-Cooled Aircraft Engines," Beisel, along with Pratt & Whitney engineers A. L. McCain and F. M. Thomas, received both the SAE Manley Memorial Medal and the Wright Brothers Medal for their work.

Beisel's star continued to rise at Vought, and in June 1935 he was promoted to chief engineer. His next major project was the SB2U, later to be named the Vindicator, and which would become the U.S. Navy's first monoplane bomber. By this time military aircraft were trending towards monoplanes of metal construction, enclosed canopies and retractable landing gear. They also trended towards either supercharged or turbo-supercharged engines that could maintain engine power in the thinner air at higher altitudes and, slightly later, pressurized ignition systems. Most, although not all, were air-cooled engines that avoided the need for heavy

Developing the Gull-Winged F4U Corsair - And Taking It To Sea

radiators, but usually with a drag penalty due to the larger frontal area of a radial engine. There was also less ambiguity within the military procurement offices, but that has to be qualified. Procurement officials and uniformed officers were aware of the above-noted aeronautical trends, but they were also cautious. And so it was that Vought entered separate and roughly concurrent biplane and monoplane competitions, and won production contracts for both the SBU-1 Corsair biplane bomber and the SB2U Vindicator monoplane bomber. Of the two, the Vindicator was the more successful, with 260 copies rolling out of the Stratford factory between January 1936 and 1941.

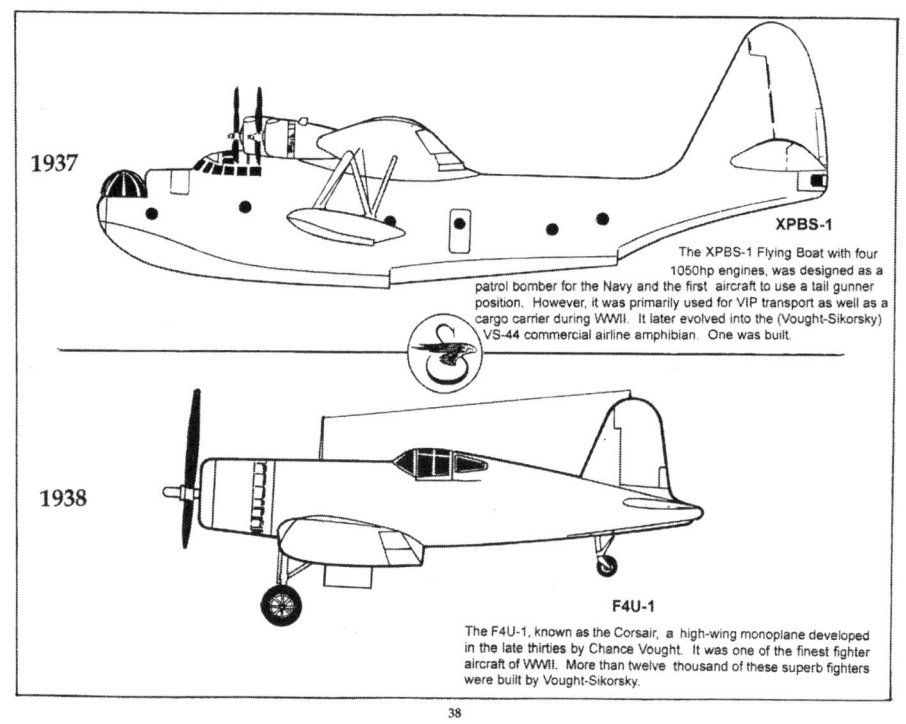

1937

XPBS-1

The XPBS-1 Flying Boat with four 1050hp engines, was designed as a patrol bomber for the Navy and the first aircraft to use a tail gunner position. However, it was primarily used for VIP transport as well as a cargo carrier during WWII. It later evolved into the (Vought-Sikorsky) VS-44 commercial airline amphibian. One was built.

1938

F4U-1

The F4U-1, known as the Corsair, a high-wing monoplane developed in the late thirties by Chance Vought. It was one of the finest fighter aircraft of WWII. More than twelve thousand of these superb fighters were built by Vought-Sikorsky.

38

The four-engine Sikorsky XPBS-1 maritime patrol bomber and the Vought XF4U-1 fighter were both conceived before the separate United Aircraft Corporation divisions merged in 1939. The XPBS-1 evolved into the VS-44 flying boat transport. Note the "bird cage" canopy on the XF4U-1. Image source/credit: Courtesy of the Igor I. Sikorsky Historical Archives, Inc.

Even before Vought relocated from Hartford to Stratford during 1939, the generally conservative procurement officials in the Navy's

Bureau of Aeronautics understood that technology was changing. They saw the war clouds that appeared over China, the Pacific and Europe, and recognized that American pilots could one day be facing far more advanced aircraft – and doing so in far-flung locations. A new generation of naval fighters would be needed, with superior performance, range and the ability to operate from aircraft carriers being the essential requirements. And as if to underscore these imperatives, the U.S. Army's Air Corp was introducing new monoplane fighters, of which the Navy's Bureau of Aeronautics (BuAer) was all too aware. Beginning in 1937, designs such as the (short-lived) Seversky P-35 and the Curtis P-36 – which quickly evolved into the Allison-powered P-40 – started to appear in the Army inventory. Even more importantly, the Army had authorized the development of Lockheed's revolutionary P-38 Lightning, an advanced twin-engine fighter. But in Vought (soon to be Vought-Sikorsky) the Navy had a firm with a good track record, and which was highly regarded for its engineering and production capabilities. So when the Navy's Bureau of Aeronautics solicited designs of an advanced new fighter in February 1938, Rex Beisel and his team of engineers were ready. But this time, Vought's chief engineer would have much more than his U.S. competitors to consider.

• • • •

The Schneider Trophy was not just a prestigious aeronautical award; it created a competition that for eighteen years would establish the fastest seaplane in the world. Established by the wealthy aircraft enthusiast Jacques Schneider in 1911, the international event was held eleven times between 1913 and 1931. As a two-time trophy winner, Great Britain would be the permanent cup holder if it won the 1931 competition. And as with teams from other nations, the British used military demonstration pilots to fly the specially designed aircraft. Flown over a 350-kilometer course, the competitions drew huge crowds and were eagerly followed by news organizations. Although it was limited to seaplanes, the unique nature of the contest ensured that the winner would be the fastest airplane in the world.

In 1931, Britain's Schneider Cup contender was designed by Reginald J. "R.J." Mitchell, the brilliant engineer who was by then the technical director for Supermarine. Designated the Supermarine S.6B, the low-winged monoplane had an open cockpit and an enormous Rolls Royce engine. Britain's goal in the event was two-fold. First, it wanted to claim the cup for the third time. Once that was accomplished, it would use one of the three aircraft that it brought to the event to make a flight at the fastest possible speed. The 1929 and 1931 events were held at Calshot Spit, a roughly mile long beach area near Southampton, England. Flight Lieutenant John N. Boothman accomplished the first goal by winning the race at an average speed of 340 m.p.h. Just over two weeks later, on September 29, Flight Lieutenant George Stainworth flew a S.6B with a 2,300 h.p. Rolls-Royce R-type engine at an average speed of 407 m.p.h., becoming the first pilot to exceed the unheard of 400 m.p.h. mark.

The phenomenal world speed record of the S.6B was all the more impressive because it occurred during the era of the biplane. But recognizing the military potential of Mitchell's design, Supermarine authorized him to develop another fast monoplane. Originally designated as the Model 300, the lightweight, land-based aircraft quickly attracted the interest of the Royal Air Force. The prototype first flew during March 1936, when Vickers (Aviation) Ltd. Chief Test Pilot Joseph "Mutt" Summers completed a short but uneventful flight at Eastleigh Aerodrome (later named Southampton Airport). Although the prototype revealed well-balanced flight controls and good flight characteristics, it was not an immediate success. Subsequent test flights revealed a lackluster level flight speed, a big surprise and disappointment. The problem was fixed two months later with an improved propeller. While not as fast as the overpowered S.6B, the superb flight characteristics, maneuverability and 349 m.p.h. speed of what was then called the Spitfire far exceeded the capabilities of current military aircraft. Supermarine received an initial Air Ministry order for 310 copies of their speedster even before initial testing had been completed; Hawker received an order for 600 Hurricanes on the same day.

That the Spitfire was a brilliant design was proven time and again while serving as Britain's premiere fighter of World War II. But the superiority of the Spitfire derived not just from its effective flight controls and low-drag profile. Mitchell was quick to adopt successful methods that had been pioneered by other aircraft, including an elliptical-shaped wing with an extremely low thickness to chord ratio, a very strong leading edge wing section, a unique boom type wing spar design and an unusually narrow, outward-retracting main landing gear. That, along with a powerful but reliable Rolls-Royce V-12, liquid-cooled engine, made the Spitfire Britain's ultimate aerial weapon. The Spitfire would undergo numerous modifications, and was the only Commonwealth fighter in production throughout the war. But it was during its early development and service (up to and including the Battle of Britain) that Spitfire Mark I and Mark II versions established the speed, acceleration and air combat maneuvering benchmarks against which Allied fighters could be judged. And those capabilities were nothing short of amazing.

Early Mk IA (circa 1938) versions of the Spitfire had a typical loaded weight of only 5,935 lbs (2,692 kg), and were powered by a Rolls Royce Merlin III engine with a de Havilland two-speed propeller. Burning the typical 87 octane avgas, the early Spitfire Mk IA's Merlin III produced 1,030 h.p. (770 kW), resulting in a power to weight ratio of 0.17 h.p./lb. Although it had less than half the power of the souped-up engines that powered the last Supermarine S.6B racers, the new fighter could still attain a maximum speed of 367 m.p.h. (582 km/hr) at 18,600 ft (5,669 m).

Britain's Air Ministry knew all along that Spitfire would do more than advance the state of the art beyond the biplane era capabilities. The Spitfire, in addition to being the United Kingdom's best fighter, would be good enough to take on any Axis Power adversary. But while Supermarine had the best interceptor aircraft in the world, the firm was woefully unprepared to produce the quantities that were needed. For one thing, Supermarine was a small company, and was already over extended due to its production of other aircraft types for the Air Ministry. A new factory was constructed at Castle Bromwich, but significant delays were encountered in constructing that plant and in getting the workers to follow Supermarine methods. Supermarine was also cautious about using subcontractors to produce components for its main factory, thereby exacerbating production delays. While production levels rose by mid-1940, the slow start meant that when the Battle of Britain began in July, Britain had far too few Spitfires.

Despite the slow start in reaching planned production levels, the combat record of the Spitfire vindicated most of the design features. Against the Messerschmitt Bf-109E, the Spitfire had a slight advantage

Developing the Gull-Winged F4U Corsair - And Taking It To Sea

in speed and could turn more tightly in a dogfight. While lacking the high altitude climb performance and having a more limited range, the Spitfire was highly effective as an interceptor. Even against the Focke-Wulf FW-190 (which appeared later in the war), the Spitfire could hold its own. One limitation that Spitfire pilots had was the use of a carburetor instead of a fuel injection system. The carburetor could not tolerate the negative-Gs encountered in an abrupt nose over, a deficiency that German pilots could exploit with their fuel-injected engines. In some cases Spitfire pilots would overcome the deficiency by rolling inverted instead of "pushing over," but the negative-G limitation was still a handicap. Then there was the landing gear.

The narrow, outward-retracting landing gear was designed so that the stress of landing would be absorbed by the strong, inboard section of the wing spar. But however desirable the narrow main landing gear was to the structural engineers, it made the Spitfire far more difficult to land. That was especially true with the Seafire, Supermarine's naval version of the Spitfire. The narrow main gear made landings aboard the pitching and rolling decks of aircraft carriers exceptionally difficult, and the long nose did not help matters either. But once airborne, the Seafire's air combat capabilities were extremely important in protecting both Royal Navy ships and convoys of merchant ships, so Fleet Air Arm pilots were forced to cope with the problem.

One area where Supermarine did make significant improvements was in the powerplant. As an interceptor, the early versions of the Spitfire had ample speed to engage incoming Luftwaffe fighters. However, the Spitfire sometimes lacked sufficient speed to catch enemy aircraft from astern. This was even true with some Luftwaffe bombers, such as the Junkers Ju-88. As a result, by the time Supermarine began producing the Spitfire Mk.5B, it was powered by Rolls Royce's newer Griffon engine. These later examples were heavier, had reduced roll rates and heavier control forces than the earlier marques. But with a typical 2,050 h.p. (1,530 kW) and a maximum speed of 448 m.p.h. (717 km/hr), the performance of the Griffon-powered Spitfires was more in line with advanced American fighters of circa 1943-5. A total of 20,351 Spitfires (all versions) were manufactured, with production continuing into 1948. Spitfires continued in military service with some nations into the 1960s, well into the jet age.

Uncharted Territory – A 400 m.p.h. Fighter

• • • •

The Supermarine Spitfire entered RAF service on 4 August 1938, but that historic aircraft was not Britain's first monoplane fighter. That honor belongs to the Hawker Hurricane, which slightly preceded the Spitfire and became the backbone of the RAF Fighter Command during the Battle of Britain. Slower and not as maneuverable as the Spitfire, it was the Hurricane that produced the greatest number of aerial victories as the Luftwaffe carried out its massive air assault on England. And every bit as much as the Spitfire, the Hurricane advanced the state of the free world's fighter aircraft beyond the biplane era.

The design of the Hurricane began in 1934, when Sydney Camm started to develop a monoplane fighter that would use Rolls Royce's new Goshawk engine. The new monoplane would be a huge advance over contemporary biplane fighters such as the Gloster Gladiator. The reduced drag of using a single wing with no external bracing, an enclosed cockpit for the pilot, a retractable main landing gear (to further reduce drag and increase speed) plus the 660 h.p. that was expected from the Goshawk engine would produce huge increases in performance and air combat capabilities. The new fighter was to be called the Hawker Fury Monoplane and, had it not been for a surprise development in powerplants, the Fury Monoplane might have come to be. But during the preliminary design process Camm, Hawker's chief engineer, learned that Rolls Royce was developing an even more powerful military engine than the Goshawk. Desiring the greater performance that the new engine – then referred to as the PV-12 – could provide, Camm shifted gears and hurriedly began a major redesign. By May 1935 the major portion of the redesign was complete and the project advanced to the prototype phase. On 6 November 1935, Chief Test Pilot P. W. S. "George" Bulman pointed the graceful new fighter down the runway at Brooklands, England, smoothly advanced the throttle of the Merlin C (as the PV-12 was then called) and accelerated rapidly. The tail wheel rose and then, with some backpressure on the stick, the Hawker Hurricane lifted gracefully off the runway. Sydney Camm had developed a winner, and fighter aviation would never be the same.

Unlike the Spitfire, which developed out of specially built racing aircraft, the Hurricane blended a state of the art engine into a retractable landing gear monoplane. These were very important, but evolutionary, advances. The result was an airplane of conventional construction that included fabric-covered wings and fuselage, a disappointing carburetor and an unimpressive fixed-pitch, wooden propeller. Not as fast or as maneuverable as the Spitfire, the Hurricane was still a tremendous leap forward in performance, becoming the free world's first monoplane fighter capable of exceeding 300 m.p.h. in level flight. But Camm's genius was also found in ways that have not always been appreciated. While the Spitfire provided marginally (but critically) better air to air combat capabilities, the Hurricane was far easier to manufacture and, when damaged, far easier to repair. Perhaps equally as important, the Hurricane was an easy aircraft to fly. Aside from rather abrupt stall characteristics and less than ideal over-the-nose visibility on landing, the Hurricane was a good aerobatic airplane and a respectable interceptor. In the hands of very young and inexperienced fighter pilots, it was a potent weapon that would often return to base despite enormous amounts of damage.

There is one more thing to consider when placing Britain's two great fighters into historical perspective. When Hitler unleashed his Luftwaffe in July 1940, he ordered more than 3,500 German warplanes to bomb and strafe Britain into submission. Against this vastly superior number, there were only 620 Spitfires and Hurricanes in service, plus some obsolete biplane fighters that were no match for the enemy. But of RAF Fighter Command's fifty-one fighter squadrons, thirty-two were equipped with Hurricanes and only nineteen squadrons had Spitfires. Spitfires were used primarily to intercept and attack enemy fighters, while the Hurricanes were tasked with shooting down enemy bombers that were unleashing terrible bomb attacks on London, other major cities, and both civil and military infrastructure. Fifty-five percent of German losses in air-to-air combat were due to the 0.303-inch Browning machine guns fired by young RAF pilots in their Hurricanes. Put another way, were it not for the availability of the splendid Hurricane, Britain would have lost the Battle of Britain. The remainder of World War Two would have been far different.

Altogether, some 14,533 Hurricanes were produced, and they were used in almost all theaters as either fighters or ground attack fighter-bombers. Some Hurricanes were used by the Royal Navy's Fleet Air Arm, where they mainly operated from aircraft carriers as interceptors.

A smaller number of Hurricanes were even modified so they could be catapulted from armed merchant ships, after which they would intercept attacking enemy aircraft. These aircraft could not be recovered on board their ships, so the pilots were forced to either ditch in the ocean or parachute towards nearby vessels. Fleet Air Arm Hurricanes also played an important role in Operation Pedestal, the 1942 mission to escort a convoy of supply ships bound for Malta. Although some ships in the convoy were lost to submarine torpedo attacks, Fleet Air Arm pilots blunted aerial bomber attacks and enabled critical supplies to reach the beleaguered island. Once again, the Hurricane – while not the fastest or best fighter in the war – was available when others were not. History has shown that when the chips were down, it was often the 340 m.p.h. Hurricane that made the critical difference.

• • • •

The mid-1930s development of the Hawker Hurricane and Supermarine Spitfire marked a sea change in fighter aircraft design, but they were not alone. In 1934, just as the Hawker Hurricane was being developed in England, the German aircraft manufacturer Bayerische Flugzeugwerke entered a competition to build a next generation monoplane fighter. The German Air Ministry had sought a replacement for its Heinkel He-52 biplane fighters, which were determined to be obsolete even as they were introduced in 1933. Of course, the Treaty of Versailles barred Germany from having a modern air force, so stealth and deception were in order. Willy Messerschmitt ran Bayerische Flugzeugwerke, and he understood what it would take to win a production contract. With his chief engineer Walter Rethel, Messerschmitt developed a prototype fighter with just a 32-foot wingspan; it was designated the Bf-109. And the aircraft that would one day be the German Luftwaffe's leading fighter during the Battle of Britain was first powered by a British-built Rolls Royce Kestrel engine of 695 h.p., which (believe it or not) the British firm tested in a German-built Heinkel He-70 flying test bed.

The interesting history of the Bf-109 continued. Judged superior to other German designs submitted by Focke-Wulf, Arado and Heinkel, Willy Messerschmitt was anxious to validate his new design. During the Spanish Civil War, Messerschmitt sent pre-production prototypes to Spain for an in-theater combat evaluation. Beginning in April 1937, production model Bf-109Bs were sent to German squadrons and, while the low-powered fighter boasted a top speed of less than 290 m.p.h., it proved to be highly effective. At this point, Messerschmitt had the right airframe but the wrong engine for his evolving new fighter. That would change. By early 1939 the Bf-109 had undergone several engine and armament changes. At that time the more powerful and reliable Daimler-Benz DB-601 powerplant was used, with the armament typically being four machine guns, two mounted in the nose and two in the wings. But the appearance of the Hurricane and Spitfire forced changes in armament and continued engine improvement by Messerschmitt, as the company was by then called.

Anticipating that speed, range and firepower would be important in any conflict with Britain, Messerschmitt's armament scheme completely changed. To match its British counterparts, all weapons would be mounted in the wing and outside the propeller arc. But most significantly, the Bf-109E-4 version would come with two machine guns and two cannon. The powerful cannon could quickly destroy an enemy fighter that came into its gunsight, although the shells could also pass through the Hurricane's fabric and inflict far less damage than a Spitfire would receive. Like the Spitfire, the Bf-109 had significant range limitations, and that would limit its effectiveness in cross Channel offensive operations. A drop tank equipped version – the Bf-109E-7 – did appear before the Battle of Britain ended, but it was unreliable and was not used in large numbers. The Bf-109 was in many ways the equal of the Spitfire but, as an escort that had to fly across the English Channel before the bombing targets were reached, the Luftwaffe had a big disadvantage. Britain's secret Chain Home radar stations and the number of Hurricanes available for attacking German bombers blunted the Bf-109's effectiveness as a fighter escort over Britain.

As the Battle of Britain drew to a close in October 1940, both Britain and Germany showed the world that they had formidable, world-class fighters. And both the Bf-109 and Spitfire would undergo changes to boost range and performance. Messerschmitt introduced the –F version of the Bf-109 in March 1941. By the time the Bf-109F airframe was married to the Daimler-Benz DB601E-1 engine (in the F-4 version), the fighter also had a much improved version of the MG 151 cannon –

vastly superior to the firepower of Allied fighters. In time, the Griffon-powered Spitfires would provide a big boost in performance over the earlier Messerschmitts, but that would change again when the later (and more powerful) Bf-109Gs entered service. Like the Spitfire, the Bf-109 remained in production throughout the war. More than 33,000 copies of the German fighter were built, making it the most common type of fighter during the conflict. And it was effective; the Bf-109 would shoot down more enemy aircraft than any other fighter during the war.

Like the Hurricane and Spitfire, the Messerschmitt Bf-109 helped advance fighter technology from the biplane era to a new world with faster, higher performance and more maneuverable monoplanes. Excluding the United States, that group of 1930s aircraft would determine the course of technology and influence the outcome of the approaching war. One more aircraft was part of that group.

• • • •

The great distance between western civilizations of the 1930s and the Far East was no greater than the cultural divide that separated the included nations. The very term Far East developed in the Nineteenth Century, when British colonial power was at its height. In the Eurocentric world of that century, the term Near Asia was used to describe the general area of the Ottoman Empire, with Middle East referring to roughly the same areas that are denoted in contemporary language, and Far East referencing the areas of the Eastern Indian Ocean and Asian Pacific territories. Japan, a critically important part of the Far East, had endured two centuries of seclusion until U.S. Navy Commodore Matthew C. Perry negotiated the 1854 Convention of Kanagawa with the Tokugawa shogunate. Also in 1854, Japan signed the Anglo-Japanese Friendship Treaty with Britain, a prelude to treaties with other nations in Europe and Asia. But despite these incremental changes, a huge cultural and economic divide remained between Japan and the rest of the world.

During the World War that ended in 1918, Japan allied itself with America, Britain, and France. In the Pacific, Japan's navy captured the Marshall, Caroline and Mariana Islands, all German territories, without encountering any military resistance. In a joint operation with Britain that became known as the Battle of Tsingtao, Japan's army landed at

China's Shandong Province, while Japan's navy launched seaplane raids from its seaplane aircraft carrier *Wakamiya*. It was the first time that an aircraft carrier was used at war. Japan's navy also patrolled the Indian and Pacific Oceans, protecting Allied merchant shipping from the German navy's East Asiatic Squadron and commerce raiders. Japan shed little blood or treasure during the World War, but it was well rewarded after the Treaty of Versailles was signed. German property and interests in China's Shandong Province were assigned to Japan, and it received mandated islands and territory throughout the Pacific Rim as a result of the League of Nations South Pacific Mandate. Japan had learned to work with the western world, but it did so on highly advantageous terms. So Japan's cultural and political separation from the western world continued, while in nearby China and Korea it favored territorial expansion. In 1931, Japan attacked and annexed the Manchurian section of China, perhaps the first overt act of what would become known as World War Two. In 1937 it attacked again in Wanping, southwest of Beijing. At this point, there was no longer any pretense of peace; Japan and China were at war.

By the very late 1930s, Japan was also in the midst of political strife at home. The expansionist political forces were dominated by senior army officers, and were aligned against the so-called peace advocates. The latter included Admiral Isoroku Yamamoto, the man who would later become known as the father of the attack on Pearl Harbor. Yamamoto was a naval aviator who had commanded the aircraft carrier *Akagi*, and was later the commanding admiral of the Imperial Japanese Navy's First Carrier Division. An astute strategist and tactician, Yamamoto had also attended graduate school at Harvard University in 1919-21. In America, the rising star of the Imperial Japanese Navy became an expert on America's industrial base, and closely followed U.S. Army Colonel Billy Mitchell's 1921 aerial bombardment tests of captured German warships. Convinced that a war with the United States would be disastrous, Yamamoto came to be regarded as a traitor by many militants and political activists. In August 1939, as the political situation in Japan deteriorated, Naval Minister Mitsumasa Yonai ordered the admiral to return to sea duty to avoid a likely assassination attempt. Japan was in a political upheaval, but the disastrous course that its militant rulers would pursue did not diminish the brilliance of its aeronautical engineering. That brilliance was in full display in what was then the world's best naval fighter: the Mitsubishi A6M "Zero."

A follow on to Mitsubishi's earlier A5M design, the Zero was designed to be a highly maneuverable, long-range carrier-based fighter. An improved fighter was badly needed. The development of the A5M began in 1934, at about the same time that Hawker, Supermarine and Messerschmitt were developing their Hurricane, Spitfire and Bf-109, respectively. But the A5M was an open cockpit, fixed-gear monoplane, and although it could operate from aircraft carriers it was 50-100 m.p.h. slower than its likely adversaries. Fully aware that the A5M would not survive in modern aerial combat, the Imperial Japanese Navy requested proposals for a new fighter.

In addition to increased speed (at least 310 m.p.h.), the IJN wanted range, endurance and maneuverability to accomplish its missions over the vast expanse of the Pacific Ocean. Because the range and endurance requirements were so strict, Mitsubishi's chief engineer Jiro Horikoshi had to keep the A6M's operational weight to an absolute minimum. As a result, the lightweight fighter lacked both an armor seat to protect the pilot and self-sealing fuel tanks. The A6M Zero was also was the first fighter to use 7075 Aluminum, a very strong alloy that Sumimoto Industries developed in 1936. Although susceptible to corrosion and expensive, the lightweight metal was strong and would easily withstand the flexing and bending that violent air combat maneuvers would often impose. With low operational weights, Mitsubishi's new fighter met the IJN's stringent range and endurance requirements. Requiring less power than evolving Allied fighters, the agile Zero was adequately served by its 950 h.p. Nakajima Sakae 12 radial engine.

The A6M entered operational status with the IJM in 1940 and quickly gained favor with its pilots. But the Zero's speed was close to that of the Hawker Hurricane and Grumman's F4F Wildcat, and slower than the Curtiss P-40 Warhawks that it would encounter over China and the Pacific. A superb dogfighter due to its high rate of climb and light wing loading, the Zero could out turn any Allied fighter at speeds below 200 m.p.h. Allied pilots were forced to use either hit-and-run dive and shoot tactics, or improvised tactical formations such as what came to be known as the "Thatch Weave." But the Zero operated in Japan's often extended backyard, and the combination of range and maneuverability made it extremely formidable until late 1943. Only a new generation of advanced Allied fighters would be decisively better.

• • • •

On 20 January 1937, Franklin D. Roosevelt began his second term as president. A former secretary of the navy and a staunch advocate of adequate naval funding, America's commander-in-chief understood that war in Europe and the Pacific was coming. But as with Winston Churchill in Britain, FDR's insights were not shared by most politicians or the remainder of the public. So slowly but surely, America began to re-arm. But aside from the Boeing B-17 Flying Fortress bomber, America was playing catch-up in aviation. Not only would the United States need new, all-metal monoplane fighters; it would need to come from behind and push the performance envelope out by more than one generation of technology. While doing that, the United States would need to ensure that new aeronautical designs were not too complicated to mass-produce, and perhaps quickly. But was all that really possible?

Aware of the formidable technological and manufacturing challenges that lay ahead, the Navy's BuAer hedged its bets. Instead of a single Request for Proposal for an advanced naval fighter, the Navy issued two RFPs: i.e., one for a single-engine and one for a twin-engine design. For the single-engine fighter, the Navy demanded the maximum possible speed, along with a stalling speed of not more than 70 m.p.h. (113 km/r) and a range of 1,000 miles (1,610 km). When Rex Beisel received the Navy's newest requirements in February 1938, he was well aware of the recent advances in fighter design around the world. Beisel also knew that other American monoplane fighters either had been, or were about to be, developed. In particular, the Curtiss P-36 monoplane that was developed for the Army Air Corps would soon evolve into the much improved P-40 Warhawk; that would be the Army Air Corps' first modern fighter to enter mass production.

The production versions of the P-40 would prove to be sturdy, and they would certainly be able to put up a fight. But with just a single-stage centrifugal supercharger, the P-40s had poor medium- to high-altitude performance. That and other limitations ensured that the Warhawk would be an interim aircraft, albeit a very important one. Likewise, Bell's unconventional P-39 Airacobra had several attributes but significant limitations in medium- and high-altitude performance. While its 37-mm cannon made it a potent ground attack aircraft, its dismal performance at altitude would severely limit its usefulness in air combat. Like the P-40, the P-39's importance to the maturing war effort derived mostly from the fact that it was available for production. Lockheed's P-38 Lightning, as revolutionary as Vought's coming design, was being developed but was not yet operational. So excluding the Army's P-38, the group of late-1930s monoplane fighters, along with the Hurricane, Spitfire, Bf-109 and Zero, were benchmarks that Beisel would have to surpass – and quickly.

Beisel and his team of engineers went to work and, to improve their chances of winning a contract, they prepared two proposals. One design proposal was based on a fighter having an existing Pratt & Whitney R-1830 Twin Wasp engine. The 14-cylinder R-1830 was well known to all military branches, as it was used to power the Curtiss P-36 Hawk. That engine would certainly satisfy the Navy's demands for reliability, but it would probably fall short of the blistering performance that the service really wanted. So Vought submitted a second proposal, which it designated as the V-166B (an internal company designation). This proposal was for a fighter equipped with the brand new, and much more powerful, Pratt & Whitney R-2800 Double Wasp engine. This was a logical move, but the unproven nature of the R-2800 made the corporate decision to submit two proposals a wise one. If the R-2800 was successful, the F4U would be far faster than any aerial opponent. The problem was with the uncertainties.

Pratt & Whitney's Double Wasp produced more power, and was substantially lighter, than the only other comparable engine – i.e., the French-built Gnome-Rhone 18L, an 18-cyclinder engine. And the Gnome-Rhone powerplant, while weighing more than 1,620 lbs, only produced 1,350 horsepower; it was wholly impractical for aircraft, and was abandoned in 1939. The R-2800 Double Wasp held considerable promise, but was still unproven. The biggest problem would be to dissipate heat from the two rows of closely grouped cylinders. To keep the cylinder head temperatures to a tolerable level, Pratt & Whitney used a radical cutting method to machine very thin fins that would dissipate heat from the cylinders. And then there was the question about power at altitude. The R-2800 initially came with a single-stage, single-speed centrifugal supercharger. In time that would be replaced with a two-speed supercharger, but would the original engine produce enough power at altitudes above 20,000 feet? Vought and Pratt & Whitney were hopeful, but until actual aircraft were built and tested no one knew for sure.

Vought's proposed V-166B was a bold design, but it offered the Bureau of Aeronautics exactly what they were looking for. In June 1938, the BuAer awarded Vought a contract to build a single prototype XF4U-1 aircraft (BuNo 1443). Every bit as radical as the Army's new Lockheed P-38 Lightning, Vought's design would be a game changer for the U.S. Navy. Pratt & Whitney's XR-2800-4 was the experimental version of the powerful new engine, and would power the prototype aircraft. And mounted at the front of the huge 1,805 h.p. radial engine was Hamilton Standard's Hydromatic 6501A-0, a giant 13 foot 4 inch, three-blade propeller. So large was the propeller arc that in order to provide adequate ground (or deck) clearance for takeoffs and landings, the main landing gear had to extend much farther than normal below the fuselage. That created a new set of engineering problems. Longer landing gear struts would have to be stronger and heavier than normal to absorb the stress of landings on an aircraft carrier. Yet the geometry of such an enlarged main landing gear would also create additional issues regarding stowage inside the wing after retraction. Beisel and his engineers instead opted for a radical, inverted-gull wing design that would reduce the distance from the wing to the ground. The wing would extend at a downward angle (anhedral) from the fuselage to the point where the main landing gear struts would be attached to the wing spar. Outward from that point, the wing would have a noticeable upward slope (dihedral) out to the wingtips. Thus was born the distinctive gull winged design. And the design innovations didn't end there.

Unlike other advanced fighter designs that would appear with radial engines, Vought eschewed either a bubble canopy or a "razorback" rear fuselage behind the cockpit. A long nose with a circular cross-section would instead lead to what was called a "bird cage' glass enclosure of a cockpit that was located back near the trailing edge of the wing. This all resulted in a big, brutish fighter, but one with a minimal fuselage cross-section. With enormous power and the minimum possible fuselage drag, the Corsair was not designed to be beautiful, just powerful and fast. But how well would this radical beast behave in the air? Would the enormous amount of torque and P-factor make the aircraft too difficult to control during takeoffs or rejected landings? And just how fast would it fly?

The job of giving this aircraft its aerial baptism belonged to Lyman A. Bullard, Jr., Vought-Sikorsky's chief test pilot. Bullard was an ex-Navy pilot, and he had several years experience testing Vought's new naval aircraft designs. But nothing like the XF4U-1 had ever existed before, so the new fighter would be Bullard's biggest challenge. The details of the design and development moved along on 10 February 1939 when – one year after the Navy's RFP had been issued – a mock-up at the factory passed its U.S. Navy inspection. With that approval, Vought-Sikorsky was able to proceed to the next step: i.e., building a prototype aircraft from scratch.

Beisel, project engineer Russell Baker, his engineering team and the flight test group all worked closely as the first (and only) aircraft took shape. The Navy had high expectations for the F4U, and was aware that the development would be extensive. But BuAer was not prepared for the plodding pace. A year after the mock up passed its Navy inspection, Vought engineers and technicians were still completing final modifications, rigging changes and pre-flight tests. There was a sense of urgency and excitement, but the details were endless. By the springtime the preparations on the prototype were nearing completion.

The first flight of an experimental aircraft is the biggest milestone between inception and production, and so it was with the XF4U-1. Not only was this a radical design; the company was betting its future on Beisel's creation. The eventful day finally came on 29 May 1940, and it was well attended by Vought officials. After careful preflight preparations Bullard taxied the yellow-winged prototype to runway 29 at Bridgeport Airport, lined up on the centerline and accelerated rapidly down the runway. The new fighter gracefully lifted off the pavement and climbed quickly into the morning sky. Bullard headed east of the airport for some preliminary tests, arriving over the Yale Bowl at 6,000 feet. But then, just a matter of minutes into the flight, an emergency arose.

Bullard encountered a severe vibration, a shaking that originated in the tail and which was very pronounced in the control stick. The cause was an aerodynamic flutter that developed in the balance tabs that trim the elevator; that flutter produced the severe shaking, which was quickly followed by an in-flight separation of the damaged structure. Bullard was able to nurse the aircraft back for a no-flap landing, but it was a close call. Vought was able to correct the problem, however, and soon test flights of the experimental aircraft continued. On July 9th, Bullard began to share the test flying with Boone T. Guyton, another former naval aviator and the man who would become the project pilot for the F4U. Guyton's love affair with the big powerful fighter began immediately, and was not diminished as the result of a weather related accident that almost destroyed the prototype a few days later. Fortunately, the experimental shop was able to rebuild the damaged aircraft within three months.

In late September the XF4U-1 flight test program resumed. By this time Vought was under considerable pressure to explore the high-speed end of the flight envelope. The Navy knew that Vought's design was not lacking in power, but actually achieving high-speed flight was something else. Would the airframe and its systems, along with the huge engine and propeller all work as planned? It was now more than two years since BuAer awarded Vought its prototype contract. The Battle of Britain raged over England and the Japanese government was acting increasingly hostile, yet the Navy knew more about the Hawker Hurricane, Supermarine Spitfire and the Messerschmitt Bf-109 than it did about its own new fighter. That would soon change.

On 1 October 1940 Lyman Bullard again climbed into the XF4U-1 cockpit and went through his prestart checklist. He had already gathered considerable data about the mid- to high-speed performance with the Pratt & Whitney XR-2800-4 Double Wasp engine, but pressure from BuAer to define the high-speed portion of the flight envelope was intense. Was the XF4U-1 prototype going to meet BuAer's performance requirements? And just how fast could the Navy's newest fighter fly? His recent tests had shown that the two rows of cylinders were producing the promised manifold pressure, with engine temperatures remaining "in the green." Now it was time to prove what the new Corsair could really do.

After an uneventful takeoff, Bullard quickly gained altitude and maneuvered the Corsair southwest of the field. A few minutes later Vought's chief test pilot crossed back over Bridgeport Airport and headed northeast towards Hartford, home to the parent United Aircraft Corporation. The Connecticut countryside quickly slid past below, and after just a few minutes Bullard was able to reduce the power setting of his 18-cylinder brute. Hartford was already behind him, and Bullard's flight data card confirmed that the Corsair's true airspeed and groundspeed had averaged just over 404 m.p.h. Two years and four months after BuAer awarded Vought its contract, the U.S. Navy had its first 400 m.p.h. fighter.

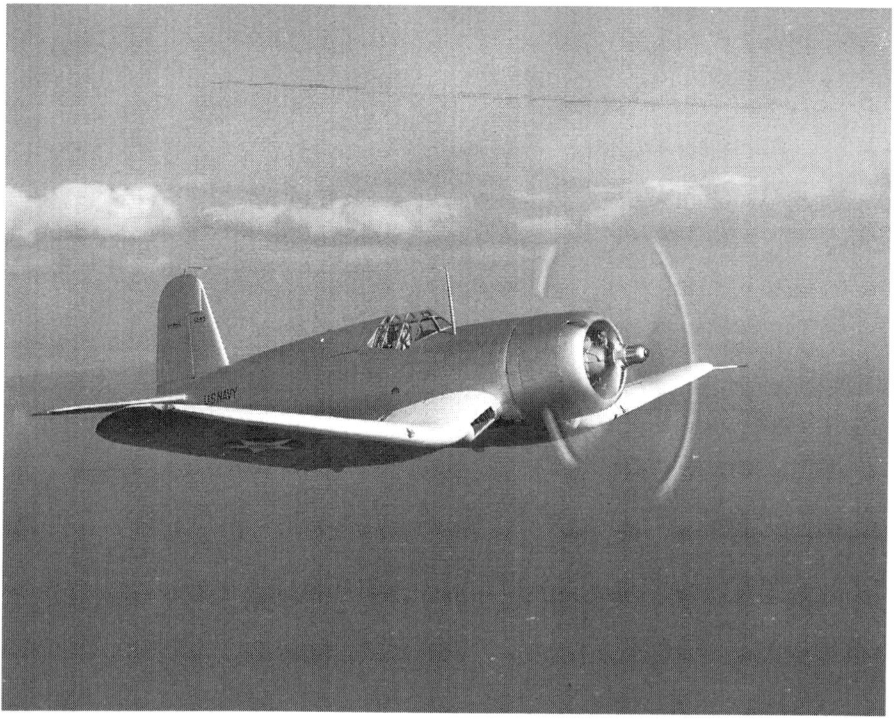
NAVY

Chapter Two

Ugly Duckling or Revolutionary Design?

The sum total of all of these innovations was a very radical aeroplane, but a revolutionary fighter . . ?

— Capt. Eric M. Brown, Royal Navy (ret.), the Fleet Air Arm test pilot who test flew the F4U Corsair, as related his book *Wings of the Navy: Flying Allied Carrier Aircraft of World War Two* (Second Edition).

Creating what would at times be the world's fastest propeller-driven naval fighter imposed some daunting technical problems on the Vought-Sikorsky engineers. The first set of problems had to do with power. The imperatives of very high speed and the capability to climb rapidly would require both an extremely powerful engine and a highly advanced propeller. The next big group of problems involved aerodynamic drag. Drag limits the speed of an aircraft, so determining the optimum size and shape of the airframe would be crucial to the success in meeting the Navy's performance requirements. As Chance Vought's chief engineer, Rex Beisel wanted to get the maximum amount of power into an airframe that would exhibit the least amount of drag. That was essential if Vought's next fighter design were to meet the Navy's performance expectations. Beisel wanted to do that, and more. But while the design problems were simply stated, the engineering solutions would not be easily attained.

For one thing, the Navy's next generation fighter would not only have to be very fast, but able to maintain a speed advantage during combat at all altitudes. And the new fighter would have to be able to operate anywhere from sea level to altitudes above thirty thousand feet, where the air was much thinner. To accomplish this, Beisel turned to a sister company. United Aircraft's Pratt & Whitney division had already developed an experimental version of its new supercharged, R-2800 Double Wasp radial engine. No American company could match the power of Pratt & Whitney's new engine and, with a mechanical, two-speed supercharger, it was expected that the R-2800 would be effective at altitudes above thirty thousand feet.

Concurrent with the design of the R-2800, Hamilton Standard – another United Aircraft company – had developed its Hydromatic A6501-0 propeller, a three-bladed aluminum monster with a thirteen foot, four inch diameter. This was a constant-speed propeller, so that as the pilot advanced the throttle in flight, the engine manifold pressure would increase – creating more power – but the propeller r.p.m. would remain constant. That was possible because as the engine produced more power, the hydraulic prop governor would increase the angle of the propeller blades to a more streamlined position. The combination of the engine's increased power and the more streamlined blade angle would minimize drag as the propeller pushed an increased volume of air through its arc. By keeping drag on the constant speed propeller to a minimum, the fighter would be able to attain the highest possible airspeed in any regime of flight. Beisel and the Vought-Sikorsky designers expected that by marrying revolutionary engine, propeller and airframe designs they would develop the world's greatest naval fighter. Working with nearby sister companies would greatly simplify the design process, logistics and cost, so Pratt and Hamilton Standard had Vought-Sikorsky's business by default. But from that point on, and despite those advantages, the marriage of the most powerful piston engine in America with a radical, low-drag airframe design would present unusual challenges.

Beginning with the circular frontal area of the radial engine, Beisel opted for a circular forward fuselage cross-section. Unlike other radial engine fighters that would follow, the Vought V-166B (which was the company's model designation) would keep a nearly constant fuselage diameter between the engine firewall and the cockpit. The tight fuselage cross-section did minimize the drag, but the big inverted-gull wing did not. Later on, other R-2800-powered

Ugly Duckling or Revolutionary Design?

fighters would appear, notably the Republic P-47 Thunderbolt and Grumman's F6F Hellcat. Both of these large aircraft had wider fuselage cross-sections and took drag penalties as a result. But even the big P-47 had a smaller wing, and that resulted in noticeably lower drag coefficient than the F4U. Several versions of the P-47 were faster than the F4U at higher altitudes, although much of that resulted from the power advantage of the P-47's turbocharger in thinner air rather than drag elimination. When it arrived in the fleet, the Grumman's F6F was noticeably slower than the F4U despite having roughly the same drag coefficient, although the Hellcat had a higher rate of climb. So Beisel's design concept of putting the biggest engine on the smallest possible airframe was sound, but keeping the F4U's weight and drag to a minimum would require a number of design innovations. And along the way, there would be a large number of changes.

The size of Hamilton Standard's Hydromatic propeller is clearly depicted in this wartime photo. Image source/credit: Courtesy of the Igor I. Sikorsky Historical Archives, Inc.

Developing the Gull-Winged F4U Corsair - And Taking It To Sea

The size and shape of Pratt & Whitney's radial, air-cooled R-2800 engine can be seen in this wartime production photo. Image source/credit: Courtesy of the Igor I. Sikorsky Historical Archives, Inc.

    One of the big changes involved armament. During the design process, the Navy decided that six Colt-Browning .50 caliber M-2 machine guns would be placed in the outboard wing sections, three on each side. Located outside the propeller arc, the positioning of this armament resulted in fuel being moved from wing tanks to a single 237-gallon fuselage tank that was placed over the wing. Placing the fuel over the wing afforded one big advantage; at any quantity of fuel, the center of mass of the fuel would be extremely close to the aircraft center of gravity. That eliminated a host of stability and control issues, but it resulted in the cockpit being moved rearward by 32-inches. That meant that instead of sitting above the wing (which is where the cockpit was located in the original version), the pilot would be seated near the trailing edge of the wing. That, along with the early model's lower seat position and "birdcage" canopy, meant that pilot visibility – especially forward over the nose – was extremely limited. This problem was most acute during low-speed, full flap landing approaches to aircraft carriers, a serious flaw that would never be fully resolved.

With most of the fuel being stored in the main fuselage tank, Beisel and Paul Baker (Vought-Sikorsky's lead engineer for aerodynamics) had to look closely at the wing design. Once again, nothing was as straightforward as even the experienced engineers might have expected. Early on it was decided that wing would incorporate a conventional, non-laminar airfoil. Typical for late-1930s fighter aircraft, the NACA 2415 airfoil would generate sufficient lift at low speeds, but without being too thick for the high airspeeds for which the F4U was being designed. With a 41-foot wingspan the Corsair would have a wing area of 314 sq. ft. and, with trailing edge flaps that could be extended downward at a sixty-degree angle, there would be lots of additional lift available for takeoffs and landings on short aircraft carrier flight decks. However, the non-laminar profile imposed significant limitations on high-speed dives due to mach effect and compressibility issues; this became a factor as aircraft velocity exceeded roughly two-thirds of the speed of sound.

The aerodynamic problems associated with compressibility and high-speed buffeting were encountered during flight tests by project pilot Boone T. Guyton. The dive tests that Guyton performed were dangerous. There was limited knowledge about aerodynamic factors at high subsonic mach numbers in 1940-44, and several manufacturers lost pilots and aircraft during high-speed dives. Working closely with William Schoolfield, Vought-Sikorsky's aerodynamics expert, Guyton was able to design a flight test regiment that pushed the Corsair well beyond 500 m.p.h. and into the regime of compressibility. The high-velocity dive tests were accomplished in July 1942, in an era before machmeters or true airspeed indicators were available; mach-trim compensators had yet to be conceived.

The F4U was the first American fighter to explore the dangerous area of high-speed compressibility, although Lockheed's P-38 and Republic's F6F would soon follow. When the F4U dive tests were completed and the data analyzed, it was determined that at altitudes above the mid-twenty thousand foot level the velocity had to be limited. In the F4U this would be where the indicated airspeed was equivalent to roughly Mach 0.72. While operations below Mach 0.72 would be more than enough for most combat maneuvering, steep dives from higher altitudes would have to be restricted to avoid loss of control due to compressibility and mach-tuck. Later fighters such as North American Aviation's P-51 Mustang mitigated this problem by using a laminar flow wing design; this delayed the onset of high speed buffeting and resulted in a higher critical mach number. But the Vought-Sikorsky wing design was pretty well established by early 1940, and the existing airfoil would be retained as the aircraft moved through flight testing, Navy acceptance tests and into production.

In selecting the NACA 2415 airfoil, Beisel's design team expected to have a wing that would produce sufficient lift at the low takeoff and landing speeds that aircraft carrier operations required. But while the F4U's airfoil was very conventional, the rest of the wing design was not. One of the first problems dealt with the geometry of the main landing gear. The typical landing gear in use during the late 1930s to early 1940s was the conventional gear – i.e., a main landing gear near the wing, and a tail wheel. This resulted in a nose high, tail low attitude for taxiing, the initial takeoff roll, and landing flare out. With this configuration, the massive Hamilton Standard propeller's size presented a problem. The main landing gear struts could not be too long; they had to be capable of absorbing highly imperfect, hard landings on the decks of aircraft carriers. Moreover, the 5.5:1 aspect ratio of the wing imposed limits on the size of the main landing gear strut, since the gear would have to fully retract within the wing. If the main landing gear struts were too long, they would be too weak and would protrude beyond the trailing edge of the wing after retracting rearward.

Unwilling to make major changes in the wing airfoil or aspect ratio, Beisel and his team adapted the now famous inverted gull wing design to ensure that while on the ground (or deck) the main gear wheels would be lower than the prop. Although revolutionary for a front-line naval fighter, the inverted gull wing configuration had been used in military aircraft before. The most famous example was the Junkers Ju-87 Stuka dive bomber, well known as a result of its service with the Condor Legion during the Spanish civil war, and even more famous when Germany invaded Poland in September 1939. Using a similar type of inverted gull wing configuration, the XF4U-1 main landing gear struts would be attached to the wing spar at the bottom of the dip in the gull wing. Attaching the gear strut to the low point of the wing would minimize the length of the strut while ensuring adequate prop clearance during ground operations, including takeoffs and landings. Then, by rotating the struts ninety degrees as they retracted in a rearward motion, the relatively short main landing gear would fit completely inside the wing in the wheel wells. So the inverted-gull wing design and the shorter main landing gear solved several problems at once, reaffirming the truism that form often follows function.

Once the overall shape of the wing was determined, the next issue was to ensure that it would be strong enough to withstand the extreme stresses of combat maneuvering and the often hard landings that occur on aircraft carriers. This began by designing a very strong center section, with the main spar extending through the center section box without interruption. Although the resulting wing center section was heavier than a more conventional design, the right angle at which the inboard wing sections joined the fuselage eliminated the need for wing fairings. The wing center section, including the inverted gull portion, was assembled as one-piece and was easily mated to the fuselage during production. At the outboard portion of the center section (i.e., where the anhedral ended and the dihedral began), a wing folding system permitted the outboard wing sections to be folded rearward for storage onboard a ship.

The F4U wing design would be the fighter's most distinguishing characteristic, but other less noticeable design features were also significant. Continuing outboard on the wing, the outer sections extended from center section to the wing tips. Just outboard from the three machine guns and ammo boxes in the outer section, many F4U versions housed 62-gallon wing fuel tanks to supplement the fuselage fuel. Unlike the fuselage tanks, the wing tanks were not self-sealing (to keep the weight down). The outboard sections had just one load-carrying spar, but it was strongly built and would prove to be sufficient. The main spar was positioned at 30% of the mean aerodynamic chord (MAC), meaning that it was three-tenths of the way back from the leading edge. Behind the main spar, the metal framework of the wing included conventional wing ribs that ran fore and aft, and a trailing edge spar.

Much of the outer wing design was very conventional, yet it exhibited an interesting mix of both old and new technology. Virtually all of the outer section skin was a fabric covering, an anachronism that would later prove to be inadequate during high speed dives in combat. The outer section trailing edge spar supported the outboard flaps and the ailerons, with the latter being of wooden construction (including a plywood surface) and a protective fabric covering. So Vought-Sikorsky's revolutionary fighter, able to dive at speeds where it was mach-limited rather than airspeed limited (and where parts of the tail would actually be supersonic), was built with liberal amounts of fabric, dope and plywood!

At the end of each wing outboard section were the wingtips, and this time the material of choice changed to something more modern – i.e., plastic. The plastic wingtips bore no structural loads, and they could easily be unscrewed and replaced. The wingtips on Corsairs that were destined for Fleet Air Arm squadrons of Britain's Royal Navy were eventually clipped by eight inches, and were less rounded. That permitted the Corsairs to be stored on Royal Navy aircraft carriers, where the below deck hangar ceilings were lower than in their American counterparts due to the armored flight decks. The clipped wingtips would be only one of several changes that the Royal Navy required for its Fleet Air Arm aircraft, as will be discussed later.

The inverted-gull geometry of the wing and the air intakes at the leading edge wing root are clearly shown in this Vought-Sikorsky image. Image source/credit: Courtesy of the Igor I. Sikorsky Historical Archives, Inc.

Ugly Duckling or Revolutionary Design?

The F4U configuration, once the cockpit was moved aft to accommodate the fuselage fuel tank, would remain relatively unchanged during its decade-long production. In this regard, the Corsair was much like other fighters. But among the single-engine fighters, the Corsair had a somewhat longer nose than most. This would significantly impair forward visibility for any ground of flight operation where the aircraft stance was the tail-low, three-point attitude of a full-stall landing, or an initial takeoff roll. The geometry of the long nose resulted in nicknames like "Hog Nose" and even less polite expressions. The distinctive inverted gull wing made the Corsair easily recognizable, although not necessarily beautiful.

Other anomalies would not be as apparent on the F4U, except perhaps to pilots and ground crews. Egress to the cockpit was accomplished by climbing onto the low point of the right wing trailing edge, walking forward on the wing walkway, and then stepping up into the cockpit. Compared to contemporary fighters, the Corsair cockpit was spacious – perhaps a little too much for shorter pilots who either couldn't reach the rudder pedals easily, or who had difficulty seeing forward. Also unusual was the lack of a cockpit floor. Anything that a pilot dropped would have a long fall, while negative G-loading could dislodge missing items such as maps, cigarette butts, and the usual debris.

Other attributes of the design were not visible, but became apparent during combat operations. The superb Pratt & Whitney R-2800 series engines were extremely rugged. Battle damage, including damage to, or the loss of, one or more cylinders would usually not stop the engine. The self-sealing feature of the fuselage fuel tank added roughly one hundred eighty pounds to the aircraft empty weight, but it would save many lives in combat. So too did the armor around the pilot seat and the areas forward of the cockpit. The ability to withstand considerable damage from enemy fire and still bring the pilot home inspires confidence in a tactical aircraft. The F4U Corsair had that in abundance.

In considering an aircraft design, one must also consider the design changes that occur during the production run. The F4U-1 version included an increase in the aileron span and the addition of balance tabs. This improved the roll capabilities and the ease of operation. Raising the pilot seat seven inches provided a marginal but important improvement in visibility, as did the replacement of the original "bird cage" canopy with the much-preferred bubble. Improvements to the main landing gear strut "de-bounced" the Corsair, a critical and necessary improvement for safe shipboard operation. An extended tail wheel strut and an improved tail wheel helped improve landing and rollout characteristics. The addition of a roughly six-inch stall strip to the right outboard wing leading edge helped to improve the often-bad stall characteristics, although it didn't lower the stall speed. That often made the difference between a safe landing and a crash into the ship's stern.

Not all of these changes originated with Vought engineers. Many were introduced as a result of demands from squadron pilots, mechanics and depot level technicians. A number of mods started as field modifications to meet immediate operational needs, and then migrated back to the factory. And then there was the giant Pratt & Whitney R-2800 series engine.

Early on, the XF4U-1 utilized the R-2800-4, with a sea level takeoff power rating of 1,850 h.p. The ubiquitous F4U-1 began with the R-2800-8, having a military power rating of 2,000 h.p. With the R-2800-8W, combat power at sea level rose to 2,135 h.p., while at 17,000 feet it could still muster almost 1,975 h.p. When the F4U-4 appeared in 1944, the R-2800-18W provided a combat power rating of 2,380 h.p. at sea level, and 2,080 at over 23,000 feet. By that time the original three-bladed Hamilton Standard Hydromatic propeller had become an even smoother running, and more capable, four-blade design. In all, several thousand design changes were incorporated into the various F4U Corsair versions during a production run that extended through two separate wars. And all of the design changes and improvements floated on a rising sea of technological change.

• • • •

By 1940, significant advances were being applied to many critical technologies. For reciprocating engines, these included multi-stage superchargers and turbochargers, constant-speed metal propellers, and hydraulic accumulators to permit propeller feathering. Aircraft manufacturing benefited greatly from improvements in machines and tool design, improved materials, advances in metallurgy, and the development of new plastics. Manufacturing methods were changing to reflect the mass production methods of the auto industry. With the cessation of civilian auto production by 1942, many automobile factories were converted to aircraft production. There was a slowly expanding body of knowledge about flight in subsonic and transonic regimes of flight; this would accelerate rapidly in the later phases of the war.

The advancement of these technologies was to a large extent driven by the necessities of war. But years before the United States formally entered the Second World War, advancing technology and increased military preparations resulted in a trio of American fighter aircraft that were revolutionary in design, critical to the war effort and historically significant. From an operational perspective, each of these revolutionary aircraft would have superior performance, and would (in mature production versions) be capable of exceeding 400 m.p.h. in level flight. Of these, only one – the Vought F4U Corsair – was a naval fighter, but to fully appreciate the F4U the significance of the other two must be understood.

The first aircraft of the American trio was the Lockheed P-38 Lightning, conceived by an executive named Hall Hibbard and the brilliant engineer Clarence P. "Kelly" Johnson. The P-38 was Lockheed's response to a February 1937 request for proposal from the U.S. Army Air Corps. The Army wanted a high-speed, highly armed fighter interceptor that would be capable of engaging in aerial combat at higher altitudes. In particular, a maximum speed of 360 m.p.h. (580 km/hr), a time-to-climb requirement of reaching an altitude of 20,000 ft (6,100m) in six minutes, and the capability of carrying 1,000 lb (454 kg) of armament were specified. February 1937 was a full year before the Navy's Bureau of Aeronautics issued its requirements for what would become the Vought F4U, and at a time when the Air Corps operated a mix of biplane and monoplane aircraft.

Lockheed began its design work immediately, and was awarded a contract for a single XP-38 in June 1937. To meet the demanding Army Air Corps performance requirements, Johnson devised a radical airframe for the single-pilot, twin-engine aircraft. Behind each of the Allison 1,150 h.p. V-1710 engines was a long boom, each of which held the General Electric turbochargers (often called turbosuperchargers) and other accessories. Besides providing a streamlined housing for the various subsystems and components, the booms provided a place to enclose the retracted main landing gears. And at their aft location, the twin booms also

Developing the Gull-Winged F4U Corsair - And Taking It To Sea

provided structural support for the very wide horizontal tail and the left and right vertical stabilizers. Once again form followed function, as it was the Army Air Corps' choice of engines and systems that resulted in the very distinction twin-boom airframe design.

There were other notable design features. One of the most notable decisions involved the induction air system for each engine. Instead of using conventional superchargers to boost high-altitude engine performance, the P-38 used turbocharger compressors (one for each engine), and the most logical placement was behind each engine in the respective boom. The turbochargers would use engine exhaust gas pressure to drive a turbine; the latter would compress incoming air so that each engine could produce greater manifold pressure (i.e., power), especially in the thinner air above 20,000 ft. The compressed air from the turbocharger's compressor would be directed to and cooled by intercoolers (basically air-to-air heat exchangers) that were initially placed in the outboard wing leading edges. The cooling system also included ethelyn glycol coolant, a tank, along with plumbing and boom-mounted coolant-air heat exchangers (each basically a radiator). It was an efficient use of available space within Lockheed's radical airframe.

The electrical system design was also important, and it resulted from trade offs. To provide electrical power to the 24-volt electrical system, the left engine drove a single shaft-mounted generator. The P-38 was a large fighter and, unlike most aircraft, the pitch of the propellers was controlled electrically, not hydraulically. Having a generator on each of the two engines would have been desirable from a systems perspective, but even in a large fighter space within the streamlined enclosures was limited. Minimizing weight was another design imperative. So Lockheed's P-38 had only one generator to power the aircraft electrical system, including the extra demands of feathering either of the Curtiss Electric propellers during an emergency. As was the case with Rex Beisel and the Vought design team, Kelly Johnson and his Lockheed engineers had to make numerous tough decisions to resolve a plethora of engineering issues.

The historical similarities did not end there. The XF4U-1 was nearly lost on its first flight when the trim tabs separated from the aircraft just minutes after takeoff. Shortly thereafter, test pilot Boone Guyton crash-landed the only existing XF4U-1 on a golf course; the plane was rebuilt although the Navy's test program was delayed for roughly three months. Lockheed also suffered from mishaps. At the end of July 1938, the Army Air Corps secretly trucked the prototype from the Lockheed plant to March Field (California). Preparations continued, and on 27 January 1939 the very first flight of the XP-38 occurred – sixteen months before the first flight of the Corsair. Although company test pilots typically make the first flight and handle most test flying of a new aircraft, in this case the Air Corps remained firmly in control. The pilot on the first flight was none other than Lt. Ben Kelsey, the uniformed Air Corps official who wrote the requirements for both the P-39 and P-38 interceptors.

Kelsey's paternalistic nature was understandable. Trained at the Massachusetts Institute of Technology (MIT) as an aeronautical engineer, Kelsey spent the first part of his Army career as then-Lt. Jimmy Doolittle's safety pilot during the latter's 1929 "blind flying" experiments. A staunch promoter of fighter aviation, Kelsey was determined to buck the extremely bureaucratic Army procurement process and push important projects at all costs. So after the maiden XP-38 flight, Kelsey had Lockheed test pilots quickly complete some additional test flights and then (with approval from General Henry H. "Hap" Arnold) scheduled himself as the pilot for an attempt at a transcontinental speed record. The record attempt was made on 11 February 1939 and involved two refueling stops on the flight from California to New York. Unfortunately, the carburetors on the XP-38's engines iced up as Kelsey was approaching to land at Mitchell Field, on Long Island, NY. The resulting crash short of the runway destroyed the aircraft (Kelsey received minor injuries), but the XP-38 crossed the United States in an impressive seven hours and two minutes flight time. The P-38 program was set back as a result of the crash, but due to the exigencies of war production orders for 667 were sent to Lockheed by the United Kingdom's U.S.-based purchasing commission. Army Air Corps orders followed, and on 16 September 1940 Lockheed test pilot Marshall Headle completed a successful maiden flight of the substantially redesigned (and much improved) YP-38. Less than three weeks later, Vought-Sikorsky's chief test pilot Lyman Bullard exceeded 400 m.p.h. in the XF4U-1 on a short dash from Stratford to Hartford, Connecticut.

The design of Lockheed's P-38 Lightning began roughly a year before design work started on Vought's V-166B, which became the F4U Corsair. The Lightning, developed to meet an Army requirement for a twin-engine interceptor, was quite different from other Army fighters, and from the F4U. Excluding the Army's Northrop P-61 Black Widow (a large, multi-crewmember night fighter that was produced in very limited numbers) and the even rarer P-70 fighter version of the Douglas A-20 Havoc bomber, the P-38 was the Army Air Force's largest fighter during World War Two. In comparison, the F4U was also a large fighter, and only slightly smaller than the Grumman F6F Hellcat, but noticeable smaller than the P-38. Both the P-38 Lightning and the F4U Corsair provided significant advances in fighter aircraft technology and performance, and did so when biplanes and fixed-gear monoplanes were still in active military service. As to the historical question as to which aircraft was the first 400 m.p.h. fighter, there is plenty of credit to go around.

Lockheed developed the P-38, and flew the initial test copy, sixteen months before the F4U took to the air. But the initial version, the XP-38, was a slower aircraft; the higher true airspeeds for which it would be capable of attaining came later. Without seeing all of the flight test data cards, one cannot say conclusively what true airspeeds each aircraft attained as of 5 October 1940. In the absence of such complete data, we can at least say that at altitudes above 20,000 ft, under standard atmospheric conditions, several models of the P-38 were capable of exceeding that significant 400 m.p.h. benchmark in level flight. In fact, at altitudes above 25,000 ft, later versions of the P-38 (with substantially higher power ratings) were able to attain a level flight velocity of roughly Mach 0.60. This would put the P-38 in a flight regime where the aircraft would tend to be mach limited rather than indicated airspeed limited, and it speaks volumes about Kelly Johnson's brilliant design, Lt. Ben Kelsey's advocacy of the Allison V-1710 turbosupercharged engine, and the exceptional job that Lockheed performed in integrating the airframe, engine, propeller and systems. So one can say that the P-38 was the first 400 m.p.h. fighter design, even if it took later versions of the Allison engine to attain that magic number. It is likely that the XF4U was actually the first fighter to exceed that threshold in level flight, albeit just barely. Vought project pilot Boone T. Guyton repeatedly claimed that the Corsair was the first fighter to actually exceed 400 m.p.h., and he was well informed on the subject. But even if Guyton was correct, the XP-38 design came first. So both aircraft deserve their share of historical credit.

Ugly Duckling or Revolutionary Design?

The other revolutionary fighter to emerge in this general time frame evolved into what came to be known as the North American P-51 Mustang. The Mustang evolved from the Army Air Corps (re-designated as the Army Air Force in June 1941) interest in using the liquid-cooled Allison V-1710 in a higher performance version of the Curtiss P-40 Warhawk. The aircraft that the Army envisioned was to be designated as the XP-46, but it turned out that developing this aircraft would have interrupted production of the P-40. Given the critical need for fighters, the Air Corps did not intend to slow down the P-40 production line. But the Air Corps did bring the concept to the British purchasing commission, with the proviso that it be manufactured by a company with production capacity to spare. The Air Corps also stipulated that the manufacturer would be able to purchase the engineering data that the National Advisory Committee for Aeronautics (NACA) had developed for a high-speed, laminar flow airfoil. The company that could meet those requirements was the relatively small North American Aviation of Inglewood, California.

Like what was then known as the Vought-Sikorsky division of United Aircraft, North American Aviation (NAA) had an rather unusual history. Formed as a holding company for airlines, it was forced to divest its airline subsidiary (except for Eastern Air Lines, which it kept until 1938) as a result of the Air Mail Act of 1934. In 1935, NAA president James H. "Dutch" Kindelberger relocated the firm from Dundalk, Maryland to the Los Angeles area to take advantage of the better weather for test flying. The firm occupied a facility of just under 160,000 sq. ft on the edge of what would later become Los Angeles International Airport, and across the street from rival Northrop. A veteran of Douglas Aircraft, Kindelberger was a good engineer and a sensational entrepreneur. NAA was able to work its way into aircraft manufacturing by building training aircraft, the most notable of which was the AT-6 Texan (known as SNJ for the Navy version, and as the Harvard by the RAF). By the time the British purchasing commission started looking for a manufacturer, NAA was highly qualified, underutilized and available. The British were very pleased with NAA's Harvard trainer, so discussions between Kindelberger and Sir Henry Self began.

From the beginning Kindelberger wanted the new British fighter to be an NAA design. A persuasive negotiator, Kindelberger convinced the British that rather than manufacture P-46s under license from

Curtiss, North American Aviation could develop a better fighter, and go into production faster with their own design. NAA purchased the NACA research data for $56,000, and development of their first fighter – designated as the NA-73X – began in earnest.

In developing what became the P-51, Kindelberger's instincts were good. North American Aviation had worked closely with NACA in developing the laminar flow airfoil technology that would prove so vastly superior at high subsonic speeds. In addition, Kindelberger knew that NAA had developed a new radiator for the Allison V-1710 engine. NAA's radiator utilized what was called the "Meredith effect" whereby hot exhaust gases were directed rearward to provide some jet thrust, thereby augmenting the engine's normal power. It took North American Aviation just 178 days to design, build and test fly their prototype. The maiden flight occurred on 26 October 1940, just three weeks after Lyman Bullard exceeded 400 m.p.h. in the Vought-Sikorsky XF4U-1, a more than a month ahead of the British purchasing commission's tight schedule. In time, the U.S. Army Air Force would adopt the fighter, although initially in a rather limited dive bombing version designated as the A-36 Apache. The P-51 Mustang designation would follow, and like the F4U and P-38 there would be improved versions, the most defining of which would be the P-51D. But the North American P-51, designed and flown before Pearl Harbor, would complete the trio of America's first, and most revolutionary, 400+ m.p.h. fighters.

Of the revolutionary trio, North American Aviation was able to move from the design phase to production with the greatest speed. Lockheed's far more complicated, twin engine P-38 took much more work before the substantially redesigned YP-38 was ready for production. Back at Stratford, Connecticut, Vought-Sikorsky struggled to make numerous changes in the main landing gear, the tail wheel, cockpit seating, canopy and cowl flaps, all of which were being done as that factory geared toward levels of production that would have been unthinkable as recently as 1938. America would soon be at war, and at the U.S. Navy's Bureau of Aeronautics, one overriding question still lingered. Would the fast but strange-looking beast with inverted gull wings prove to be a revolutionary performer in fighter squadrons, or a big and expensive mistake? Much test flying and developmental work remained as the calendar advanced into 1941. And as the Navy awaited its answer, major changes were sweeping across the factory floor.

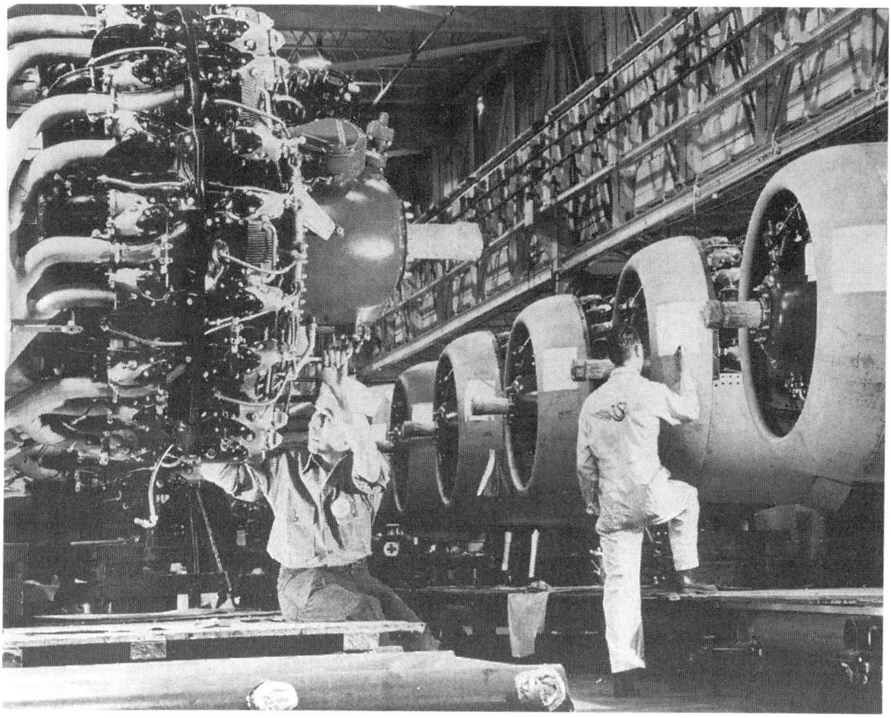

Chapter Three

At the Factory – Winning Through Mass Production

> *During the past year, American production capacity for warplanes, including engines, has risen from approximately 6,000 planes a year to more than double that number, due in greater part to the placing of foreign orders here. Our immediate problem is to superimpose on this production capacity a greatly increased additional production capacity. I should like to see this nation geared up to the ability to turn out at least 50,000 planes a year. Furthermore, I believe that this nation should plan at this time a program that would provide us with 50,000 military and naval planes.*
>
> – President Franklin D. Roosevelt, in his speech entitled 'Ominous Day,' delivered to a joint session of Congress on 16 May 1940.

In 1939, Chance Vought Aircraft temporarily morphed into the Vought-Sikorsky division of United Aircraft Corporation (UAC). Concurrent with that reorganization, preparations for war were already taking place at American factories. Driven by the confluence of technological advances, economic necessity and public policy, changes were being made at mills, factories and distribution centers – changes that were in some cases as radical as Rex Beisel's F4U design. The move towards wartime production was necessary to ensure that the huge quantities of aircraft, ships, tanks and other materials of war could be produced rapidly, using available materials, and at acceptable quality. Aircraft would no longer be handcrafted; that meant large facilities and the widespread use of assembly line methods of mass production. At the end of the Great Depression, American workers – men and women – wanted and needed jobs, so they went to work. As much as America's uniformed servicemen, their efforts in the factory would contribute to winning the fast approaching war.

Vought-Sikorsky, as a division of UAC, was fully engaged in the effort to ramp up to full wartime production. The Stratford factory complex, barely a decade old when the F4U first flew in May 1940, had already been expanded to accommodate the then merged divisions of UAC. When the two divisions merged in 1939, there was still sufficient room for Sikorsky operations and the existing Vought production lines, albeit just barely. In addition to the rapidly growing F4U program, the Stratford factory supported the development and production of other Navy aircraft, such as the SB2U-1, the OS2U-2 Kingfisher and the newer XTBU-1 torpedo bomber. A limited amount of scarce floor space was also made available for the V-156B1 (a dive bomber funded by the British purchasing commission) and the Navy's super-secret V-173, an experimental twin-engine flying wing. All of this was in addition to Igor Sikorsky's XPBS-1 amphibian, a four-engine naval patrol bomber and Sikorsky's experimental helicopters, the most famous of which was the VS-300. The XPBS-1 lost the design competition to the Consolidated PBY Catalina, and only three civilian VS-44 versions were ever produced. But the complex, which would be further expanded until 1944, would not support all of the full production of all of the aircraft types that it was developing.

As Sikorsky's seaplane business came to an end, his helicopter activities continued. By 1942, as the F4U-1 entered production, the Sikorsky R-4 helicopter – America's first production helicopter – was being readied for production. It was clear that the F4U and other Navy projects would by themselves use up all of the Stratford factory's space and capacity. So in January 1943 Vought and Sikorsky were again separated into their own divisions, with Chance Vought Aircraft remaining at the Stratford factory and Sikorsky Aircraft moving to its new South Avenue plant in Bridgeport. There, at its nondescript factory by Long Island Sound, Sikorsky Aircraft would manufacture the R-4. The R-4 proved to be an important success for rescue, medical evacuation and liaison missions in the Burma, China and Pacific theaters. The fabric-covered helicopter was primarily sold to the Army

At the Factory – Winning Through Mass Production

Air Force, but the U.S. Navy and Coast Guard also received some, as did the Royal Air Force and Royal Navy in Britain.

Even with a major expansion, the Stratford plant would have to give up more than the Sikorsky Aircraft operation in order to accommodate F4U development and production. By 1942 the XTBU-1 torpedo bomber, powered by the same Pratt & Whitney R-2800 that was used by the F4U, was running far behind schedule. Although it was an impressive design that boasted superior performance for a torpedo bomber, the U.S. Navy's Bureau of Aeronautics assigned production of the XTBU-1 to Consolidated Aircraft. Consolidated eventually built the aircraft under the designation TBY (Sea Wolf) at a new factory in Allentown, Pennsylvania, and critically needed floor space at Stratford was saved. With the completion of the two new experimental hangars, the top-secret V-173 was located away from production areas, and far out of view of even most military visitors to the plant.

Then there was the V-156B1 dive bomber. A limited number of these aircraft, originally destined for France, were acquired by the Royal Navy's Fleet Air Arm as SBU-2 Chesapeakes. These underpowered aircraft were also used briefly by the U.S. Marine Corp, where they were known as Vindicators. Unfortunately, the Chesapeake was completely unsuitable for use aboard Royal Navy aircraft carriers due to its very long takeoff distance. Realizing that the Chesapeake could pose a greater threat to Fleet Air Arm pilots than to the enemy, the aircraft was soon relegated to target-towing and training duties by the Admiralty. In a final bit of ignominy, the SBU-2 was replaced by the fabric-covered Fairey Swordfish II biplane, a much slower torpedo bomber but an aircraft that could be used on aircraft carriers at sea. As a result of the termination of Chesapeake/Vindicator production, more manufacturing space became available in available in Stratford.

The result of all these changes was that Vought would become focused on the mass production of the F4U and the OS2U-2 Kingfisher. Development of the single XF4U-1 into the F4U-1 production version would be protracted, a circumstance that kept the airplane's development chronologically aligned with the wartime plant expansion. And along with the expansion of the physical plant, there would be a much larger and more diverse workforce.

The Home Front

Even before the F4U-1 was ready for production, the tempo of the then Vought-Sikorsky division was ramping up. By the end of 1940, the factory employed approximately 4,450 workers, including production workers, plant and technical support personnel, professional design and engineering staff, along with a growing administrative staff and managers. 1940 was also the year the military conscription of young men resumed, so getting the right workers was not always assured. On the positive side, there were still substantial numbers of unemployed and under-employed workers. In 1939, the nation's unemployment rate was still an extremely high 17.5%. In 1940, as the nation ramped-up for war, the rate remained at 15%. There would be a large pool of available workers as the F4U project moved through its development phases and into production.

Vought-Sikorsky's preparation for the anticipated F4U-1 production further benefited from its location. The Bridgeport area was a center of manufacturing, and had been since the nineteenth century. Major employers included General Electric, Remington Arms, Bridgeport Brass, Jenkins Valves, Bridgeport Machine, Inc. and Bullard Machine Tool Co. There was a high level of knowledge of machinery and factory work in the community, even among some of the unemployed. And the manufacturing base of the city was heavily biased towards metal forming, millwork, machine and tool design and armaments. From 1938, Bridgeport Machine began producing what became the world standard small to medium sized vertical milling machine. Even earlier, Bullards became a world leader in the design and construction of vertical turret boring mills. While much of the F4U was constructed using aluminum (in contrast to iron, steel and heavier metals), the availability of workers with machine or tool knowledge was a big advantage.

Also with the ramp-up to production, many women began to apply for jobs at factories. In fact, during the war years the number of women working in the non-agricultural labor force rose by 50%. Vought-Sikorsky was no exception, and enjoyed the benefits of this trend. While most women applied without the benefit of apprenticeship training or experience building aircraft, many could be trained to operate machinery, install components and sub-assemblies, rivet structural components and spot-weld. With many young men enlisting or being drafted into the military, there were abundant job opportunities for women. There were also some interesting surprises; many women who were excellent at seemingly unrelated tasks (e.g., sewing) had good dexterity and became excellent assemblers, riveters and welders. In one instance with which the author is aware, a young teacher resigned her position to take a better paying job as a welder at Vought-Sikorsky.

By the time production peaked in late 1943, employment at what was once again Chance Vought Aircraft had roughly tripled from the already high 1940 levels to almost 13,450 workers (including professional staff and management).

Three women employed in the engineering department, located across Sniffens Lane from the main plant. Many women left jobs as teachers, librarians and retail clerks for the better pay and opportunities that the war effort provided. Morale soared as women joined the rapidly expanding company, as did production rates. Image source/credit: Courtesy of the Igor I. Sikorsky Historical Archives, Inc.

Of course, all workers had lives outside the workplace, and lifestyles during the war were affected by the national emergency. Rationing Boards restricted consumption of food, gasoline and textiles, and all civilian automobile production had ceased. So strict were the regulations that women had to do without silk stockings. Two-piece bathing suits became popular, as the design minimized the use of badly needed fabrics. Civilian travel that was not local in nature became more difficult. Strains were placed on personal and family relationships as many men (and some women) began military service, while others served the war effort by working in a critical occupation. As the nation went to war, Vought-Sikorsky and its employees were immersed in the war effort, the major lifestyle changes that it brought, and a new national psyche.

Materials and Machines

Despite the pressing needs of the Navy, the development of the F4U was protracted. Some of this was caused by the crash of the only prototype on 11 July 1940; that set back the program by roughly three months. The damaged aircraft was rebuilt and flying by October, but much of the flight testing and pre-production developmental work continued throughout 1941 and into 1942. The development of the F4U roughly coincided with significant changes that were imposed on defense contractors, many of which involved the control (and occasional rationing) of strategically important materials. The timeframe in which the physical plant was expanded to meet wartime needs was a factor in the F4U's development, as was the radical nature of the design itself. In the XF4U-1 and the production versions that followed, Vought was greatly expanding the limits of airspeed, altitude, g-loading and payload capacity. It was doing this with new materials and manufacturing processes at a plant complex with no direct rail links, and in a period where interstate turnpikes did not exist.

Because of the drastic changes that wartime production would impose on defense contractors and their suppliers, it was quickly realized that priorities had to be established for the use iron, steel, aluminum, copper, titanium, magnesium and other scarce materials.

This was initially the responsibility of the Supply Priority and Allocation Board. The Office of Production Management was responsible for ensuring that factories were adequate for war production needs, and that production output matched the myriad wartime requirements. After the attack on Pearl Harbor, America was officially at war and the federal government tightened its grip on production still further.

On 16 January 1942, President Franklin D. Roosevelt signed Executive Order 9042, thereby replacing the foregoing entities with an even more powerful War Production Board. Even aircraft manufacturers were affected, so design innovations based on the availability of materials became a norm. Although much of this federal control was anticipated before the attack on Pearl Harbor, the engineering decisions about which materials to use would not always be easy. For aircraft manufacturers like Vought-Sikorsky (and then Chance Vought Aircraft), decisions involving the use of aluminum and other materials were important.

Very strong yet weighing just one-third of an equivalent volume of steel, aluminum was the metal of choice for airframes. One of the boron group of elements, aluminum provided a strength-to-weight ratio (i.e., tensile strength/density) that exceeded that of any other metal. Aluminum structures could also withstand the stresses and pressures that even violent maneuvering could impose, a critical requirement for a fighter. Being corrosion resistant and easy to cold work, aluminum sheets could be stretched and worked into complex shapes having compound angles. Those properties were important, but the miracle metal was part of a larger technological development in aircraft design.

Until just before World War Two, it was common to design tactical aircraft with cross-sectional frames and longitudinal members that would carry the in-flight aerodynamic loads. These fuselage shapes were typically covered by a high grade of cotton or similar fabric, which formed the skin when it was stretched around the underlying structure. (Even the fairly recent Hawker Hurricane featured this method of construction.) But a newer method came into practice; engineers would design a semi-monocoque fuselage with pre-stressed skin that would carry much of the loads. In a semi-monocoque structure, the frames and stringers would mainly be used to maintain the form of the structure and, as a result, they could be much lighter than the frames in earlier aircraft. The worked aluminum sheets with internal stiffeners would provide a stronger and lighter fuselage, and do so with reduced aerodynamic drag. The drag reduction could be carried even further if rivets (including flush rivets) could be eliminated. This was all wonderful, but by the early 1940s (and when its availability was critical to the war effort) aluminum was in short supply.

    The root causes of America's aluminum shortage were disputed, although some parties contended that it resulted from a monopoly by Pittsburgh-based Alcoa. Of course, Alcoa was in the business of producing aluminum, which it accomplished by taking bauxite ore and then treating it through an electro-chemical process (the Hall process). Alcoa was regarded as being the leader in process efficiency, but concerns about the company's very high market share had existed for years. In 1937 the Justice Department brought a 130-count lawsuit against Alcoa under the Sherman Antitrust Act. The complaint alleged that Alcoa was operating as an illegal monopoly and asked a federal court to dissolve the company. The trial began in the Southern District of New York on 1 June 1938 – the very month that Vought received its Bureau of Aeronautics contact to develop the XF4U-1 prototype. In fact, when the United States entered the war on 8 December 1941, the Justice department was still seeking to have the federal court dissolve the nation's leading producer of a strategically important war material!

At the Factory – Winning Through Mass Production

Vought-Sikorsky workers fabricating sheet metal for an F4U fuselage. Notice the compound angles of the skin. Image source/credit: Courtesy of the Igor I. Sikorsky Historical Archives, Inc.

It would have been useful if at this juncture a settlement in the case could have been reached, especially with both the War Production Board and the War Department clamoring for more aluminum. And presumably the trial judge, whose courtroom was not far from the Brooklyn Navy Yard and Floyd Bennett Field, was aware of the ongoing world war. In the end, Alcoa won at the trial court but then lost on appeal due to a narrow reading of the law. But the litigation didn't end until many years later during the Korean War; by then the facts that were presented in the cause of action were moot. Alcoa may have survived because of the critical need for aluminum and its success in quickly adding wartime capacity. That, and the plodding legal system, bought it time. In fact, aluminum was so critical to the war effort that in 1942 two German U-boats delivered eight saboteurs to the United States; they were tasked with damaging or destroying major aluminum plants. Perhaps for good reason, the captured saboteurs were tried before a military tribunal rather than a civilian court.

So Alcoa, along with its competitor Reynolds Metals, were able to substantially increase aluminum output during the war years. Aluminum production climbed from 146,000 short tons per year in 1939 to roughly 800,000 short tons by the end of the conflict. But supply constraints early in the war were real, and neither aircraft manufacturers nor the war effort could wait. While this author is unaware of any archived decision documents, it would seem likely that Vought engineers considered various material options for the F4U. But the rationale for some decisions remains unclear.

Could some portions of the outboard wings and flight controls use fabric skin to save precious aluminum? Or was fabric used as a weight saving measure? The answer may never be known. But for whatever reason, fabric-covered wood was used instead of aluminum in building the ailerons. Fabric was also used as skin for the aft portion of the outboard wings, the elevator and rudder. Although not known at the time, there were drawbacks to the use of fabric. One of the biggest problems was that during high speed flight the fabric would bulge slightly, thereby increasing aerodynamic drag. But fabric did serve the most important need, which was getting Corsairs down the production line.

Similar supply problems arose with other materials, such as rubber. When America formally entered the war on 8 December 1941, Japan controlled most of the natural supply of rubber. Since rubber was an essential war material, synthetic rubber substitutes would have to be used. There were several examples of synthetic rubber from the 1930s, including DuPont's polychloroprene (now commonly know as Neoprene®), Goodyear's Chemigum® and BF Goodrich's Ameripol®. But once again, there was a supply problem: i.e., synthetic rubbers that were usable for tires, O-rings, engine gaskets and other components did not exist in sufficient quantities. And as if that weren't bad enough, the United States was falling far behind Nazi Germany in annual production of synthetic rubber. In 1941, Germany produced roughly 70,000 tons of synthetic rubber, almost nine times the total production of the United States.

Aware of the dire consequences of running out of rubber, the government created the U.S. Rubber Reserve Company in June 1940. This entity coordinated research, development of new polymers and production, with different rubbers being labeled with different 'GR' (for Government Rubber) prefixes. By the end of the war America had become the world leader in synthetic rubber production, with a total output of 845,000 tons. But it was a close call. Rubber was a critical material in engine mounts, gaskets, landing gear and tires, and a failure to quickly develop and produce synthetics would have crippled American war production.

The manufacturing process was also affected by the Navy's "buy-in" to Vought's basic design philosophy. Aware that the powerful F4U would be a relatively large fighter, the Bureau of Aeronautics was completely on board with Rex Beisel's design mandate of minimizing drag. This went far beyond the selection of a circular fuselage cross-section. Even with a minimal fuselage cross-section and a fully retracted landing gear, a substantial amount of drag could be created at the boundary where the aircraft surface met the passing airflow. As metal began to replace fabric skin in the 1930s, the process of riveting became the norm. Riveting aluminum sections of skin to the internal support structure was mechanically acceptable, but the exposed heads of rivets added to the parasitic drag. This was not a big problem with biplanes or slow monoplanes, but it would detract from the performance of a high-speed fighter.

Aluminum, the material of choice for most of the F4U's fuselage, empennage and wing structure, all but eliminated rivets and flush rivets in the skin; this would yield incremental but important drag reductions. This in turn meant that there would be a lot more welding. In general, welders require a considerable amount of specialized training and practice. But welding was increasingly being used for shipbuilding, automotive and truck applications, construction and (most recently) aircraft, so interest in the new welding technologies was keen in the Navy's BuAer. And as the F4U was being developed, the technology of welding was changing.

In 1939, General Electric's Floyd C. Miller published "Properties of Brazed 12% Chrome Steel" which focused on the mechanical properties of brazed joints. Two years later, Northrop Aircraft and Dow Chemical developed their Gas Magnesium Arc-Welding (GMAW). Then, in 1942, Northup's G. V. Pavlecka and Russ Meredith invented the process of Gas Tungsten Arc-Welding (GTAW). Many of the benefits of GTAW came later, but the technology could be used for welding magnesium, and later stainless steel and aluminum in the construction of military aircraft. GTAW is more commonly known as TIG welding (for Tungsten Inert Gas), or Heliarc. But while Northrop was looking for an ultimate metal and manufacturing process, Vought-Sikorsky – working closely with the Bureau of Aeronautics and the Naval aircraft factory (at Philadelphia) – kept it simple.

Spot-welding replaced rivets in many surface areas. Note the localized area of the weld. Image source/credit: Courtesy of the Igor I. Sikorsky Historical Archives, Inc.

With the F4U, fuselage sections were fabricated from relatively large sheets of aluminum. The sheets were pre-formed at the factory prior to assembly, and made extensive use of stiffeners on the inside. The external surface of the reinforced skin was strong but very smooth, all of which was possible by spot-welding the stiffeners on the inside and practically eliminating rivets. Much like a modular home that has plumbing and wiring pre-installed into each section, the fuselage panels had flight control and other subassemblies pre-installed on the inside of the skin panels. Also important was the size of the panels.

Larger fuselage panel sections eliminating issues that might arise while joining sections of different sizes and shapes to the frame. All of this contributed to the all-important need to minimize boundary airflow drag in every conceivable way.

Another external change that would impact the development of the Corsair's multi-role capabilities happened outside the factory, and largely went unnoticed. Technological advances in metal forming resulted in a new type of rolling mill, a watershed event that would permit the manufacture of improved radomes, antenna and components for airborne radar. Radar would be important to the F4U-2 aircraft that would be dedicated night-fighters.

Rolling mills are metal forming machines that can significantly reduce the thickness of metals. In general, rolling processes can be subdivided into "hot rolling" (done above the recrystallization temperature of the metal), and "cold rolling" (often at room temperature but always below the recrystallization value). Rolling mill machinery consists of rollers that are mounted to rigid metal frames which are typically aligned above one another, and which can progressively squeeze the metal to reduce its thickness. Hot and cold rolling enable mills to produce a variety of metal products including steel beams, galvanized steel bars, rolled brass and copper for electrical applications, and aluminum sheets for aircraft manufacturers. By the time that the F4U was being developed, the leading producer of these mills in the United States was the American Rolling Mill Company, Inc., of Middletown, Ohio – better known as Armco.

Armco's mills were in widespread use in a variety of industries, and were instrumental in the rapid expansion of American production capacity for the war effort. Then, in October 1940 – the month that Lyman Bullard pushed the XF4U-1 past the 400 m.p.h. benchmark – leading scientists secretly began work on a special project at what was called the Radiation Laboratory at the Massachusetts Institute of Technology (MIT). A direct result of collaboration with Britain, the Radiation Lab (often called the "Rad Lab") was responsible for developing a high frequency, microwave wavelength radar system as quickly as possible.

At this point in the war, fighter aircraft had no radar. In some areas (such as England), ground-based radar could detect enemy aircraft, at which point ground controllers could relay intercept information to squadron pilots. But such radar was usually not available, and pilots relied on good eyesight and constant scanning to detect enemy aircraft. A small, high-resolution radar that could be installed on a fighter would enable a pilot to detect enemy aircraft and intercept them at night – or in reduced visibility. The U.S. Joint Chiefs of Staff were aware that a decisive factor in the Battle of Britain had been ground-based early warning radar, so there was considerable military interest in such a device. By this time the British had invented a multi-cavity magnetron that was very promising. The magnetron was small and light enough for use on an aircraft, and capable of producing microwave emissions at wavelengths in the order of ten centimeters. The Rad Lab arranged to have Bell Laboratories design a production unit based on a proven eight-cavity configuration. But then a problem developed.

In order to work properly the magnetron required a very high voltage transformer, which in turn required incredibly thin sheets of silicon steel. The technology to make such thin steel did not exist; it seemed as if the Rad Lab had run up against a dead end. Determined to move their proven radar technology into production, the Rad Lab sought outside help. They first contacted Westinghouse, a leading manufacturer of electrical and electronic devices. Westinghouse in turn referred the Rad Lab to Armco, which confirmed that such ultra-tin silicon steel had never been rolled before. But Armco was soon able to develop (under license) a new mill that could roll silicon steel down to 0.002-inch thickness. With that capability, transformers for new microwave airborne radar could be manufactured. Along with Grumman's night fighter version of the F6F Hellcat, the Vought F4U-2 night fighter led America into a new realm of aerial warfare in the Pacific.

In the end, the design of the F4U cannot be separated from the selection of materials, or the manner in which they were used. One of the most interesting aspects of the Corsair design is that while it made use of pre-stressed aluminum panels and spot welding, its use of wood and fabric were a throw back to an earlier era that was obsolete. As the reader will see later, the extensive use of fabric skin would have some very undesirable effects in certain regimes of flight. But by the time that the limitations of fabric skin in a high-speed fighter were realized, the F4U was busy fighting a global war.

At the Factory – Winning Through Mass Production

Stratford Factory Complex Circa 1942-5: Assembly Lines, Mass Production and the Flexible Factory

As America slid towards war, President Franklin D. Roosevelt envisioned America as an arsenal of democracy. At the Stratford plant there was an interesting mix of change and constancy as Vought-Sikorsky, in lockstep with other defense manufacturers, marched to the president's beat. Some of the biggest (and most important) changes were in the physical plant.

In May 1939, United Aircraft Corporation approved the construction of a new engineering building at the Stratford plant. The two-story concrete and brick structure provided over 5,300 square feet of space for design, drafting, general engineering, and experimental labs. Soon to follow was an additional 64,500 square foot manufacturing area. Completed in July 1939, this addition contained a new boiler room, employee cafeteria, employee locker room and first-aid station. Then, on 21 August 1939, UAC announced a major ramp-up of its three most critical divisions. In particular, UAC directors had just approved a major expansion of the physical plant at its Pratt & Whitney, Hamilton Standard and Vought-Sikorsky divisions. Pratt & Whitney would see a 1.5 million square foot increase in manufacturing space at its East Hartford plant, located at the perimeter of Rentschler Field. Hamilton Standard, also in East Hartford, would receive another bay that would run longitudinally along the length of the building. At Stratford, UAC planned to roughly quadruple the size of Vought-Sikorsky's main manufacturing building. When completed, the wartime expansions would drive the total footprint of the complex to over 1.6 million square feet.

The massive expansions would radically alter the way in which Vought-Sikorsky operated, and would be undertaken expeditiously. To ensure that these projects proceeded on schedule, UAC retained the renowned architect Albert Kahn. Kahn was well known around the world as the designer of Ford Motor Company's mammoth Highland Park factory, within which mass production began with the Model T production lines. As America prepared for World War Two, Kahn and his engineers designed and oversaw the construction of 20 million square feet of manufacturing facilities, including

Ford's huge Willow Run plant in Ypsilanti, Michigan. At the Willow Run plant, Ford mass produced B-24 Liberator bombers using automotive assembly line methods. At its peak rate of production in 1944, the Willow Run plant was building 650 B-24 bombers per month – an astonishing airplane every hour, around the clock. It was a methodology that Vought would seek to replicate for the F4U, with only partial success. Kahn died in 1942, the year that his biggest Vought-Sikorsky project (Building B-2) was completed on the north side of the Stratford complex. Like most other Kahn projects, it was completed on time.

The build-out of the plant resulted in both qualitative and quantitative improvements to the manufacturing process. By 1941, north side additions included (in addition to assembly line and work cell areas) a new paint shop, a sandblast area, a new hammer shop and a deflector shop. As the expansion proceeded, two pads were installed as bases for new transformers, along with a new fire suppression tank and a pump house.

The large expansion of the factory in 1942, especially Building B-2, enabled Vought-Sikorsky to introduce a modern production line for the F4U. With the new assembly line and adjacent work cells, Vought finally moved from building handcrafted aircraft to mass production. A similar assembly line was set up for the Navy's OS2U-2 Kingfisher, a scout and rescue aircraft that was launched from cruisers and battleships by stern-mounted catapults. But despite the size and scope of the changes, much of the daily work routine remained the same – or nearly so. Piston-engines were still being mounted to airframes, airplanes were still being painted, and wheel & brake assemblies were still being installed to landing gear. The engineering and drafting departments were still there, although each was growing in its brand new building. To these constants was the one overriding change: i.e., many more workers were building many more airplanes, and doing this in a larger and faster moving process.

Among the most important process upgrades during the transition to mass production was the construction of the assembly lines for the F4U and the OS2U-2 Kingfisher. Installed in the new Building 2, the F4U production line began with sub-assembly lines for the various sections of the aircraft. The lines moved the assemblies on a conveyor system of tracks which, after a final curve, merged into the final assembly line. The sub-assembly lines were important. For example, on one of the sub-assembly lines the forward fuselage section (which extended forward of the cockpit to the firewall) was mated to the wing center section. The main spar carried through the fuselage, and was directly underneath the firewall, thus simplifying the assembly process.

The VS-44 marked the climax of Sikorsky flying boats. The size of the aircraft is a clear reminder of why Igor Sikorsky chose a factory site next to a river. Had the short-lived VS-44 program continued, additional production space would have been needed. Even when the 1942 plant expansion was complete, Sikorsky was spun off as a separate division and moved to a new factory in Bridgeport. Later in the war, production of the new Sea Wolf torpedo bomber was also moved as the Navy would not allow F4U production to be impeded. Image source/credit: Courtesy of the Igor I. Sikorsky Historical Archives, Inc.

Developing the Gull-Winged F4U Corsair - And Taking It To Sea

With the end of Vindicator dive bomber production early in the war, Vought-Sikorsky was able to concentrate on manufacturing the F4U Corsair and the Kingfisher. The Kingfisher was catapult-launched from U.S. Navy cruisers, and had a distinguished combat record as a scout and rescue aircraft. Image source/credit: Courtesy of the Igor I. Sikorsky Historical Archives, Inc.

On a separate line, the mid-fuselage section (beginning near the rear end of the cockpit and end ending forward of the stabilizers) was jointed to the aft-fuselage section. The entire tail section was built up, with the vertical and horizontal stabilizers being added. As the aircraft progressed down the final assembly line, hydraulic lines, control rods, electrical wiring, cockpit interior and other items were added. The long final assemble line ran parallel to the front of the complex (facing Main Street) and headed towards the end of the building, which faced Sniffens Lane. But the end of the line, the engine, accessories, propeller and outboard wing sections had been added, along with all of the other items needed to complete the airplane.

The F4U production line ended at the south end of the factory. There, completed Corsairs were rolled out of the building, inspected, and then towed across the street to the airport. From the Vought flight operations area on the Bridgeport Airport, each of the new aircraft was carefully test flown by one of the production test pilots. It was, by late 1942, a fast paced work environment, and more so in 1943 when production markedly accelerated. Yet even in the demanding work environment of the factory, human engineering was evident. In addition to a spacious new cafeteria and locker area for workers, music was played over loudspeakers. Providing a little peace in the wartime work environment was important.

Along with the new production lines, there were many new fixtures, jigs, presses and other machines; many had been installed in advance of the Pearl Harbor attack. Much of the new equipment was needed to expand and improve metal forming, machining and finishing processes, with considerable attention being directed towards aluminum alloys. There was also considerable outsourcing; many subassemblies with built by subcontractors and shipped to the Stratford plant, where they were assembled.

One point that should be made about the Vought-Sikorsky manufacturing plan is that of integration. Since UAC had its Pratt & Whitney and Hamilton Standard divisions involved in the F4U program, there was a large amount of vertical integration. That was essential, as the use of the R-2800 powerplant and the big Hydromatic propeller were integral parts of the F4U design. The same was not true with airframe subassemblies and other components. Here, outside supplies played an important role in fabricating portions of the wing and fuselage. UAC and the Navy's BuAer all recognized that with the F4U, Vought-Sikorsky was transitioning from a relatively small manufacturing operation to a very large one. To attempt to impose vertical integration on the entire manufacturing process would have been unworkable. The fact that other licensed manufacturers were brought in to the Navy's production scheme make this clear.

Other changes appeared in the manufacturing plan. A growing number of new Vought workers had to learn metal-forming skills for the aluminum sheets that would be shaped into cowlings, wing sections and fuselage panels. Considerable work was done near the assembly lines in work cells, an arrangement that was far more important than in automotive assembly. In several ways, Vought and other manufacturing companies were introducing some lean manufacturing methods fifty years before lean process design became common. But even with the huge expansion and the introduction of mass production processes to the factory, Vought was still operating with circa 1941 technology. And limitations of machine and tool technology had a definite impact on wartime manufacturing.

By late-1941, the F4U was roughly midway between the maiden flight and full production. It was almost a decade before even the most basic numerically controlled (NC) lathes and milling machines were available. In the pre-NC age of manufacturing, blueprints were used instead of programs and files; the widespread use of templates, cams and servo-driven machinery was the norm. Machine set up for repetitive operations was important, and required some level of experience, and the need for experienced draftsmen was acute. Blueprint reading was a must for skilled workers. So even with the addition of new employees, as the factory floor moved from pre-production prototypes to early production aircraft, all but the most basic tasks on the new F4U assembly line required considerable in-house training.

Some of the in-house training of new workers paid big dividends. For example, the elimination of most rivets from the aircraft skin reduced that application for riveting (although rivets were used internally on structures). But as Vought production managers realized, the use of pre-stressed stiffeners on the inside of the aluminum skin panels required a completely different skill: i.e., spot-welding. Spot welding is a technique that requires a considerable amount of skill and precision, but in a manufacturing environment it can be taught to workers having the requisite aptitude. So Vought was both a factory and a training school for assemblers, machine operators and both skilled and semi-skilled workers. It is a testament to the quality and dedication of Vought workers that the aluminum metal forming and welding technique were acquired and used with great success.

Vought was also able to compete effectively for workers. One production worker who was hired to work on the Vindicator dive bomber in 1941 left a job at a wire mill in Bridgeport. The wire mill paid $0.25/hour, a typical wage for a new worker at the end of the Great Depression. Upon arrival at Vought-Sikorsky, his hourly wage immediately jumped to $0.55/hour. By 1942 the Vindicator production ended, and workers were reassigned to either the Kingfisher or Corsair line. A six-day workweek became standard, and some Sunday shifts were necessary. With overtime pay on a typical sixty-hour workweek, Vought workers could maintain a solid, middle-class standard of living.

If 1942 is to be considered as a year of rapid expansion and the development of new skill sets, 1943 was the year that Vought's relatively new workforce matured. The flow of work on the newly created assembly line, along with the use of work cells, were especially important. There was a significant digression from lean manufacturing principles: i.e., the absence of *poka yoke*, or rigid quality control. However, the demands of the military were such that the production line had to keep moving. As the reader will see, some modifications (including high priority fixes) were accomplished on the assembly line, but many were also done at operating squadrons.

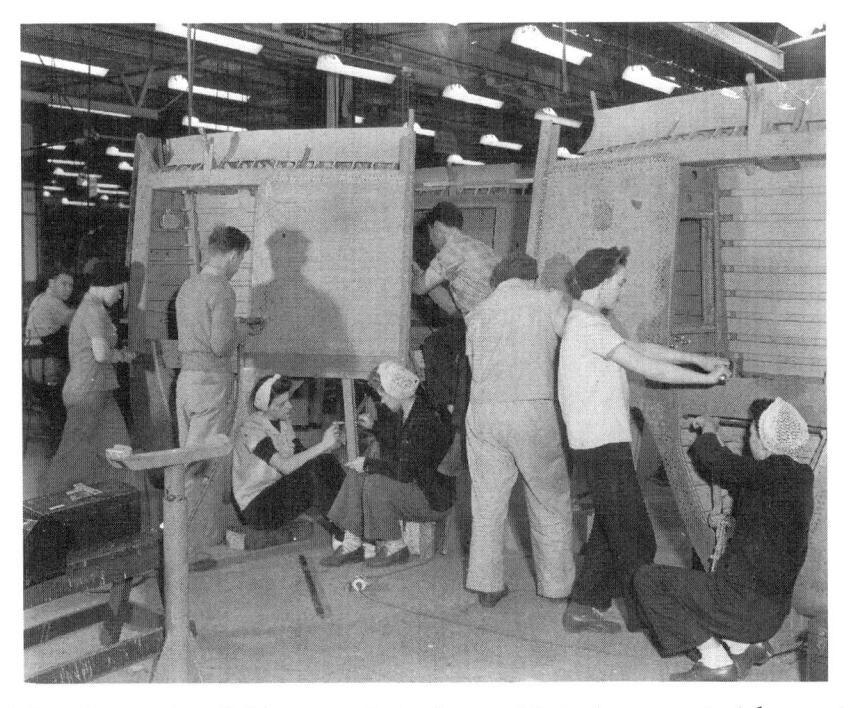

Workers in a work cell. These specialized assembly tasks supported the nearby production line, and were put into practice decades before lean manufacturing was studied in detail. Most production workers could hear the music that was played over the loudspeakers in the main assembly areas. Image source/credit: Courtesy of the Igor I. Sikorsky Historical Archives, Inc.

Within the Stratford complex, one of the major subassembly areas was devoted to the wing center section. The curved main spar (including the spar caps and web); the forward torque-box; the trailing edge spar, plus the stringers, stiffeners and ribs, and flaps all had to be fabricated and assembled into the center section. Since the main landing gear would join the wing at the low point of the main spars anhedral, it had to be built up and then joined to the wing at the main spar. Then the completed wing center section would be joined to the fuselage center section, and the F4U would begin to look like more and more like a completed airplane.

Other areas were used to prepare the already assembled Pratt & Whitney Double Wasp engine (with its accessories) for installation onto the airframe. And, of course, the big Hamilton Standard Hydromatic propellers had to be installed on the prop shaft as the airframe moved towards the latter portion of the final assembly line. So work cells supported the assembly line, and were kept in close proximity to the conveyor. Many of the structural sub-assemblies that required riveting, such as the box into which the landing gear would retract, were built up in work cells and then moved to the assembly line when completed.

Aside from the constraints of space, numerous minor – and some not so minor – design changes were incorporated right on the factory floor. For example, changes to the landing gear oleo and the right outboard wing stall strip, were largely imposed at the factory after field modifications were performed at operating squadrons. These seemingly minor changes would have significant effects during operation, especially in the critical approach and landing phases of flight.

Overall, the ramp-up to full production was far slower than the Navy desired, despite Vought-Sikorsky's wartime expansion and the transformation of the factory. Hence, the effort to keep up with the BuAer's production demands was pervasive. BuAer was well aware that producing all sub-assemblies and components at just one location would be too much to expect. As the reader will soon see, other large manufacturers would be licensed to take up some of the Navy's F4U production needs.

Workers swarm over an F4U at the eastern end of the main plant. Image source/credit: Courtesy of the Igor I. Sikorsky Historical Archives, Inc.

Radar: Incorporating New Technology During Production

As previously mentioned, the development of radar during the war would affect some of the F4U's varied missions. Interest in radar began as the U.S. Navy was bringing new technology to its warships. In fact, early radars had been tested on a U.S. Navy destroyer as early as 1936. But it was the January 1939 testing of radar aboard the battleships U.S.S. New York and the U.S.S. Texas during fleet maneuvers that made the big difference. So successful was the radar tracking of surface vessels, projectiles and distant aircraft that the Navy began ordering CXAM series radars, which evolved into a standard early warning radar for its capital ships. The development of the combat information center (CIC) on warships soon followed.

By the time that the XF4U-1 flight test program ramped up in 1941, the Navy realized that the potential uses of radar were enormous. Radar could be developed for tracking ships (ASV radar) and incoming aircraft; fire-control radar to aim a warships guns and AA defenses (the latter generally FD-series radar), and aircraft-mounted air intercept (AI) radar. The sharing of secret knowledge was helped when Prime Minister Winston Churchill sent the British Technical and Scientific Mission (the Tizard Committee) to the United States in 1940. One of the persons who became extremely interested in Britain's progress in radar was Rear Admiral Harold Bowen, director of the Naval Research Laboratory (NRL) in Anacostia, Maryland, and the former head of the Bureau of Engineering.

Bowen had been instrumental in the U.S. Navy's research in radar since 1935. In April 1937 the admiral made the service's radar program its highest priority; this paved the way for successful sea trials of experimental radar on a destroyer. This was further developed into the XAF radar prototype that was tested on the New York in 1939. After meeting with the Tizard Committee, Bowen realized that with microwave radar and multiplexing, a practical AI radar for fighters was within reach. Then, on 27 March 1941, an experimental radar installed on a B-18 bomber being utilized by MIT's Rad Lab was able to detect the outline of Cape Cod and numerous nearby vessels during an in-flight test. Of course, Vought was unaware of the details of AI radar development, but the NRL and the Navy's BuAer were privy to the top-secret advances at MIT's Rad Lab. So in November 1941, the month before the attack on Pearl Harbor and more than seven months before the first F4U-1 production aircraft was delivered, the Navy asked Vought to study the feasibility of producing a night fighter version of the Corsair. Then came the devastating attack at Pearl Harbor, with an immediate ramp up of activity.

The night fighter study was quickly completed in January 1942, as was a full-scale mock up. In due course this led to the conversion of thirty-four F4U-1s into F4U-2s (the night fighter version), with two more aircraft being converted to the night fighter configuration in the field. These special aircraft came with improved cockpit instrumentation (including a radar altimeter); an autopilot; flame retardant exhaust system modifications, and either an APS-4 or APS-6 radar. The radar was pod-mounted beneath the outboard section of the right wing, an asymmetrical location that resulted in one of the machine guns and some ammo being removed from the left wing so as to keep the aircraft balanced.

The final factory modification to the F4U-2 night fighter configuration occurred in April 1943; it was an extended process that was superimposed on the existing F4U-1 production schedule. To avoid interruption of the assembly line in Stratford, existing production aircraft were modified into F4U-2s with help from the Naval Air Factory in Philadelphia. This was perhaps the most important example of the marriage of a new technology with the existing F4U airplane to develop a new type of weapon system. Yet in a bit of irony, the installation of AI radar would produce an air intercept capability that would be better utilized in the Corsair's next war.

Vought Flight Ops: Experimental and Production Test Pilots

While physically separated, the Vought flight operations benchmarked the beginning and the end of the F4U production line. In experimental flight test, the test pilot performs the tasks that are necessary to validate a design before it is committed to production. Production test pilots, on the other hand, validate the service effectiveness and performance of manufactured products – each and every one – prior to delivery to the military. So they serve opposite ends of the production process.

As the F4U project developed Boone T. Guyton, still a lieutenant j.g. (junior grade) in the Navy Reserve, became the F4U project pilot. Once the F4U moved into production and the workload increased, the flight test department grew to a peak of twenty-three pilots, six of whom were in experimental flight test.

Guyton's autobiography *Whistling Death: The Test Pilot's Story of the F4U Corsair*, provides the best look inside the experimental flight test program. And Guyton is the one who took the biggest risks doing (among other things) the dangerous stall and spin tests, the high-speed dive tests, and the validation of the control system modifications, especially the ailerons. Guyton survived two flight test accidents, but just barely. Test pilot Bill Boothby was killed in March 1944 while trying to "bail out" of his F4U over Trumbull, Connecticut after an engine fire. Test pilot Dick

Burroughs died after the war, in July 1946. The engine of his F4U-5 failed, and he attempted a dead-stick landing at the Tweed-New Haven Airport. He was unable to make the runway. There were many close calls, but fortunately no other fatalities.

Group photo of Vought test pilots, taken in front of the flight test hangar on 22 August 1945, just before the end of the war. John French is the third from the right, with no signature. Some pilots were not present, such as Boone Guyton and Bill Horan. Photo courtesy of Sue French and the Connecticut Air and Space Center, Stratford, CT.

Getting test pilots during the war years was not easy, as most medically qualified men in their twenties and thirties were subject to military service. But some qualified civilian pilots were able to work their way in, and provided very good service. Bill Horan and Charlie Sharp, both local flight instructors, advanced from production testing to experimental test flying during their years at the program. John R. French, another local instructor, proved that perseverance paid off.

A flight student of Horan and Sharp, French went from being a student pilot in 1937 to a flight instructor for Army and Navy cadets at Turner Falls, Massachusetts in 1941. Having been a plumber for Vought-Sikorsky, French returned to become a security official at the Bridgeport Airport in 1943. French continued flying and was hired into Chance Vought's flight test department in early 1945, by which time he had logged a total of 1,591 flight hours. After a number of local flights in a Vultee military trainer, John French made his first Corsair flight on 11 February 1945.

All of French's production flight test hours were logged in the F4U-4 version of the Corsair, the most advanced version to see action in the Pacific. But by this time the war in Europe was about to end, and the war in the Pacific, while still very deadly, was entering its final months. F4U production was drastically cut at the end of the war and, as with most production test pilots, John French's relationship with the Corsair soon came to an end. His last flight in the F4U-4 was on 30 September 1945.

Many of the F4U test pilots remained in the area after the F4U program wound down, while others moved out of the area. Some remained active as pilots, while many pursued other careers. Boone Guyton continued flight-testing Vought aircraft for several more years, including the company's first jet – the F6U Pirate. He later held other positions with United Aircraft divisions. Charlie Sharp and Bill Horan became successful corporate pilots, with Horan becoming the chief pilot for Great Lakes Carbon Corporation. He spent many years flying DC-3s and a Convair 580 for GLC. Connie Grasso managed the nearby Monroe Airport for many years; he was the instructor who checked out this author in the J-3 Piper Cub. Grasso also held a job with Connecticut's Department of Motor Vehicles, convincing evidence that general aviation flying careers were not lucrative in the post-war era. John French continued his career with Vought, returning to his pre-war position as a plumber. Jim Malarky, who ran Vought flight ops as a non-pilot manager, later became the airport manager at Tweed-New Haven Airport. While at Vought, Malarky ran the flight schedule, supervised the new control tower operators and superintended Vought's massive new hangars at the Bridgeport Airport. It was a smooth running operation, and a great preparation for his career as a airport manager.

F4U being towed across Main Street from the final assembly area to the flight test hangars at Bridgeport Airport. Image source/credit: Courtesy of the Igor I. Sikorsky Historical Archives, Inc.

Corsairs Built Under License by Brewster Aeronautical Corp.

Well before the F4U was ready for production, the Navy recognized that even the expanding Vought-Sikorsky factory in Stratford would not have the capacity to meet wartime production needs. The co-location of both Vought aircraft production and Igor Sikorsky's helicopter activities was one of several problems. In addition, even if Sikorsky helicopter activities were moved (as they eventually were) and all other Vought projects were to disappear (and they wouldn't), the Stratford plant would still be unable to meet wartime needs. In addition, Vought had never managed a large production run for the U.S. Navy. So following what became a standard practice of assigning aircraft production to more than one supplier, the Navy made similar plans for the F4U. The result was that on 1 November 1941 the Navy designated

At the Factory – Winning Through Mass Production

Brewster Aeronautical Corporation of Queens, New York as an associate producer of the Corsair.

Brewster-built Corsairs would have the designation of F3A-1 (to identify Brewster as the manufacturer); this was concurrent with the Navy's first official use of the name Corsair in describing the F4U series aircraft. Unfortunately, the selection of Brewster as a licensed manufacturer was problematic from the start. The young company had some experience building aircraft for the Navy, notably the SBA-1 dive bomber and the notorious F2A-2 Buffalo. A monoplane fighter that had beaten out a competing Grumman proposal, the F2A-2 was Brewster's big hope for the future. But the Buffalo – often regarded as the worst fighter of the Second World War – proved to be far too slow and ineffective as a dogfighter; it was quickly withdrawn from frontline service. In addition, the fighters' main landing gear could not withstand the hard deck landings that were typical while operating aboard an aircraft carrier.

Despite the dismal performance of the Buffalo, Brewster was thought to have potential as a licensed manufacturer of another company's design. With a pressing need to build more Corsairs using Vought's existing design, the BuAer awarded the F3A-1 contract to Brewster Aeronautical Corp. What followed were a plethora of graft, mismanagement, labor strife and shoddy workmanship issues, with production badly lagging. By early 1942, Brewster defaulted on its obligation to produce the Buccaneer dive bomber for the Navy. President Franklin D. Roosevelt became personally involved, using his wartime authority and ordering Navy Secretary Frank Knox to take control of the firm.

Time passed, but there was little improvement. By March 1943, nearly a year later, not a single F3A-1 Corsair had been accepted by the Navy. A major part of the problem centered on the poor relationship with union officials, particularly Tom DeLorenzo, the combative president of the United Auto Worker's local chapter. Strikes (including wildcat strikes) and slowdowns plagued the firm at both its New York factory (in Queens, near LaGuardia Airport) and its satellite facility in Pennsylvania. The slowdowns were crippling production, but shoddy workmanship was equally bad.

The abysmal performance by Brewster Aeronautical occurred when the Navy was desperate for more fighters for the use in the Solomon

Islands and the Pacific. After the short tenure of a caretaker chief executive, the Navy installed a former Westinghouse executive named Frederick Riebel, Jr. as president. Unfortunately the labor unrest and production problems continued. In June of 1943 the first two F3A-1 Corsairs were finally accepted by the Navy, but at the peak of wartime production Corsairs would only occasionally emerge from Brewster assembly lines. In October, the Navy replaced Riebel with west coast industrialist Henry J. Kaiser as the next president of Brewster. In pressing Kaiser to take over the firm, the Navy was using its last best shot.

Henry J. Kaiser was one of America's greatest industrials, although his name was not as well known as others such as Henry Ford. Originally from upstate New York, Kaiser moved west as a young adult, eventually establishing himself as a contractor. After completing several municipal road-repaving contracts, Kaiser became a subcontractor on a $20 million road construction project in Cuba. It was not an easy assignment. The master contract was to build a 200-mile portion of the Central Cuban highway in that nation's Camaguey Province. Kaiser completed that job in 1927, and it positioned him for other major projects. Kaiser's firm played important roles in the construction of the Hoover Dam (1931), Bonneville Dam (1934) and the Grand Coulee Dam (1937). But as impressive as these accomplishments were, it was at his Kaiser Shipyard in Richmond, California that Henry Kaiser's manufacturing genius caught the attention of the U.S. Navy.

Kaiser Shipbuilding (plus its sister shipyards in Portland, Oregon and Vancouver, Washington) became world leaders in the wartime construction of transport ships (known as Liberty ships). Kaiser utilized modular components and lean manufacturing methods so that the ships could be quickly assembled at the shipyard. In fact, Kaiser was able to reduce the production time for some large vessels to under five days, to the delight of the Navy and President Roosevelt. The Navy even used Kaiser to build smaller escort carriers based on his record of performance. A great multi-tasker, Henry Kaiser also founded Kaiser Steel and later Kaiser Aluminum.

The Navy may have had yet another reason for wanting Kaiser to take over a company that was succumbing to labor strife. Kaiser was well liked by his workers for being one of the first major contractors to provide economical health coverage to workers and families. Kaiser's

At the Factory – Winning Through Mass Production

bold plan for a health maintenance organization (HMO) reached critical mass when he was a contractor on the Grand Coulee Dam project in 1938. He expanded this in early 1941 with his shipyards in California. By 1945, this would become the famous and highly successful Kaiser Permanente Foundation. So in October 1943, when the U.S. Navy wanted to give Brewster Aeronautical Corporation a last chance to perform, Kaiser acquiesced and accepted the service's plea for help.

Kaiser did significantly improve Brewster production, which increased from 14 aircraft during October 1943 to 123 during April 1944. But his efforts came too late. By mid-1944, Vought and Goodyear production lines were operating at peak capacity, and with no major quality issues. Although appreciative of Kaiser's efforts and his results, the Navy had had enough with Brewster. Kaiser, who worked without salary as a favor to the Navy, resigned in May; he had had enough as well. In July 1944 the Navy terminated all Brewster contracts.

Brewster Aeronautical Corporation has often been judged to have been the worst performing defense contractor of the war. In total, the firm produced some 735 F3A-1 Corsairs. A number of the Brewster-built Corsairs were sent to the Royal Navy's Fleet Air Arm, although most were accepted by the U.S. Navy. Yet once in squadron service, the sorry saga continued. Poor workmanship plagued many of the F3A-1s and was blamed for numerous operational problems, including some in-flight wing failures. Aerobatic maneuvers had to be banned in some of the F3A-1s, an enormous indictment of shoddy workmanship, but a necessary action even in the middle of a world war.

Corsairs Built Under License by Goodyear

The Navy's experience with Goodyear was the exact opposite of the turmoil at Brewster. Goodyear's factory was located in Akron, Ohio, and it was awarded subcontractor status in December 1941 – the month after Brewster Aeronautical received its designation. On 25 February 1943 the first Goodyear FG-1 made its maiden flight. The event occurred just ten days after the Navy's VF-17 received its first F4U-1 from Vought. By April, Goodyear was delivering aircraft to the Navy. By the end of 1943, Goodyear delivered 377 Corsairs, nearly triple the number of Brewster. Many of the FG-1s had a fixed, non-folding wing.

This saved weight and simplified construction, an important benefit when Corsair squadrons were restricted to land bases by the Navy.

Goodyear built a total of 4,006 FG-1 series aircraft by 1945, almost one-third of all Corsairs that were built by the end of production in early 1953 (during the Korean War). Because of its proficiency, Goodyear was selected to build the F2G series of the Corsair. The latter version was the standard airframe and the massive, four-banked Pratt & Whitney R-4360-4 that was designed to produce 3,000 h.p. for takeoff. The F2G-1 was to be the land-based version and the F2G-2 had the folding wing for carrier operations. The end of the war resulted in the cancellation of this aircraft; only five copies of each were built. It is a testament to Goodyear that the firm was selected to manufacture this extremely powerful Corsair. In fact, many of the last flying Corsairs were built at Goodyear's Akron, Ohio factory.

• • • •

In all, roughly 950 design changes were incorporated in the F4U design. Vought, its parent United Aircraft Corporation, along with the Pratt & Whitney and the Hamilton Standard divisions, were at the leading edge of technology. All three companies also pushed technology from design and development functions to the manufacturing processes, with significant impact on Vought's workforce and factory floor. The Navy's Bureau of Aeronautics appreciated all this, but also saw the bottlenecks and limitations that developed as the companies mobilized at the end of the Great Depression. The use of Brewster Aeronautical and Goodyear as associate producers under license, and the separation of Sikorsky operations into a separate United Aircraft Corporation division in 1943, all contributed to the Bureau's demanding production requirements. But the improvement and increased utilization of the F4U by the services was not entirely driven by the manufacturer. Vought technical representatives, working with U.S. Navy and Marine Corps squadrons, plus those of the Royal Navy's Fleet Air Arm, developed modifications in the field that corrected some of the glaring problems that became apparent in operational service. The feedback to the factory from tech reps and the squadrons, and the commitment from Vought management to make things right, was the final step in getting the F4U Corsair ready for war.

At the Factory – Winning Through Mass Production

Back In Time – Images of the Growing Factory Complex

Information is important, but factual data alone provides a barren form of history. Most people benefit from visual perceptions, and this is especially important when one wants to appreciate what past events were like at the time. The images below were provided courtesy of the Connecticut Air and Space Center, in Stratford, Connecticut, and the Igor I. Sikorsky Memorial Archives, Inc. Note that the Chance Vought Aircraft division of United Aircraft Corporation was briefly known as Vought-Sikorsky between 1939-43. After that, the divisions were again separated, with Chance Vought Aircraft (CVA) remaining at the Stratford plant until 1948.

This image was taken from the Vought property on the west bank of the Housatonic River. The shoreline extension provided addition space for building the ever-growing factory complex. The mouth of the river at Long Island Sound is in the distant background. The factory complex lies behind the photographer. Photo courtesy of the Connecticut Air and Space Center, Stratford, CT.

Developing the Gull-Winged F4U Corsair - And Taking It To Sea

The expanding factory complex greatly altered the landscape in the Lordship section of Stratford. Pictured above is one of experimental hangars (right side), with the recently completed Building 2 addition in the background (left side, background). Notice the residential buildings in the left side of the picture, situated between the photographer and Building 2 (background). Photo courtesy of the Connecticut Air and Space Center, Stratford, CT.

This image shows the early stages of expanding the two-story main factory. Note some of the residential buildings in the background. This view is facing north from the north side of the complex. Photo courtesy of the Connecticut Air and Space Center, Stratford, CT.

At the Factory – Winning Through Mass Production

The two-story factory extension nears completion. This is on the north side of the complex. Photo courtesy of the Connecticut Air and Space Center, Stratford, CT.

Early construction continues on the test hangar. Note the vintage of the vehicles. Photo courtesy of the Connecticut Air and Space Center, Stratford, CT.

Developing the Gull-Winged F4U Corsair - And Taking It To Sea

The size of the test hangar is apparent as the building nears completion. Photo courtesy of the Connecticut Air and Space Center, Stratford, CT.

By late-1943 the three-story office area that fronted on Main Street was nearing completion. This was during the period of peak manufacturing, during which time Vought (then known as Chance Vought Aircraft) and U.S. Navy Bureau of Aeronautics (BuAer) representatives were busy overseeing production schedules and approving the numerous engineering changes. Out of view behind the photographer were the newly constructed flight test hangars on the Bridgeport Airport property. Photo courtesy of the Connecticut Air and Space Center, Stratford, CT.

At the Factory – Winning Through Mass Production

Repositioning F4U Corsair with crane after final assembly. Image source/credit: Courtesy of the Igor I. Sikorsky Historical Archives, Inc.

Developing the Gull-Winged F4U Corsair - And Taking It To Sea

Working on an F4U engine and accessories. Note the double-row of cylinders of the R-2800 powerplant. Note also the size of the aircraft; it was considered a large fighter for its day. Image source/credit: Courtesy of the Igor I. Sikorsky Historical Archives, Inc.

At the Factory – Winning Through Mass Production

Spraying was one of many mundane but important jobs at the factory. This worker is spraying in the area of the firewall and the self-sealing fuselage fuel tank. Note the smoothness of the fuselage skin. Image source/credit: Courtesy of the Igor I. Sikorsky Historical Archives, Inc.

Developing the Gull-Winged F4U Corsair - And Taking It To Sea

Pictured above is a company assembly at Vought-Sikorsky's Stratford, Connecticut plant. The men and women who appeared at the assembly built the F4U Corsair, earning several awards – including the coveted Army-Navy 'E' for Excellence production achievement award. They were part of the world's most productive workforce, and helped make that victory possible. Image source/credit: Courtesy of the Igor I. Sikorsky Historical Archives, Inc.

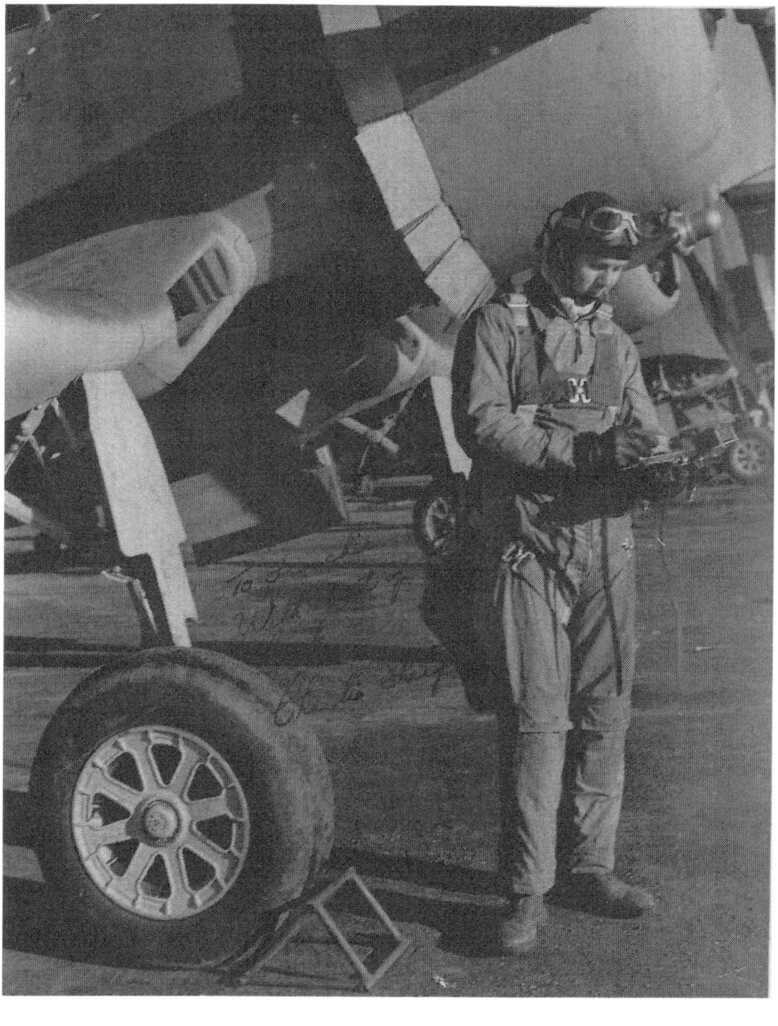

Chapter Four

The F4U Corsair Goes To War

Pearl Harbor has now been partially avenged. Vengeance will not be complete until Japanese sea power has been reduced to impotence. We have made substantial progress in that direction. Perhaps we will be forgiven if we claim we are about midway to our objective!

– Fleet Admiral Chester W. Nimitz, Commander-in-Chief, U.S. Pacific Fleet, after the U.S. Navy defeated a superior force of the Imperial Japanese Navy in the Battle of Midway, June 6, 1942, in CINCAPAAC Communiqué No. 3.

Day-to-day fighting in the South Pacific has proven the Corsair decidedly superior to all models of the Japanese Zero.

– Fleet Admiral Chester W. Nimitz, in a May, 1943 telegram to Vought employees at the Stratford, Connecticut factory.

Getting the Vought F4U Corsair into the Second World War involved much more than meeting the demanding performance standards of the Navy's Bureau of Aeronautics (BuAer). In fact, a complex constellation of circumstances, events and conditions would have to come into proper alignment before the F4U would be squadron ready. And even then, the early F4U Corsairs – despite their spectacular performance – revealed significant operational deficiencies. The effort to correct those significant problems would be time consuming, and involved both the manufacturer, the Navy and Marine Corps. Had Vought failed, the production of the F4U would have likely been short-lived, as Grumman's very impressive F6F Hellcat would quickly become available.

During 1941, the rapidly expanding Vought-Sikorsky complex in Stratford strained to get the XF4U-1 ready for acceptance by the U.S. Navy. BuAer was closely monitoring new weapon systems such as the Corsair, and the progress of the flight test program was critical. Although the early speed tests of the XF4U-1 were very encouraging, the aircraft would have to be cleared for flight throughout the entire flight envelope to meet U.S. Navy requirements. Unless the flight test program could validate all of those requirements, there would be no F4U production. And BuAer, while optimistic, had good reason for keeping a close watch on the program.

The months that preceded the Pearl Harbor attack were part of a critical period for the U.S. Navy. The Second World War was underway in Europe. France, Poland and Austria had fallen to Nazi Germany, and Great Britain had come within a whisker of losing the Battle of Britain. Meanwhile, storm clouds loomed large over eastern Asia and much of the Pacific as Japan expanded its footprint in that region. War with Germany and Japan was coming, and Navy admirals, BuAer and fleet fighter and bombing squadrons all knew it. Yet as war drew close, the Navy had huge problems with its existing fighter programs.

The Navy's problems began with the Brewster F2A-3 Buffalo, which was proving to be wholly inadequate for its planned role as a shipboard fighter. Although early versions were wonderful aerobatic aircraft (several pilots would later relate that the maneuverability was close to that of Japan's A6M Zero), the small fighter had grown in weight. With that significant weight increase came a noticeable decrease in performance, a critical flaw for a fighter. And the F2A-3's very weak main landing gear, something that was only revealed after shipboard squadrons began operations at sea, resulted in numerous accidents. The landing gear problem became severe at a critical time. On 3 December 1941 – just four days before the attack on Pearl Harbor – VF-2, enroute to Pearl Harbor aboard the *U.S.S. Lexington*, advised BuAer that due to main landing gear structural failures it had stopped flying the Buffalo on routine operations. The communiqué from a fighting squadron when war was imminent could only be considered as a strong rebuke of the F2A-3's acceptance by the bureau.

Fortunately, the Navy had another new monoplane fighter. Yet the Grumman F4F Wildcat, which was being rushed into service to replace the disastrous Buffalo, fell far short of the F4U's blistering speed. And while the F4F was not as maneuverable as the Japanese Zero, it was easy to fly off a carrier and was very rugged. In the early part of the war, the Grumman F4F Wildcat would give a good account of itself against difficult odds, but it was an interim airplane. These events unfolded throughout 1941, but months before Pearl Harbor BuAer and Navy brass knew that they had a major problem with their fighter programs. That Brewster's initial production order (for the F2A-2) was issued on 11 June 1938, the same day that Vought received its initial contract to build and test the XF4U-1, was not lost on the bureau.

Aware that it was being closely watched, Vought's experimental XF4U-1 went through a standard but rigorous flight test regiment. The flight test program was more than a process to validate the basic design, identify problems and then demonstrates fixes. The process was a bridge that would take the experimental XF4U-1, and develop it to where the F4U-1 production version could be authorized by BuAer. So the Navy had a lot riding on the F4U program, but it had reason to be optimistic. By late 1940, the experimental XF4U-1 had established its 400 m.p.h. speed capability and basic flight traits. During 1941, Vought-Sikorsky (as it was then called) and the Navy wanted to complete the flight tests and acceptance flights, and then move the aircraft into production. But while the Corsair was fast in the air, its development plodded along.

As the flight test program progressed during 1941, it was found that some old standards from the biplane era would have to be relaxed by the Navy. These included a power on, ten thousand foot vertical dive requirement, and a recovery from a ten-turn spin. Both of these changes were necessary, but unfortunately each one delayed the program. And while a power-on, ten thousand foot vertical dive requirement had to be eliminated for modern fighters, terminal velocity dive tests were still *de rigueur*. Then there were the spin tests. Although the Corsair exhibited an abrupt wing drop at the aerodynamic stall, the problem with prolonged spins was a separate issue – and a big one.

Flight tests showed that the Corsair's spin behavior was conventional until after two turns. After that, the results ranged from unpredictable to unrecoverable, at least by use of the aircraft flight controls. On an early spin test that went to thirteen turns and was unrecoverable, it was the availability of a spin-chute that saved Boone Guyton's life. Additional spin tests were ordered, but invariably Guyton had to rely on the spin chute to affect a recovery after the spins flattened out. The Navy agreed to relax the spin requirement, but only after consulting with Vought managers and engineers from the National Advisory Committee for Aeronautics (NACA). Thereafter, a prohibition against intentional spins in the Corsair became sacrosanct, although recoveries from incipient spins were routine.

In April, Guyton successfully demonstrated the XF4U-1 to BuAer at NAS Anacostia (in Maryland, next to Washington, D.C.) and NAS Dahlgren (in northern Virginia). A laundry list of essential changes that would be needed on production models was developed, and on 30 June 1941 Vought-Sikorsky received a production order for 584 F4U-1 Corsairs. The changes that BuAer required – and which would later be added to the laundry list – would be critical to the success of the F4U, both as a carried-based airplane and as a weapon system. Although the resulting production airplane remained recognizable as the gull-winged F4U, the modifications that were imposed were significant.

Beginning with the configuration, the most obvious alteration was in the fuselage. BuAer decreed that the F4U-1 would be armed with six .50-calibre machine guns, and that the guns and their adjacent ammo boxes would all be in the outboard wing section (where they would fire outside the propeller arc). That, in turn, required the relocation of the wing fuel tanks to a single 237-gallon tank in the fuselage. In the interest in keeping the fuel tank as close to the aircraft center-of-gravity (c.g.) as possible, the fuselage tank was placed over the wing. Later, the tank was made to be self-sealing, with a 177 pound weight increase; this afforded greater protection if the tank was hit by enemy fire. The movement of the fuel load into the fuselage produced another big advantage in combat: i.e., a much higher roll rate.

The placement of the fuel tank over the wing, while in some ways desirable, required that the cockpit be moved rearward by 32-inches. That change resulted in the pilot being roughly over the wing trailing edge. While the new configuration did not create any c.g. problems, the somewhat longer nose greatly reduced the forward visibility on take-offs and landing approaches. Being unable to see a runway (or even a ship, like an aircraft carrier) immediately became a major problem in landing, especially for shipboard operations. A slightly later change in raising the pilot seat by eight inches was designed to improve forward visibility, but that offered no more than a minor improvement. When Lt. Eric Brown of the Royal Navy's Fleet Air Arm (FAA) tested the F4U, he famously remarked that the only adequate visibility from the cockpit was when he looked straight up.

Another change that the Navy's BuAer insisted on was an aileron modification to improve lateral control and roll rates. To be sure, the aileron effectiveness of XF4U-1 at low carrier approach speeds, while not great, was no doubt adequate. Still, there was considerable room for improvement, and any improvement in the production version would be desirable; improved lateral control at low speeds could save lives in an unforgiving shipboard environment.

In addition to lateral control, the Navy test pilots who did the BuAer flight evaluations had something else in mind. The F4U was a large fighter, and its likely aerial adversaries had superior roll rates. In his outstanding autobiography *Whistling Death: The Test Pilot's Story of the F4U Corsair*, author Boone Guyton makes the interesting note that the timeliness of the Navy's request suggests that the service may have been privy to information about the roll capabilities of the A6M Zero. If so, both the source and existence of such information would have been highly classified. In any event, the aileron modifications involved considerable trial and error, with each change requiring additional flight tests.

Bill Schoolfield was the engineer in charge of the aileron project, and the culmination was a new aileron with greater lateral span, a retrimmed aileron nose and the addition of trailing edge balance tabs to reduce stick force on the unboosted flight control. Guyton claimed on various occasions that on the improved F4U-1, the maximum roll rate exceeded 180 degrees per second. This author is unaware of other reports of roll rates that high, but it is clear that production F4U-1s with balance tabs had superior roll rates with minimal stick forces. Perhaps most important, at speeds above 200 knots the large F4U could out roll and out turn the nimble A6M Zero. It was a worthwhile result from an engineering and flight test process that continued to the end of 1941.

Other deficiencies in the basic Corsair had to be worked out, and many of these were initially done on an *ad hoc* basis with operational squadrons. Among the additional changes that were fairly straightforward were changes in the instrument panel layout in the cockpit; adding a jettison control and jettison capability to the "birdcage" canopy, and the upgrade from the original Pratt & Whitney XR-2800-4 to the R-2800-8, the first version to deliver the full 2,000 h.p. at takeoff. Still other important changes came about because of field modifications and demands from operational squadrons of the Marine Corps, Navy and the Fleet Air Arm. The first of these involved leakage of hydraulic fluid from the upper cowl flaps, a problem that resulted in the accumulation of fluid on the windshield.

Fourteen small cowl flaps regulated airflow through the cowling that surrounded the large, double-row radial engine. Essential for an air-cooled engine like the R-2800, the movable flap surfaces at the trailing edge of the cowling could be extended or retracted by means of small hydraulic actuating cylinders. Leakage from the lower and side flap cylinders, while not desirable, did not impair pilot vision. But the leakage from the cowl flaps forward of the windshield was another matter. The movable upper flap was eventually eliminated, but not before field modifications were accomplished. In the FAA, this was done by mechanically locking the movable panels, and later replacing them with the fixed type. Similar field modifications were done on Marine Corps and Navy aircraft until the changes filtered back to the production line. Feedback to the factory in Stratford did not just travel through military channels; Vought technical representatives in the field helped to push the changes through company channels.

The original birdcage canopy was another problem. Being relatively low and having structural members that inhibited the pilot's view, the birdcages were replaced by "bubble" canopies. The new canopies provided a much needed improvement in visibility. Unfortunately, the change occurred only after the F4U-1 was in production, with many Corsairs being deployed to operational squadrons with the much disliked birdcage canopy. Despite the greater height of the bubble canopy, the aircraft suffered no loss of airspeed.

The original tailwheel was also a source of trouble. An improved tailwheel that raised the tail and slightly reduced the "three-point" attitude of the airplane improved forward visibility and directional control on landings; the latter was a major problem that would delay the arrival of Corsairs on American aircraft carriers. Material issues and the design of the tailwheel itself were also improved. The tailwheel issue alone would make carrier operations impractical. "A bouncy undercarriage led to skipping over arrester into the safety net ahead" confirmed retired Royal Navy Capt. Eric M. Brown, one of the Fleet Air Arm test pilots who evaluated the F4U's shipboard landing traits.

Without a doubt, some of the biggest problems that the Corsair faced in active military service were those that could result in loss of control on the latter portions of a carrier approach, and after the aircraft arrived on the deck. One of the inherent dangers in being a naval aviator is the need to approach the carrier slowly enough so that at the proper time the aircraft can be safely "recovered." Approaching the ship's stern, the Corsair would be configured for landing with the landing gear and arrester hook down, and landing flaps selected. The aircraft would be flown at a slow approach speed, slightly above the stalling speed at which point the aircraft would cease to fly. The abruptness of the stall, always unexpected and accompanied by a sudden wing drop, would often prove fatal at the low height at which they generally occurred.

To provide a more docile stall characteristic (i.e., less wing drop) experiments were done with different types of leading edge spoilers. Often called stall strips, the triangular-shaped wooden strips would be attached to the leading edge of the right outboard wing. While not actually lowering the stall speed, the stall strip would cause the wings to exceed their critical angle of attack at roughly the same time, thereby avoiding a deadly wing drop. Experimentation was done with different sizes, shapes and locations at both at the factory and in the field. In the end, it was the Navy's VF-17 "Jolly Rogers," experimenting and flight testing their home grown stall strips in the field, that developed the form which the factory finally adopted.

Taking care of the asymmetrical wing dropping did not solve all of the stalling issues. In the landing configuration, there was little pre-stall buffet prior to the aerodynamic stall. A stall warning light on the instrument panel was designed to provide some warning, but it was calibrated to illuminate just a few knots above the stall. Even in completely still air, that warning would be very late, especially for a brand new aviator with limited hours in the airplane. In many cases, the fact that the long nose – extending roughly fourteen feet forward in front of the pilot – produced such an absence of visual cues that a pilot, intent on watching the Landing Signal Officer (LSO) at the stern, could inadvertently get too slow. The resulting increase in the angle of attack (i.e., the angle at which the passing airflow met the wing) could quickly result in a fatal, low altitude stall. But the problem didn't end there. If the carrier's LSO signaled a "wave off" the pilot would immediately apply full power – or close to full power – and risk rolling inverted to the left, a situation from which recovery would be impossible at low altitude and airspeed.

One of the most unfortunate aspects of the F4U's fine overall history was the frequency with which approach and landing accidents occurred. This was especially true during initial qualification in the aircraft by inexperienced pilots who received their initial assignment to a F4U squadron. But even when the pilot arrived safely at the carrier's stern "in the groove" the risks were not over. Most landing approaches that received a "cut" signal from the LSO rather than a "wave off" would result in the Corsair's arrival on the deck. But when the throttle was cut, the heavy nose of the nearly stalled Corsair had a tendency to drop. The inertia of the heavy airplane impacting the deck would typically produce a bounce, some being rather dramatic, and others more subdued.

Aside from developing an ideal throttle technique and a sense of how much back pressure to hold on the stick, the landing gear – not just the pilot – would affect the outcome of the landing. Early Corsairs were prone to bounces, one of the many issues that both the Navy and the Fleet Air Arm found highly unacceptable. Even without a bad bounce, Corsairs that arrived on the carrier deck and "caught a cable" often encountered directional control problems due to an uneven touchdown (i.e., a bank) and the close proximity of the flap trailing edge to the deck. The latter problem directly derived from the small and very low tail wheel assembly. So there were myriad ways to get into trouble with a Corsair, even if the magnitude of the error was not great. Even experienced pilots were not immune. And Corsair pilots operated during daylight and nighttime conditions, usually with a pitching or rolling flight deck due to sea conditions, and often in rain or reduced visibility. It thus becomes clear why in naval aviation lingo aircraft are launched and recovered during shipboard operations.

That the Navy would have ordered a naval fighter with so many deficiencies might seem unbelievable, especially considering the problems with the quickly retired Brewster Buffalo. Yet the F4U embraced a plethora of new technologies and, quite frankly, the Vought test pilots handled approaches and landings at the Bridgeport Airport without difficulty. So the correction of the Corsair's laundry list of problems was not unlike a shakedown cruise of a new warship, where problems to be worked out are first revealed and then addressed. Hence, it is not surprising that many of the more egregious handling problems were discovered by the Navy during actual shipboard landings. Unfortunately, many of these problems would not be corrected until 1943, a situation that necessitated that most production Corsairs would go to the Marine Corps for use from land bases. That was fine with the Marine Corps, which could immediately use the fighters at Guadalcanal and other bases in the Solomon Islands region.

Some of the teething problems with the Corsair were more easily remedied. After the attack on Pearl Harbor, security at the Stratford plant was tightened and the push to get the Corsair ready for squadron use went into overdrive. In mid-January 1942 Guyton flew the XF4U-1 to the Naval Air Factory (NAF) in Philadelphia for its initial carrier suitability trials. The tests were to be flown by a Navy test pilot on a mock carrier deck. At this point, Vought-Sikorsky had yet to design a rugged and capable tailwheel and arrester hook. The Rube Goldberg-like contraption that formed the arrester hook was intended to reduce the Corsair's development time, but the ill-conceived mechanism disintegrated on the first arrested landing. It would be the first of many disappointments.

As 1942 progressed, the urgency of getting the Corsair squadron-ready continued to rise. The Battle of the Coral Sea (4-8 May 1942, near the Solomon Islands) proved that aircraft carriers would be the principal capital warships in the war with Japan. That sea battle blunted the Japanese advance near Australia, an important result in a war that had been going badly for America and her Allies. Then, from 4-7 June 1942, American and Japanese carrier fleets battled again, at the Battle of Midway. The American victory turned the tide of the war, but the war was still in its early stages. In both of these naval engagements, the U.S. Navy had to make due with its Grumman F4F Wildcat fighters. Yet despite the imperative of time, it wasn't until 25 June 1942 that the first production F4U-1 made its maiden flight. With its much longer nose and repositioned cockpit, the new fighter had the look of a racer. But when the next carrier suitability tests were held in September, it was clear that major approach and landing issues remained unresolved.

On 25 September 1942 Lt. Cdr. Sam Porter began official U.S. Navy carrier trials using the seventh production airplane. The ship that was used for the trials was the escort carrier *U.S.S. Sangamon* (CVE-26), a converted tanker that had a small, 502-foot long, 81-foot wide flight deck. *Sangamon* was in Chesapeake Bay, having returned from Operation Torch in support of the North Africa landings. *Sangamon*, like other CVEs, would have a distinguished combat record with the Navy; its smaller dimensions were the price that was paid to manufacture and deploy the large number of escort carriers needed for the war. As such, the ship was a good test of the F4U which, unfortunately, performed poorly. Porter experienced most of the F4U's bad traits: i.e., poor visibility due to the birdcage canopy, the Corsair's long lose, and leaking hydraulic fluids that collected on the windshield. The abrupt stall and wing drop during the recoveries were experienced, as was the pronounced bounce and difficulty in maintaining directional control on the flight deck. After just four takeoffs and recoveries, Porter halted the trial.

The failed carrier trials occurred three months to the day after the first flight of the F4U-1 production version of the Corsair. Significantly, Vought test pilot Boone Guyton discovered that the wing drop tendency at the stall was even more pronounced on the production version of the airplane than on the original XF4U-1 experimental version. But during September 1942 Guyton was busy with high-speed dive tests that would take the production aircraft in the regime of transonic flight. It would be 1943 before many of the chronic problems with the F4U-1 would be rectified, or at least minimized. In the meantime, production ramped up despite the deficiencies; the Navy needed an air superiority fighter that could defeat the Japanese Zero in the skies over the Pacific. With land, air and sea battles for control of Guadalcanal underway, production of the Corsair would not be delayed.

Often overlooked in discussions of the failed carrier suitability trials was an important detail to the fighting on Guadalcanal. In addition to the land and naval battles on and around that island, there was an immediate and ongoing need for air defense against enemy air attacks. Japanese pilots quickly learned that they needed to circumnavigate islands where Australian coast watchers could detect (and report on) their southbound flights towards Guadalcanal. To provide early warning of unobserved air attacks, three SCR-270 radars were sent to the island; the first unit arrived just five days before the F4U's dismal performance aboard the *Sangamon*. Two SCR-268 radars followed almost immediately. The delicate air war over Guadalcanal was about to change.

The bulky SCR-270s operated at a 3-meter wavelength, and were able to detect incoming aircraft at ranges up to 125 miles. The SCR-268s operated at a 1.5-meter wavelength; they had a much shorter operating range, but could display the approximate altitude of incoming aircraft. Lt. Lewis C. Mattison (USNR) headed a small contingent of fighter director officers (FDOs) who were specially trained in coordinating radar plots with airborne interceptors; he arrived on Guadalcanal shortly after the first radars came ashore. Once the SCR-270s and SCR-268s were operational, it was realized that the practice of keeping fighter interceptors aloft over Henderson Field around the clock was no longer necessary. This provided a huge tactical advantage, along with significant logistical advantages, as far less fuel and maintenance were needed. So important was this finding that Lt. Col. Walter L. J. Bayler, the last marine to leave Wake Island before its capture, was quickly placed in command of Cactus air defense (Cactus was the code name for Henderson Field).

Radar would completely change the course of the war in the Pacific, as would the F4U. But in 1942 radar was aboard many America warships and ashore at Guadalcanal, while the Corsair had yet to enter the war. So the F4U, which would initially be banished from American aircraft carriers, would be going Guadalcanal and the Solomon Islands, where it was needed the most. There, with its superior speed and good rate of climb, F4Us would bolster air defenses and become a major factor in taking the air war to the enemy. It could do what the F4F, P-39/400 and P-40 could not do. But first the F4U had to get into the Solomon Islands. That effort soon centered on two fighting squadrons, the U.S. Navy's VF-12 and VMF-124 of the Marine Corps.

Developing the Gull-Winged F4U Corsair - And Taking It To Sea

The Vought-Sikorsky F4U-1 "Corsair" shipboard fighter, said to be the fastest and most powerful airplane of its type in the world, is in quantity production for the U.S. Navy. Powered with a 2,000 h.p. Pratt and Whitney Double Wasp engine and equipped with a Hamilton Standard Hydromatic propeller, the Corsair possesses the speed, maneuverability and firepower to take the measure of the best the enemy can produce.

VOUGHT-SIKORSKY AIRCRAFT
DIVISION OF UNITED AIRCRAFT CORPORATION
STRATFORD CONN.

Souvenir of Visitors' Day — December 6th, 1942.

Despite the F4U's developmental problems, Vought-Sikorsky regarded the Corsair as a fully capable shipboard fighter. This is evidenced by its 6 December 1942 Visitor's Day brochure. Image source/credit: Courtesy of the Igor I. Sikorsky Historical Archives, Inc.

VF-12, the "Peg Legs," was an established Navy fighting squadron that was commanded by Lt. Cdr. Joseph C. "Jumping Joe" Clifton. Clifton, once a star fullback at the Naval Academy and an experienced F2A Buffalo pilot, was well suited to command the Navy's first F4U squadron. VMF-124 was a new Marine Corps squadron that was quickly established in September 1942. Commanded by Maj. William E. Gise (a Pensacola classmate of test pilot Guyton), it would be the first squadron to deploy to combat with the F4U. VMF-124 was formed a month after the Marine Corps assaulted Guadalcanal, and when the outcome of that battle remained uncertain. That the Marine Corps was rushing VMF-124 into combat was well understood, so in early November 1942 Vought sent Boone Guyton to San Diego. The pilots were stationed at nearby Camp Kearney and it was there, while Guyton was lecturing to young squadron pilots, that he fully realized the predicament that Vought was in.

By November 1942 it was nearly two and a half years since the first flight of the XF4U-1, and more than sixteen months since the production contract was signed with BuAer. In Stratford, construction of the addition at the north end of the complex was on schedule; that would more than double the footprint of the factory floor, permitting a sharp increase in production rates during 1943. 1943 would also be the year that many of the "fixes" and design changes would appear in the new F4U-1s. But the war wasn't stopping; Vought had to immediately fix the most pressing issues that could derail the F4U deployment. As Guyton lectured the young marine pilots at Camp Kearney, Col. Stanley Ridderhoff directed an *ad hoc* "fix it" detail that included squadron maintenance personnel, Vought's project engineer Russ Clark and service manager Jack Hospers – the man who created the "fix it" program with Ridderhoff. Gise made it very clear to Guyton and the other Vought representatives that VMF-124 was about to deploy, and if the urgent fixes were not accomplished the squadron would ditch their Corsairs and take F4F Wildcats instead. VMF-124 deployed during the first week of January 1943, and managed to hold onto their Corsairs, but just barely.

VF-12 also received Vought's attention, and visits from Guyton. Like VMF-124, VF-12 was working up for deployment in the San Diego area, at NAS North Island. Because of VMF-124s deployment schedule

Developing the Gull-Winged F4U Corsair - And Taking It To Sea

and the needs of other Marine Corps squadrons, new F4U-1s were slow to arrive at VF-12. VF-12 suffered fourteen fatalities during its workup and westbound deployment aboard the *U.S.S. Enterprise* (CV-6, the "Big E"). Although Clifton and his squadron liked the F4U's performance, the poor safety record with the Corsair was considered along with the fact that supplying the F4U with spares and product support would be difficult aboard the *U.S.S. Saratoga* (CV-3, and the ship upon which VF-12 would be operating in the combat theater). As a result, VF-12 relinquished its Corsairs and transitioned to the more docile F6F Hellcat. However, VF-12 did reveal yet another problem with the F4U before the change; the rather weak pneumatic tire on the small tailwheel assembly was not up to the stress of hard carrier arrivals. It was yet another problem to be added to Vought's long laundry list.

Lt. Cdr. Joseph C. Clifton discussing tactics with pilots of VF-12 in early 1943. VF-12 later switched from the F4Us to the Grumman F6F Hellcat. Image source/credit: Courtesy of the Emil Buehler Library Collections of the National Museum of Naval Aviation, from the Commander Joseph C. Clifton Photographic Album, Accession Number 1977.031.084.081.

As a result of VF-12's transition to the F6F, the first U.S. Navy squadron to take the F4U into combat was Lt. Cdr. John "Tommy" Blackburn's "Jolly Rogers." Blackburn commissioned VF-17 at NAS Norfolk on 1 January 1943, shortly after returning from combat with VGF-29, which he commanded during the invasion of North Africa. Blackburn, a Naval Academy graduate and a perfectionist when it came to flying, was largely able to hand pick his squadron pilots. Unfortunately, it would be mid-February before the first of the squadron's F4Us was ready, so Blackburn began working up his squadron with an assortment of trainers. As Corsairs became available Blackburn drilled his pilots relentlessly. Fully aware of the F4U's limitations for shipboard use, Blackburn began using a curved approach that enabled him to keep the LSO in sight; he would roll wings level and align with the flight deck very close to the stern, a practice that was not official Navy doctrine. Despite numerous bounces and blown tires, not one VF-17 pilot was lost coming aboard ship.

Blackburn deserves significant credit for identifying deficiencies that would affect squadron operations, and then developing fixes. Working closely with his squadron maintenance officer, Lt. (j.g.) Butch Davenport, the unit established a dialog with Russ Clark and Vought field service rep Ray DeLeva. Among their more notable accomplishments were a design for a wedge-shaped spoiler to mitigate the wing drop at the stall, a method for modifying the main gear oleo struts for de-bouncing purposes, and an alert to BuAer about defective tail hooks. VF-17 also pushed for a bubble canopy, modifications to cowl flap actuating system; many of the changes that VF-17 pioneered appeared in production aircraft later in 1943 and 1944.

One serious problem that had to be corrected with both field modification kits and production changes involved failures of the pressurized ignition system. At higher altitudes, it was essential to pressurize the ignition system to prevent a loss of power. Other World War Two fighters encountered the problem, including the Grumman F6F Hellcat. In the case of the Corsair, the root cause was not a design deficiency, but a failure of a supercharger on the Pratt & Whitney R-2800. The problem would only manifest itself at altitudes near thirty thousand feet, and above. Unfortunately, a VMF-124 Corsair flown by Lt. Kenneth A. Walsh lost all of its power on a high altitude flight over the Solomon

Islands. Walsh, a future Corsair ace and Medal of Honor recipient, became the first pilot to ditch a Corsair at sea.

An F4U from the VF-12 'Jolly Rogers' shown during carrier qualifications aboard the U.S.S. *Charger* (CVE-30) in 1943. This image shows that aircraft engaging one of the arrester cables. The delicate but abrupt transition from flight to arrival on the flight deck is why the process is known as the 'recovery' of aircraft. Courtesy of the Emil Buehler Library Collections of the National Museum of Naval Aviation, from the Robert L. Larson Photograph Collection, Accession Number 1996.253.7144.015.

The enormous effort to play catch-up and correct significant problems with the F4U no doubt saved Vought's contracts with the Navy. It also ensured that by early 1943 the Marine Corps had the best possible naval fighter. VMF-124, VF-17 and countless other Navy and Marine Corps squadrons distinguished themselves in combat in the Solomon Islands. The big additions to Vought's Stratford plant, along with licensed production by Brewster Aeronautical Corporation and Goodyear (especially Goodyear) kept the supply line filled with new airplanes. By the summer of 1943 Fleet Air Arm squadrons began to form in the United States; they too would make significant contributions to the process of improving the design. But even as the production ramped up and the F4U-1 design matured, Corsair pilots faced some new challenges. The first 400 m.p.h. naval fighter was pushing into even newer and more dangerous aerodynamic frontiers.

• • • •

Prior to embarking on the *U.S.S. Bunker Hill*, VF-17 pilots were required to complete a high altitude vertical dive maneuver. This was part of a familiarization syllabus and a mandate from the commanding officer, Lt. Cdr. Tommy Blackburn. In particular, the maneuver was designed to provide pilots with some exposure to the F4U's performance in dives from high altitudes, including vertical acceleration, high-speed roll rates and expected G-forces in a recovery to level flight. Using one of the squadron's brand new F4U-1As, Lt. Chuck Pillsbury (the squadron's operations officer) dutifully rolled inverted at thirty-thousand feet, pulled back on the stick and brought the nose to a vertical attitude. Upon initiating his recovery, Pillsbury was unable to pull the positive-G forces necessary to raise the nose at the expected rate. Pillsbury was able to affect a recovery – but just barely. Upon examination of his aircraft, the fabric skin of the elevators was badly tattered; Pillsbury was lucky to have survived.

Suspecting that a defective elevator had been installed on a new airplane, Blackburn repeated the maneuvers in his own airplane, with an almost identical result. The presented multiple problems. For one thing, could the design of the fabric-covered elevators be deficient? Moreover, if those terrifying dive recoveries were the result of an encounter with a little understood sonic phenomenon, what flight limitations would have to be imposed? And how would these limitations affect tactics and combat operations against Japanese fighters? Blackburn lacked some of these answers, but VF-17 would soon be engaged in aerial combat over the Solomon Islands. As a quick and dirty measure to protect his pilots, Blackburn banned vertical dives at altitudes above twenty thousand feet.

VF-17's ban on high-altitude vertical dives was imposed roughly eleven months after Vought test pilot Boone Guyton carefully pushed the Velocity-G-load frontier of the F4U-1's flight envelope. Numerous high-speed dives were accomplished, with Guyton pushing the Corsair past subsonic speeds into the transonic regime of flight. These risky maneuvers were used to establish the critical mach number for the F4U, a previously unheard of metric for an airplane with a high-lift NACA 2415 airfoil and fabric covered control surfaces.

Just what were the F4U's limiting mach numbers? Without flight test data cards or telemetry data to review, accurate values are elusive. In his carefully researched book *America's Hundred Thousand: U.S. Production Fighters of World War Two,* author Francis H. Dean (an experienced engineer and meticulous fact checker) included a reference to the critical mach number of the XF4U-1. The value given is 0.73 Mach, as established by Vought-Sikorsky dive tests during January 1941. That raises a question about Vought's data. In early 1944, the Royal Aircraft Establishment (RAE) flight tested three USAAF fighters at the request of the Eighth Air Force. In his autobiography *Wings On My Sleeve,* Capt. Eric Brown (RN, ret.) refers to tactical mach and critical numbers. Brown's opinions are important, since he performed most of the dive tests while assigned to the RAE by the Fleet Air Arm. The dean of Royal Navy test pilots later clarified how that nomenclature applied to those military fighters in a mach-limited environment.

"Our test aircraft had machmeters" Brown elaborated. "We determined tactical mach numbers (maximum at which the aircraft can conduct combat) and the critical mach number (the limit beyond which control will be lost, and noted the flight characteristics warning that these limits are being approached. Such characteristics could be heavy vibration, severe buffeting or varying degrees of nose-down changes of trim."

The flight tests at the Royal Aircraft Establishment did not include the F4U, which was primarily intended for use in the Far East (China-Burma-India) and Pacific Ocean theaters. The tactical mach numbers cited by Brown for the Lockheed P-38 Lightning and the Republic P-47 Thunderbolt were, respectively, Mach 0.68 and Mach 0.71. Interestingly, Boone Guyton notes in his book *Whistling Death: The Test Pilot's Story of the F4U Corsair* that on a dive test in which he reached Mach 0.71, the local airflow at the tail was determined to be a supersonic Mach 1.05. So sme notes on the nomenclature over time are useful.

In jet aircraft, the critical mach number (M_{CRIT}) is typically slower than the maximum operating mach number (M_{MO}). However, the World War Two fighters encountered their limiting mach numbers and conditions in steep, high speed dives from relatively high altitudes. The dives were intended to either close on an enemy aircraft that as being attacked, or to escape from a pursuing aircraft. The tactical mach number that Brown elaborated on would provide a limit for combat maneuvering, not just pure speed. In addition, the critical mach number that Brown referred to would be an aerodynamic limit determined without tactical maneuvering considerations.

From the foregoing (and available data that remains, the critical mach number for maneuvering in the F4U-1 may have been in the neighborhood of Mach 0.67, with a maximum velocity of Mach 0.73 (similar to M_{MO}). That would mean that at 30,000 feet the Navy's first 400 m.p.h. fighter would not be able to dive as fast as the North American P-51 Mustang, the Messerschmitt Bf-109 or the Focke-Wulf Fw-190. Interestingly, there appears to be little available hard data as to the altitude at which the F4U became mach-limited as opposed to being airspeed limited.

In looking at the risks that naval aviators faced in taking the F4U into combat, a formidable list emerges. The U.S. Navy, U.S. Marine Corps and the Royal Navy's Fleet Air Arm were all actively engaged in improving deficiencies in the landing gear, tailwheel and tailhook assemblies, canopy, pilot seat height, cowl flaps and the undesirable stall characteristics. That the F4U entered these services before the major problems were corrected speaks to how badly that highly imperfect airplane was needed. By the end of the war, the Navy and Marine Corps Corsairs would fly 64,051 sorties, over which 9,581 were from aircraft carriers. The Corsair would destroy 2,140 enemy aircraft in aerial engagements while suffering the loss of 189 aircraft, an impressive 11.1:1 kill ratio. This was second only to the 19:1 kill ratio achieved by pilots flying Grumman's F6F Hellcat.

Looking a little further, some 349 Corsairs were lost in combat due to anti-aircraft artillery (AAA) fire. Compared to the total of 538 Corsairs that were lost due to enemy fire, another 230 were lost due to accidents during combat missions. In addition, 692 Corsairs were lost during accidents on non-combat missions (including training). So the young Navy and Marine Corps Corsair pilots faced a far greater risk of death in a Corsair accident than from air-to-air combat, or from being shot down over a target. The same risks applied to pilots in the Fleet Air Arm and the Royal New Zealand Air Force.

Then there were the pilots themselves. In their late teens to late-twenties (and older for many career officers), Corsair pilots served in an environment that was in many ways unique, even among military aviators. Often with just two hundred hours flight time, they were expected to quickly master their powerful Corsairs, or at least be ready to fly them into combat. They were ready, willing, and for the most part able, to takeoff and land aboard aircraft carriers in an airplane (the F4U "Ensign Eliminator") that had significant limitations in a shipboard environment. The young naval aviators did this in all kinds of weather, lighting and sea conditions, knowing full well the risky, unforgiving nature of their missions. They hand flew their aircraft with almost no radio navigation aids, often venturing hundreds of miles over the ocean to spend a relatively few minutes in life or death encounters with enemy aircraft or flak, often with the risk of mid-air collisions. And they did still more.

That these young F4U pilots also ventured to very high altitudes when little was known about the physiological effects of high-altitude flight in unpressurized aircraft. They flew aggressively, even when high-speed dives to intercept enemy formations below could be deadly. They had no way of knowing, at a given altitude, whether their Corsair was mach-limited or airspeed limited. They flew without ejection seats, flight directors, VOR navigation systems, machmeters or mach-trim compensators; these aids would evolve in the years and decades that followed. And, at the end of each mission, the young pilots who deployed aboard aircraft carriers had to be able to land their aircraft aboard their ship. For many Corsair pilots, that was the biggest risk of all.

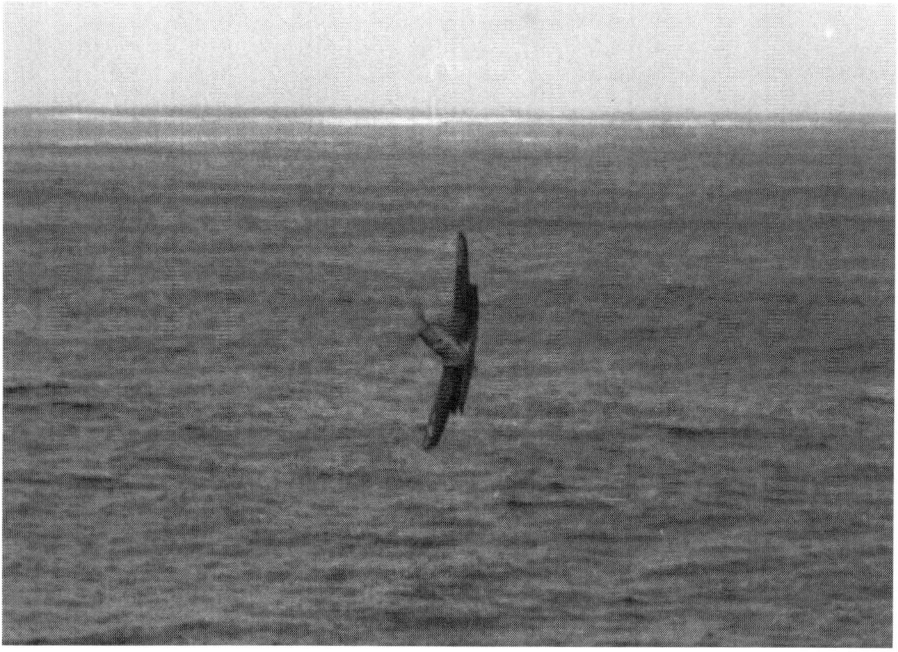

Chapter Five

Fleet Air Arm Methods – Taming the Ill-Mannered Beast

Every landing of a fighter aboard a carrier was in itself an event fraught with far greater possibilities for error and disaster than any airfield landing. The results of getting it wrong could be immediate and dramatic.

– Test pilot Jeffrey Quill, who evaluated aircraft carrier landing techniques of the Spitfire and the F4U Corsair for the Royal Navy's Fleet Air Arm, as related in his autobiography *Spitfire: A Test Pilot's Story*.

A curved approach was very necessary if the pilot was to have any chance of seeing the carrier, let alone the batsman!

– Capt. Eric M. Brown, the Royal Navy Fleet Air Arm test pilot who evaluated aircraft carrier landing traits of the F4U Corsair, as related in his book *Wings of the Navy: Flying Allied Carrier Aircraft of World War Two*.

The U.S. Navy's difficulty in adapting the F4U for shipboard duty was part of a larger problem involving long-nosed naval fighters. Landing these Second World War fighters aboard an aircraft carrier involved visual maneuvering at speeds that would be considered dangerously slow under other circumstances, and at which control effectiveness of ailerons was degraded. Approaches at airspeeds that were only a little above their minimum flying speed were necessary, however. The aircraft would have to "land" – actually, arrive on the deck

Developing the Gull-Winged F4U Corsair - And Taking It To Sea

and be "trapped" by the arrester hook and cables – where the margin for error was nil. Even fighters that had good carrier landing traits (e.g., the Grumman F6F Hellcat) could only mitigate the risks of shipboard operations, one reason why naval aviators have always been a special breed of aircrew.

It is instructive to note that two of the greatest fighters of World War Two – the Supermarine Spitfire and the Vought F4U Corsair – each encountered their greatest operational challenges not with enemy fighters, but with shipboard operations. In the case of the Spitfire, this is somewhat understandable since the aircraft was designed as a land-based fighter interceptor. With limited range and a narrow landing gear, it was not well suited for carrier work. But the critical need to put into service a faster interceptor than the Hawker Hurricane resulted in the development of the Seafire for the Royal Navy's Fleet Air Arm, a naval version of Britain's greatest fighter. The F4U, however, was designed from the beginning as a naval fighter. So despite the Corsair's status as the fastest naval fighter of the war, it's deficiencies as a carrier-based fighter – especially during the first two-thirds of the war – are an important part of its operational history.

In the case of the F4U, the basic fuselage and wing configuration remained unchanged throughout the conflict. While the two rows of cylinders in the Pratt & Whitney R-2800 did not extend as far aft as the Spitfire's Rolls-Royce Merlin or Griffon engines, the rearward movement of the cockpit (to accommodate the 237-gallon fuel tank) ensured that the F4U would always have extremely poor visibility on landing approaches. Improvements to the main landing gear struts and the tailwheel, the addition of a stall strip on the right wing, along with a better canopy and higher cockpit seat were all incremental changes, but the cumulative effect was positive. In April 1944, after extensive trials aboard the *U.S.S. Gambier Bay*, the U.S. Navy finally approved the F4U for shipboard operations. April 1944 was also significant for two other important milestones. First, that was the month in which Vought, Goodyear and Brewster together produced 569 Corsairs, the highest monthly production of the war. And on 3 April 1944, Royal Navy Fleet Air Arm Corsairs flew top cover during the daring daytime attack on the German battleship *Tirpitz*. The Fleet Air Arm was the first service to use the Corsair operationally aboard aircraft carriers, leading the U.S.

Fleet Air Arm Methods – Taming the Ill-Mannered Beast

Navy by nine months. And as a result of pressing the Seafire and the Corsair into shipboard service, the Fleet Air Arm had the most experience of any naval service in learning the secrets of landing long-nosed aircraft aboard ships. So an important part of the Corsair's development into a well-rounded naval fighter came not from America, but from Britain.

In the United Kingdom, as with America, the ramp up in war preparations came too late. One of Britain's many problems was to develop an effective force of fighters for aircraft carrier duty. But after September 1939 Britain was at war, and German U-boats were sinking far too many freighters bound for England. At this time the British purchasing commission was buying a number of different fighters from America, but despite shortages of materials caused by the U-boat the island nation pressed ahead with domestic production. In the case of the Supermarine Spitfire, that meant the creation of a second factory at Castle Bromwich to build aircraft under license. As was the case when a portion of F4U production was assigned to the Brewster Aeronautical Corporation, mismanagement, shoddy workmanship and labor strife affected the Castle Bromwich factory. Finally, in May 1940 Lord Beaverbrook (the first Minister of Aircraft Production) forced a change in management to ensure better cooperation with Supermarine. All of this delayed the Seafire version of the Spitfire, so the Royal Navy pressed a navalized version of the Hurricane and Grumman F4Fs into service. From here, the timelines get interesting.

On 27 July 1940 an initial order of the export version of the Grumman F4F Wildcat was reassigned to Britain after the fall of France to the Germans. By November 1st, a total of 81 Grumman Wildcats (initially named the "Martlett" by the Fleet Air Arm) had been delivered. It was still nearly two years before the Corsair would enter Fleet Air Arm squadrons, but Britain was rapidly moving into the monoplane era of naval fighters. The biggest problem, aside from insufficient numbers, was in performance. Both the Hawker Hurricane and the Grumman Wildcat were inferior in speed to enemy fighters such as the Messerschmitt Bf-109 and Bf-110. This was brought home during Operation Pedestal, 10-15 October 1942, when a heavily escorted supply convoy to the island of Malta suffered devastating air attacks. Even the Hurricanes were at a speed disadvantage against Bf-110s, which could use that advantage to escape after a convoy was attacked. By this time Seafires were arriving in Fleet Air Arm squadrons, but not in sufficient numbers.

Due to production constraints and other wartime priorities, serious consideration of the Seafire did not begin until December 1941. During that month, Lt. Cdr. H. Peter Bramwell, commanding officer of the Fleet Air Arm's Service Trials Unit, completed suitability testing of the Seafire. This included simulated carrier operations at a specially designed area at RNAS Arbroath, and concluded with takeoffs and landings aboard the carrier *H.M.S. Illustrious*. Although Bramwell's report was generally favorable, he strongly recommended that a curved landing approach be used so that pilots could keep the carrier and the all important landing signal officer (called Deck Landing Control Officers, or "batsmen" by the Fleet Air Arm) in sight. The curved landing approach had not been the standard doctrine, but it was judged necessary due to the restricted forward visibility caused by the Seafire's long nose. Bramwell also questioned whether the aircraft was suitable for fleet use aboard smaller escort carriers. Despite that reticence, acceptance of the aircraft was by then assured, and on 15 June 1942 Seafires began to enter the Fleet Air Arm inventory. Just ten days later the F4U-1, the first production version of the Corsair, would make its first flight in Stratford, Connecticut.

Once the Seafire arrived in Fleet Air Arm shipboard squadrons, it quickly enhanced the defensive capabilities of the Royal Navy. The Seafire had enough speed to catch and then shoot down enemy reconnaissance aircraft, and it could take on any enemy fighter that might be encountered. The next question was whether the aircraft could in fact be safely used on CVEs, the smaller escort carriers. Bramwell was doubtful in his service trial report, but the Fleet Air Arm had to be sure. So on 11 September 1942, Lt. Eric M. "Winkle" Brown began deck landing trials on the escort carrier *H.M.S. Biter* using a Seafire IB from No. 801 Squadron. It was an important time in the development of the Seafire, and in developing approach and landing methodology.

A highly capable test pilot, Brown took on his assignment in earnest. It was widely reported that Brown completely disregarded Bramwell's admonition and flew a rectangular pattern around the *Biter*, culminating with a straight-in final approach. To maintain visual contact with the ship on the close-in final approach, Brown used what he termed a "crabbed approach." Using this method he yawed the nose of the aircraft to the right, counteracting the yaw by slightly lowering his left wing. This was highly unorthodox; Brown's technique involved uncoordinated flight and airspeeds that were only slightly above an aerodynamic stall. Any misuse of the controls or unexpected turbulence could result in a stall at an altitude from which there would be no recovery. Brown was comfortable with this unorthodox landing approach, and used it consistently and without difficulty. But there was more to the story about landing the Seafire aboard aircraft carriers than is sometimes reported.

"The curved approach in deck landing really occurred in the Royal Navy with the advent of the Seafire in late-1941" according to Brown. "This aircraft had poor visibility ahead at 1.1 Vs (stalling speed), the recommended deck landing approach speed, but it had mild stall characteristics and good lateral control at low speeds. The Royal Navy's normal method of deck landing was to turn in a final straight approach at 200 feet and set up a constant airspeed/constant rate of descent — which gives a constant attitude, which is what satisfies the LSO."

So Brown was no doubt following established Fleet Air Arm doctrine in that his curved approach had a short straight-in short final, during which his "crab" enabled him to keep the DCLO (or LSO) in sight. Most significantly, the Seafire's use aboard the CVEs was approved and, despite the aircraft's limitations, it significantly improved the Royal Navy's shipboard fighter capabilities. In contrast, just two weeks after Lt. Brown's deck landing trials aboard the *H.M.S. Biter*, the new F4U Corsair failed similar trials aboard the *U.S.S. Sangamon*.

The failure of the F4U in the initial U.S. Navy carrier trials did not slow down the Fleet Air Arm. The rapid addition of Seafires to the fleet CVEs was important to the Admiralty, and urgently needed in advance of Operation Torch. Operation Torch, the Allied invasion of North Africa, was set to begin on 8 November 1942, so getting squadrons worked up (i.e., combat ready) had to proceed expeditiously. That the Seafire would enjoy some measure of success was not in doubt after Brown's report, yet Seafire accidents at sea remained all too common. Many non-combat accidents occurred during the final portion of the landing approach, or during the actual landing on the deck, and with the loss of far too many pilots and aircraft.

The low point in shipboard landings of the Seafire came during Allied invasion of Salerno, Italy between September 9 and October 6, 1943 (Operation Avalanche). Seafires aboard the escort carriers experienced 73 deck landing accidents while flying a total of 713 sorties. Because of the high accident rate, by the dawn of the third day of the operation the number of available Seafires had decreased from 100 to just 39. Contributing to the problem was the limited speed of the escort carriers (only about 17 knots) and lack of wind during the operation; this combination reduced the wind speed over the deck and necessarily resulted in higher touchdown speeds. Still, the accident rate was appalling for an aircraft that was in its second year of shipboard operations. So Operation Avalanche prompted a much more detailed look at how Seafires should be operated aboard ship.

Britain's Fifth Sea Lord, Rear Admiral Sir Denis Boyd, decided that he wanted an informed opinion on the problem from a qualified Spitfire pilot, but one who was further removed from the service than his own line officers. Boyd asked Supermarine test pilot Jeffrey Quill if he would accept a temporary Fleet Air Arm reserve commission as a lieutenant commander, immediately after which he would receive an abbreviated course in carrier flying. From there Quill would investigate the Seafire's approach and landing problems, a process that would include flying duties with operational squadrons.

Quill spent five months on active duty with the Fleet Air Arm and accumulated over one hundred carrier landings, mostly on *H.M.S. Ravager* and *H.M.S. Pretoria Castle*. Most of his operational flying was done with Seafire squadrons, but he also flew Grumman F4Fs and F6Fs from carriers. He even spent time as a pilot with an F4U Corsair squadron. The latter experience enabled Quill to prepare a report on the suitability of the F4U for Royal Navy escort carriers, but his most important work was a report that he submitted to the Admiralty on 29 February 1944. That report summarized the principles that governed safe approaches and landings on straight-deck aircraft carriers, and spoke to specific methods that had proven to be effective. The impetus for the report was the Supermarine Seafire, but the salient points would apply equally to the F4U Corsair – and any other long-nosed fighter where the forward visibility was restricted during landing. Included in Quill's report, which was received by the Fifth Sea Lord, were four main factors that would affect the successful outcome of an approach and landing aboard a carrier. According to Quill, the first and foremost factor was the method of approach. That could be considered with his second factor, which was the view from the cockpit.

Quill's methodology for the Seafire landing approach was not unlike that which existed within the Fleet Air Arm, but he established a formality and rigor that had previously been lacking. To Quill, the critical nature of carrier landings – especially by newly trained naval aviators with limited flight time – required that the method that he articulated be applied on every approach.

According to Quill, there were eight "reasonable rough rules for a Seafire deck landing." In a simple form (with some paraphrasing for the benefit of non-pilot readers), they were:

1. Circuit (traffic pattern) height should be 300-400 ft.
2. Enter the circuit (pattern) by flying upwind (i.e., with the ship on left side of the aircraft). 10-15 seconds after passing the ship's bow, make a left turn to enter the downwind leg on the ship's port side.
3. Keep the circuit (pattern) small.
4. Configure the aircraft for landing (i.e., gear, flaps & arrester hook down) before passing abeam the carrier on the downwind leg.
5. Prior to passing abeam the ship, slow to an intermediate approach airspeed (for Seafires, use 80 knots). Watch the carrier closely to best judge the point at which to start the turn back towards the stern of the passing ship.
6. When passing the ship's port quarter during the inbound turn towards the stern, establish the final approach airspeed (70-75 knots for a Seafire); maintain a steady rate of descent; closely monitor both the indicated airspeed and the Deck Landing Clearance Officer (DLCO, but known as a Landing Signal Officer – or LSO – in the U.S. Navy), and "make up your mind that you are going to arrive from the port quarter, and not the starboard quarter."

7. "If you have difficulty seeing the batsman [DLCO] lean your head over the port side of the cockpit."
8. Wear Mk. VII or Mk. VIII goggles.

The foregoing formed Quill's methodology. In the summary of his report, he did not use the term "curved approach," but that is exactly what he described. Unlike a rectangular traffic pattern, Quill's close-in circuit would require a continuous turn that would terminate close to the fantail of the carrier. The low circuit height was necessary to ensure there would be just a modest descent gradient from the circuit altitude to the deck of the carrier, typically about 70 feet above the waterline. A shallow to moderate bank would be sufficient; at the reduced airspeed of Quill's approach, the turn radius would be relatively tight at speeds below 80 knots. During darkness or very reduced visibility, that proximity to the ship would help young, low time pilots maintain visual contact and avoid spacial disorientation.

It is noteworthy how Quill succinctly but firmly emphasized how critical it was to use the turning maneuver as a means of not overshooting an extended centerline of the deck. For one thing, the DLCO closely monitored each arriving aircraft, and used hand held batons and gestures to guide to pilot to the "cut," the point where the pilot was to cut the throttle to idle for the landing (or trap). In cases where the approach was dangerous or otherwise lacking, or where the landing zone was not clear, the DCLO would signal a "wave off." Only by keeping the DCLO in view could the pilot see the signal to "cut" or execute a wave off. If the pilot accidently crossed the extended centerline and ended up to the starboard (right) side of that line, a close-in turn to the left would be needed. Erratic close-in maneuvering could place the DCLO completely out of view when that officer absolutely had to be seen.

In addition, close-in maneuvering – especially where the arriving aircraft had to maneuver back onto the centerline following a wide turn – created a very significant risk that if a wave off were not signaled (or if a wave off signal were missed) the aircraft would contact the deck with an excessive sideload, or with a misalignment. A crash on the deck would often result from such an error, which if minor might cause a landing gear failure or a bent prop. But in many cases such a crash on the deck could rip off a wing, sever the fuselage, or send the aircraft skidding off the port side of the deck and plunging into the ocean. Such crashes were almost always fatal.

After the method of approach, the second factor that Quill listed which governed the success of carrier landings was "the view from the aeroplane." That the pilot needed to keep the carrier and the DLCO in sight was well understood, but doing that would not be possible unless the pilot could look to the side – way from the nose – to maintain that visual contact. Keeping everything in sight was also essential to control the geometry of the turn. Unlike the land-based pilot approaching a stationary airport and using a rectangular traffic pattern, the carrier pilot would start a circular approach with the banked turn continuing almost to the stern of the ship. Significantly, the aircraft carrier would be steaming away from the arriving aircraft; this is not as simple as approaching a land airport. In fact, the speed of even a slow escort carrier through the water (let's say at 16 knots) would be more than twenty percent of the final approach of a Seafire. This relative movement would have to be compensated for throughout the landing approach; the more distant the ship became as it steamed away, the flatter the approach. So a good view from the cockpit was essential.

As if all that weren't enough, the pilot could be distracted by rolling and pitching motion of the deck, and the need to maintain the proper interval with the aircraft ahead. That was often the case, with time intervals between arriving aircraft as low as thirty seconds. It is not hard to understand why so many carrier approaches lacked the requisite precision, despite the often deadly consequences. So Quill's "view from the aeroplane" was an essential factor, to the point where the use of proper goggles and leaning to the side of the open cockpit near the end of the approach could make a critical difference.

F4Us on the deck of the *U.S.S. Attu* (CVE-102) at the end of the war. From this close view the reader will appreciate the very small size of an escort carrier's deck. Image trying to land on a deck this small at sea, often during poor visibility or night – and in an aircraft where the pilot's forward view is blocked by the nose! Image source/credit: Courtesy of the Emil Buehler Library Collections of the National Museum of Naval Aviation, from the Robert L. Lawson Photograph Collection, Accession Number 1996.488.035.002.

The third main factor that Quill listed as essential to successful carrier landings was "the speed controllability of the aeroplane." One can easily see why this was so critical. Unlike a landing at an airfield ashore, the naval aircraft approach path (if all went well) would terminate at a point where the arresting cables crossed the deck. Upon arrival at that point the aircraft would be "trapped" by the arrester hook snagging a cable, at which point the aircraft would abruptly cease to fly. This was completely different from landing within a touchdown zone within the first third of a large land runway. And during the Second World War, there were no angled flight decks on aircraft carriers. In fact, there was a substantial barrier placed across the deck immediately beyond the landing area. If the arriving aircraft failed to stop (by hooking onto the arresting cable) it would crash into the barrier, which would prevent the plane from destroying other aircraft that would have been moved to the forward deck after landing.

The need to land firmly at the desired point on the deck required that the arriving aircraft be only slightly above its stall speed; that would preclude "floating." This would not happen unless that aircraft were close to the desired airspeed, so airspeed control was another critical factor. In the case of the Seafire, the pilot enjoyed excellent controllability about all three axis and very straightforward stall characteristics. But excellent controllability is different from stability.

In designing a highly maneuverable dogfighter, R. J. Mitchell gave up a substantial degree of stability. The Spitfire or Seafire pilot could command rapid rates of roll, and pitch rapidly towards the vertical – and well beyond, as in a loop. But the qualities that made the Spitfire a great interceptor also made it not so nice in other areas, as for example in instrument flying. Quill, one of the Spitfires greatest admirers and advocates, was also very direct about the lack of pitch stability. That was emphasized in his report, where he used the term "fore and aft stability." The problem of poor pitch stability reared its ugly head in three major ways during an approach to an aircraft carrier. This applied to the Seafire, but the principle was equally valid for other long-nosed, single engine fighters like the F4U.

The first such problem was the all important speed control. Even relatively small pitch changes could cause an unacceptable increase or decrease in airspeed, and with less pitch stability inadvertent errors could easily occur. The second problem was that of maintaining a relatively constant pitch attitude so that the aircraft would be ready to land at the "cut." The curved approach began on the downwind leg and was completed near the ship's stern, so the aircraft needed to be in a pitch attitude from which the pilot could respond to the DCLO's signal to "cut" the power and snag an arresting cable. With poor pitch stability, the naval aviator might unknowingly allow the nose to get too high or too low while turning back towards the carrier. So the young naval aviator would be flying his aircraft, judging his turn radius, looking for the batsman's signals, and doing this in all kinds of visibility, lighting and sea conditions. Sometimes this would be done in a battle damaged aircraft. So deviations from the desired pitch attitude and airspeed could easily occur.

The third problem would be the potential for pilot-induced-oscillations. Coming around the curved pattern towards the deck, the pilot would have to make any adjustments to turn radius, airspeed, or rate of descent as he was drawing closer and closer to the deck. The risk of overcorrecting to salvage an imperfect approach was real, especially when an aircraft was low on fuel and a "wave off" would make the situation critical.

Quill also addressed the matter of aircraft configuration as it related to speed control. One problem with the aerodynamically clean Seafire was that even with its gear and flaps down the Seafire has less than the optimal drag for good speed control. The F4U, on the other hand, had massive amounts of drag; its large flaps could be extended downward some sixty degrees. The main landing gear (including its doors) produced a further addition of drag. Of course, all of that drag became a problem if the airspeed deteriorated or if the pilot received a wave off close to the deck, but it did help in keeping the airspeed under control during the landing approach.

Quill's February 1944 report to the Admiralty came as the Fleet Air Arm was working up its squadrons in preparation for Operation Dragoon, the Allied invasion of France (D-Day, 6 June 1944). The report also followed the Fleet Air Arm's use of carrier-based Corsairs during the 3 April 1944 attack on the German battleship *Tirpitz*. No. 1834 Squadron, flying off the *H.M.S. Victorious*, provided fighter top cover for the attacking aircraft, although there was no aerial engagement. But Fleet Air Arm operations up to that point did not directly benefit from Quill's report. The succession of incremental improvements, skillful flying and the imperatives of war resulted in the overall success of the Royal Navy Seafire and Corsair squadrons.

April 1944 was also the month that Vought's improved "longstroke" main landing gear struts established an improved landing capability. With this modification, a very thorough landing evaluation aboard the *U.S.S. Gambier Bay* resulted in the U.S. Navy's decision to allow the F4U to serve aboard aircraft carriers. But the U.S. Navy, and not without some very good reasons, delayed that authorization until the latter part of the war. The F4U had enjoyed considerable success as a land-based fighter up to that point. In addition to being the Marine Corps frontline fighter, F4U-2 night fighters with the Navy's VF(N)-75 squadron had demonstrated the Corsairs ability to perform radar-guided nighttime intercepts.

The first successful intercept at night occurred while operating over New Georgia Island in late October 1943; this validated the importance of radar. In March 1944, the month after Quill's report was submitted to the Fleet Air Arm, the U.S. Marine Corps began using the F4U as a dive bomber. This was especially important in the Pacific theater, and was further evidence of the Corsair's multi-role capabilities. And with the Grumman F6F Hellcat proving its worth as a fighter with shipboard squadrons, the U.S. Navy had every reason to delay shipboard approval for the Corsair.

The extension of F4U operations to shipboard operations was also derived from feedback within stateside U.S. Navy channels. The incremental modifications to the main landing gear, tailwheel, canopy and height of the pilot's seat, plus the addition of a spoiler to the right outboard wing, did not provide enough of a cumulative improvement until the spring of 1944. So as late as March, the chief of operational training at NAS Jacksonville regarded the deck landing characteristics of the F4U as dangerous. This concern, born out by a high accident rate for pilots training in the F4U, involved more than loss of control during the final stages of the landing approach. Even when the Corsair made a successful approach and cut, engaged the cable and arrived on the carrier deck, it was then prone to swerving and bouncing. It was the improved main gear oleo that finally provided sufficient improvement to overcome the widespread concerns. Once the *Gambier Bay* landing trials (with 113 landings) demonstrated a marked improvement in handling, the F4U was ready to go to sea. By mid-May 1944, the U.S. Navy went even farther. It determined that the F4U was the best all-around naval fighter. Thereafter, even existing squadrons would transition to the Corsair.

The acceptance of the F4U for shipboard operations did not change one underlying fact. The Corsair, the U.S. Navy's fastest and most capable fighter towards the end of the war, still had very undesirable handling traits while approaching and landing on a carrier. The most egregious handling problems had been mitigated, but bringing an F4U safely aboard a ship at sea would always be challenging. Royal Navy Lt. Eric M. Brown (later captain) flew the Corsair on land and sea and, despite being impressed with the range and performance, still found its landing characteristics to be deficient.

"It had its own nasty and vicious characteristic if a pilot undertaking a deck landing got too slow on the final stage of the approach" noted Brown. He added that if the pilot then "gunned the throttle . . . this caused the aircraft to rotate around the huge propeller and crash inverted into the carrier's stern, always with fatal results."

Risks to pilots were also present at greater altitudes. In the landing configuration with an approach speed of 80 knots, Brown discovered that with minor changes in the wings angle of attack the F4U could enter a stall abruptly. Entering the stall the right wing on Brown's test aircraft would drop suddenly, and a spin entry could immediately follow. If such a stall were entered at (e.g.) a height below 200 feet, the recovery would have to be initiated immediately and positively.

Brown's opinion carries a special weight. As a leading test pilot in the Royal Navy, he flight tested every Fleet Air Arm aircraft of World War Two, including the Corsair. Brown also set the record for the most landings on an aircraft carrier of any naval aviator, an incredible 2,407. Eric Brown's special skills at carrier landing resulted in his extensive experience landing aircraft on carriers during and after the war. Yet his comfort zone for carrier landings was badly breached by the F4U.

One thing that both Eric Brown and Jeffrey Quill agreed on was the need for Corsair pilots to fly a curved approach to the ship's stern. That was the only way to keep both the carrier and the DLCO (or LSO in the U.S. Navy) in sight while flying at the correct pitch attitude and approach airspeed. Yet even on a curved approach, both the ailerons and elevator were found be sluggish. And this dismal view was just for the approach. After the "cut" Brown lamented how the nose would drop heavily, often resulting in a bounce. Vought's improved main gear oleos mitigated the problem of bouncing, and an improved tailwheel design also improved directional control problems once the Corsair was on the carrier deck. An objective evaluator, Brown did praise the aircraft's inflight stability, ruggedness and its rapid acceleration. So once Vought's numerous improvements were made (either at the factory or in the field), what were originally extremely poor handling traits during approaches and landings became tolerable, albeit barely so.

By the time U.S. Navy carriers began using the F4U in large numbers, the experience level of pilots and operational squadrons had dramatically increased. That helped to reduce the accident rate, but landing the Corsair aboard a carrier was always a demanding task. And the U.S. Navy never really copied Fleet Air Arm methods, instead using a slightly flatter approach and slightly higher "cut."

"The U.S. Navy had a different technique" Brown confirmed, "approaching straight and descending to about 50 feet above the deck, then leveling off some 50 yards from the ship's stern. The LSO would normally give the 'cut' as the aircraft crossed the stern, and the pilot would then push forward into the arrester wire area.

"There was a spell shortly after the end of World War Two when the Royal Navy adapted the American deck landing methodology in the interest of facilitating cross-operations, but this proved very unpopular with the British, whose accident rate increased as a result."

So the ship landing doctrines and methodology between the Royal Navy and the U.S. Navy were different, but there is yet another twist to this story. Many U.S. Navy pilots seemed to have adopted the curved approach and, while they may have rolled out to a straight in final, the final approach was often quite short. The use of this technique minimizing the time that the view of the LSO was restricted by the Corsair's long nose. The curved approach with a very short final has been revealed in photographs of approaching F4Us, and also by then-Lt. Cdr. "Tommy" Blackburn. In his first shipboard landing in a Corsair, Blackburn approached the *U.S.S. Charger* in Chesapeake Bay using a curved approach. Flying at a low airspeed – and very close to the 1.1 V_s velocity used by the Fleet Air Arm – Blackburn rolled onto a very short final just one hundred yards astern of the ship.

Late in the war, American fleet carriers with night fighter squadrons utilized AN/APS-4 "Snapper" radars to aid both pilots, the Snapper control officer, and the Landing Signal Officer (LSO) at the stern. Under ideal conditions, Snapper – usually a qualified pilot working with radar operators at the ship's port beam – would "call the turns" so that the pilot would be radar guided to a downwind leg roughly

1,600 yards off the ship's beam. Snapper, who could communicate with the pilot, the bridge and the LSO using split phones, could also reduce pilot workload by calling the final turn back towards the ship. This would ideally have the pilot "in the groove" just 100 yards from the "cut" at the ships stern.

So it was the Royal Navy's Fleet Air Arm that first made effective use of the F4U as a shipboard fighter. The Fleet Air Arm also deserves credit for establishing the doctrine of the slow, curved approach with a constant gradient to the "cut." Some American squadron commanders, like Lt. Cdr. Tommy Blackburn of VF-17, apparently used the method, albeit informally. Yet in the incomplete history of the Corsair there is an unknown number that does not appear in the statistics of aerial victories, missions flown and battles won. That unknown is the number of pilots who safely returned to their ship, but who might otherwise have been lost while flying the "Ensign Eliminator." Developing procedures to enable young Corsair pilots to be on a stabilized approach and "in the groove" in all types of weather, lighting and sea conditions, was an important part of taking the ill-mannered Corsair to war at sea. In meeting that critical need, the quiet heroes of the Royal Navy's Fleet Air Arm led the way.

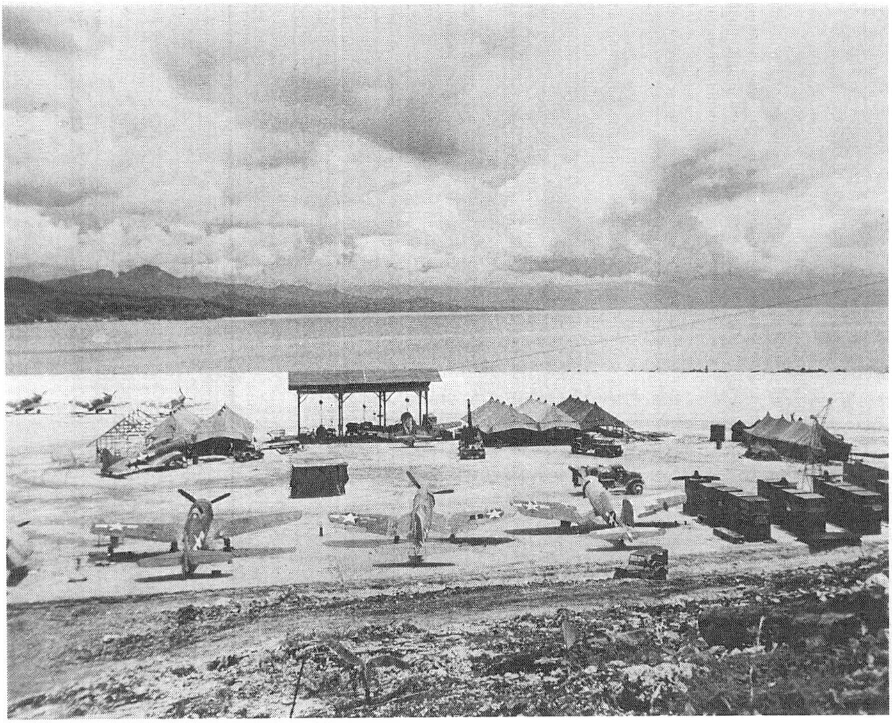

Chapter Six

F4U Corsairs of the U.S. Navy and Marine Corps

> ... *Separated from his escort group when he encountered approximately 50 Japanese Zeros, he unhesitatingly attacked, striking with relentless fury in his lone battle against a powerful force. He destroyed 4 hostile fighters before cannon shellfire forced him to make a dead-stick landing off Vella Lavella where he was later picked up. His valiant leadership and his daring skill as a flier served as a source of confidence and inspiration to his fellow pilots and reflect the highest credit upon the U.S. Naval Service.*
>
> – From the Medal of Honor citation for 1Lt. Kenneth A. Walsh, of Marine Fighting Squadron 124, for valor in action against overwhelming enemy forces in the Solomon Islands area on 30 August 1943. Walsh was the first F4U ace of the war.

It was an unfinished airfield on remote Guadalcanal Island, yet it resulted in the first Allied offensive campaign in the Pacific. Located off the northeast coast of Australia in the British Solomon Islands, Guadalcanal was strategically important. By mid-1942, Japan had already captured and occupied Thailand, Burma, Singapore, Malaya, the Philippine Islands, the Dutch East Indies, Guam, and Wake Island. It also occupied the northern portion of Papua New Guinea, and was positioning ground forces for an attack on Port Moresby. Guadalcanal was strategically important to Japan, since it could be used as an air base to gain air superiority over the ocean near Australia, New Zealand, and the surrounding sea-lanes. Occupied by Japanese forces in July 1942, the unfinished airfield was equally important to the Allies. Admiral Ernest King, the U.S. Chief of Naval Operations, became the leading pro-

Developing the Gull-Winged F4U Corsair - And Taking It To Sea

ponent of an attack on Guadalcanal. King overcame opposition from General George C. Marshall, and plans for an amphibious assault were quickly prepared. On 7 August 1942, a force that was spearheaded by U.S. Marines invaded the island and quickly captured the unfinished airfield. So began the six-month long Guadalcanal Campaign, and some of the bloodiest fighting of the Second World War. The captured airstrip was named Henderson Field in honor of Major Lofton Henderson, the first Marine Corps pilot to be killed in action during the war.

The decision to allocate F4U production to the U.S. Marine Corps occurred during the Guadalcanal Campaign. Here, the timeline tells the story. On 25 September 1942, the F4U failed its initial carrier landing trials aboard the *U.S.S. Sangamon* (CVE-26). That failure occurred less than two weeks after the crucial battle at Bloody Ridge, when the Marines 1st Raider Battalion repelled an assault by Japan's 35th Infantry Brigade near the Lunga River. Henderson Field on Guadalcanal remained in American hands, but just barely. America's Joint Chiefs of Staff knew that more battles would follow, including Japanese air attacks and the deployment of additional troops at night by the "Tokyo Express," the name given to the Japanese destroyers and submarines that transported troops to the island under cover of darkness. In October, with Guadalcanal and its all-important Henderson Field still under American control, the Japanese began major counterattacks. The Battle of Cape Esperance resulted in a naval defeat for the Imperial Japanese Navy off the north coast of Guadalcanal, but not before Japanese transport ships landed several thousand reinforcements on the island. On 23 October 1942 the reinforced Japanese forces on Guadalcanal began a three-day battle to retake Henderson Field. Even before that battle began, the Navy – fully aware of the strategic importance of the Solomon Islands and the need for better fighter aircraft – began to allocate brand-new F4Us to the Marine Corps. On 26 October, VMF-124 received its first Corsairs.

The failure of the F4U during its carrier landing trials was disappointing to officials at the Bureau of Aeronautics and at Vought, but it led to a fortuitous turn of events. The U.S. Marine Corps, although a naval service and part of the Department of the Navy, usually operated its naval aircraft from shore bases. After the Marines assaulted Guadalcanal (and nearby islands) on 7 August 1942, Allied tactical air operations were established on the island and referred to as the Cactus Air Force (until the end of 1942, when it was redesignated as AirSol). From Henderson Field (and various satellite airstrips), Cactus Air Force fighters – mostly U.S. Army Air Force P-400s (a faster version of the Bell P-39), Curtiss P-40s and Grumman F4F Wildcats – began defensive and offensive missions. These aircraft were critical to the defense of Guadalcanal since the ninety-mile long island had not been secured.

The use of P-400s, P-40s and F4Fs was only a stopgap measure. The P-400's nose-firing 37-mm cannon and wing-mounted 50-calibre machine guns could be devastating against enemy landing craft and attacking ground forces, so the marines and soldiers did have some close-in air support. Moreover, the P-400 was wholly inadequate for air-to-air combat, especially at altitudes above fifteen thousand feet. The Curtiss P-40 Warhawk and the Grumman F4F Wildcat were far more capable as fighters, but still inadequate. So the marines and soldiers on the ground at Guadalcanal would have to fight with what they had. And they fought hard, with six Marine Corps pilots receiving the Medal of Honor for valor in the skies over the Solomon Islands.

By the beginning of 1943 the Japanese High Command, recognizing that Guadalcanal had been lost to the Allies, began to withdraw its troops from the island. The American victory was the equivalent of the naval victory at the Battle of Midway, after which the Imperial Japanese Navy lost its offensive advantage. American marines and soldiers on Guadalcanal would continue to endure air raids as they secured other parts of the island, but they still lacked a long-range multi-role fighter that was superior to those of the enemy. The F4U would change that.

Whatever its limitations in carrier landings, the F4U could certainly operate from land airfields. So during October 1942, with combat still raging on and over Guadalcanal, the Marines transitioned the newly organized VMF-124 (under Major William Gise) from F4F Wildcats to F4U Corsairs. The first F4U-1s began arriving on 26 October, just one month and a day after the unsatisfactory carrier trials. There were just a few weeks to teach the young Marine pilots the basics of flying the Corsair and de-bug the aircraft.

The hectic pace continued. Then, on 28 December 1942 VMF-124 with its twenty-two Corsairs was declared operational. In early January 1943, with hardly any break, the unit sailed from San Diego bound for Espiritu Santo (in the New Hebrides archipelago). From the staging and maintenance airbase at Espiritu Santo, VMF-124 flew into Henderson Field, arriving on Guadalcanal on 12 February 1943, just days after the Guadalcanal Campaign officially ended. But while one campaign had ended, the tempo of the war did not change. Within just an hour of the squadron's arrival, VMF-124 flew its first mission – it escorted a PBY Catalina on a 230-mile rescue mission to pick up two downed pilots at Sandfly Bay, Vella Lavella. No fighter opposition appeared, but that did not matter. Two years and four months after Lyman Bullard first coaxed the XF4U-1 past 400 m.p.h. in level flight, the Vought F4U Corsair had gone to war.

VMF-124 arrived at Henderson Field as the Guadalcanal Campaign was drawing to an end, but it was a useful base from which to begin combat operations. In particular, the use of the F4U for operational sorties and the tempo of combat operations enabled the Marine Corps and Vought to identify maintenance issues and other problems that would only be corrected with modifications. Some of those issues derived from the aircraft configuration. The F4U-1s of VMF-124 had the original "birdcage" canopy, and the restricted visibility that resulted from the low canopy and low seat position were not helpful during combat air patrols. The original tailwheel and strut also created problems while landing at Henderson Field, since the three-point touchdown attitude was decidedly nose-high. So the process of correcting problems with the F4U and providing feedback to the Navy in Washington and Vought at its Stratford, Connecticut plant continued. That feedback came from squadron pilots and operations officers, non-commissioned officers (NCOs) involved in squadron level maintenance, and also from Vought tech-reps who were deployed in the combat theaters. Due to the haste with which VMF-214 departed from San Diego, fly-away kits were hurriedly sent to the Southwest Pacific for installation at Espiritu Santo. In reality, corrective maintenance continued even after the squadron was operational at Henderson Field. Feedback from operational squadrons (e.g., power loss at high altitude due to inadequate pressurization of the ignition harness) resulted in de facto modifications on the factory floor, kits for in-service repair and successive model changes. The process of improvement, beginning with the February, 1943 arrival of VMF-124 on Guadalcanal Island, would continue throughout the war.

Despite the limitations of the birdcage cockpit and short tailwheel, the first F4U-1s to enter combat had the improved ailerons that noticeably increased the roll rate; this improvement was very important to a fighter that would have to engage the nimble Japanese Zero. The -1 also had the improved slotted flaps, which offered a marginal improvement for slow approaches to aircraft carriers and short runways. The early -1 Corsairs had the -8 version of the R-2800 Double Wasp. The -8 had just a single-stage supercharger and lacked the water-injection system of the -8W version; the latter would later add another 250 h.p. for up to five minutes. Aside from the above-noted ignition harness issue, the simple engine configuration of the first Marine Corps Corsairs simplified squadron maintenance. Along with the learning curve for maintenance, Marine Corps pilots were learning how to best use their new and potent weapon.

The first fighter escort mission of VFM-124 occurred on 13 February 1943, and was uneventful. The next mission was not. On 14 February VMF-124 was part of the fighter escort for a group of PB4Y Privateer (the naval version of Liberator) bombers that attacked Japanese shipping near Kahili Aerodrome on Bougainville Island. The target area was some three hundred miles north of Guadalcanal, and well within the range of the fighter escorts. The bombardment of 14 February 1943 was to be a repeat of the previous day's raid, except that this time the attacking force was met by approximately fifty Imperial Japanese Navy A6M Zeros. At the end of the aerial engagement, only three Japanese fighters were lost versus eight American fighters, including two F4Us, two P-40s and four P-38s. The raid was dubbed "The St. Valentine's Day Massacre" and it had a sobering effect on Cactus Air Force morale. However, Allied pilots quickly developed tactics that could defeat the Zero (and other Japanese fighters) in most aerial encounters.

Even with the early single-stage supercharger, the F4U-1 had more than adequate level flight speed to take on its adversaries in a dogfight. With its improved ailerons, the Corsair could out-roll and out-turn the nimble A6M Zero as long as it kept its speed up. Another key element was to begin an encounter with an altitude advantage. Flying top cover for attacking bombers, the F4U would be considerably slower than its desired engagement speed. By starting an engagement with an altitude advantage, the aerodynamically clean F4U could rapidly accelerate and force the adversary to fight on its terms. Using its speed advantage, the F4U could often disengage from, and then re-engage, enemy fighters. So early detection and starting with an altitude advantage were important. VMF-124 pilots quickly learned how to engage the enemy, and in air-to-air engagements they would repeatedly use that advantage.

Once acclimated to their new theater of operations, the pilots of VMF-124 and other F4U squadrons were also able to exploit the multi-role capabilities of the aircraft. Defensively, the Corsair could act as an interceptor. And unlike the F4F Wildcat, the Corsair was an effective air superiority fighter. It had the range, speed, altitude, and maneuvering capabilities, plus the necessary firepower, to establish dominance over any adversary. As would also soon be established, the F4U could be highly effective in ground attack roles, operating in offensive strike packages, harassing hostile positions by strafing, and close-in support of friendly troops. In time dive bombing, night interception (using radar-equipped F4U-2s) and photo reconnaissance would become additional mission capabilities. To see how the growing numbers of F4Us were deployed in these various missions, it is helpful to look at the theater of operations.

First Lieutenant Kenneth A. Walsh of Brooklyn, New York, America's No. 2 ace with 20 Japanese planes downed over Guadalcanal, Russell Islands and Munda, stands outside his hut at his fighter base. Two old propellers bear miniature Japanese flags, one for each plane.

Mild-Mannered Marines and Tough Corsairs Prove Deadly Combat Combination

"WE WERE badly outnumbered, fighting between 50 and 60 Zeros. . . . The strong construction of our planes got us out uninjured. . . . The engines and propellers really came through for us. . . . My engine was badly hit and I had to fly 135 miles with only 40 pounds oil pressure. . . . Many of the boys came back with many hits in their engines. . . . I had 20mm shells through the propellers and the engine. . . . The Corsair brought us through some tough fighting. . . . I've seen the boys come back with up to 100 cannon and bullet holes in their planes."

These graphic remarks of four Marine Corps fighter pilots, just returned from the Southwest Pacific war zone, highlighted their appearance before employees of Chance Vought, Pratt & Whitney and Hamilton Standard divisions as they reported on the achievements of the battle-tested Vought Corsair.

First To Fly F4U in Combat

Members of VMF 124—first squadron to take the Vought Corsair into combat last winter—and of VMF 112, which followed it by only a few weeks, the quartet returned to this country ten months later with 20 weeks of combat service recorded. They spoke before employees of both shifts at a Navy Day rally in the Vought plant at Stratford and a few days later addressed a capacity audience of P & WA and HSP employees at the Bushnell Memorial auditorium in Hartford.

Their public appearances followed tours of the three main plants responsible for production of the fighter in which they had set a new pace in enemy fighter destruction.

The youthful visitors, whose famous outfits were responsible for the downing of more than 150 Japanese planes were: First Lieutenant Kenneth A. Walsh of Brooklyn, New York, America's No. 2 ace with 20 Japanese planes shot down; Captain Joseph F. Quilty, Jr. of Boston, Massachusetts, operations officer and Captain Louis R. Smunk of Flushing, Long Island, all members of Squadron 124, with 68 enemy aircraft "certains" and 25 "probables" against a loss of only three pilots and Captain Joseph P. Lynch of Hyde Park, Massachusetts, whose Squadron 112, better

SEPT.-OCT.-NOV. 1943   PAGE NINE

Lt. Kenneth A. Walsh was an enlisted pilot before receiving his USMC commission. One of the highest scoring aces, Walsh received the Medal of Honor for his exploits in the Solomon Island region. Image source/credit: Igor I. Sikorsky Historical Archives, Inc.

Naval Air War in the Pacific, 1943

The Japanese defeat at Guadalcanal and the surrounding islands put the Empire on the defensive. Yet the change in the initiative did not alter the fact that Japan still had established air and naval bases stretching from the northern Solomon Islands to its main island of Honshu, as well as Burma, Indochina and Manchuria. In addition to its army and marine forces, Japan's air and naval assets were still formidable, despite the loss of four aircraft carriers during the Battle of Midway. Allied air assets on and near Guadalcanal would thereafter be used for both defensive purposes and offensive operations. In visualizing the geographical area of operations, it is helpful to bear in mind just how far south in the Southwest Pacific Guadalcanal and the Solomon Islands are. Situated just east-northeast of Australia and southeast of Bougainville, Rabaul and the Admiralty Islands, Guadalcanal is over three-thousand miles south of the Japanese home islands and roughly thirty-four hundred miles from Tokyo. In fact, Guadalcanal is closer to the Indian Ocean than Hawaii. From that very distant starting point, Allied forces would move progressively closer to Japan.

In June, 1943, the Allies implemented Operation Cartwheel. The impetus of the Allied offensive was to isolate Japan's very significant forward base at Rabaul (on New Britain Island, east of New Guinea), and thereafter adopt an island-hopping campaign that would take the Allied forces close to the Japanese home islands. In addition to long-range bombers, long-range fighters such as the F4U, P-38 and P-47 would play a crucial role. The northward advance of the Allies meant that land bases would be available for land-based fighters, including the F4U. Rapidly increasing F4U production ensured that Marine Corps squadrons would all get the F4U as replacements for the slower and less capable Grumman F4F Wildcat. Putting large numbers of Corsairs into Marine Corps squadrons during 1943, and not the delay in qualifying the aircraft for aircraft carrier operations, would have the biggest impact on the naval air war in the Pacific. By the end of the year, some 2,471 Corsairs had been produced by Vought, Goodyear and Brewster Aeronautical. Besides VMF-124, early Marine Corps squadrons that operated the F4U (including Goodyear or Brewster versions) included VMF-121, VMF-112, VMF-122, VMF-213, VMF-214 and VMF-221. In addition, VMF(N)-532, a night fighter squadron operating the F4U-2, was commissioned at MCAS Cherry Point. But while the U.S. Marines were the first to take the F4U into combat, the U.S. Navy was playing catch up.

VF-12 had been the first Navy squadron to qualify in the F4U, transitioning at NAS North Island in San Diego at the same time that VMF-124 was at nearby Camp Kearney. But the transition to the F4U was difficult. VF-12 sailed from San Diego to the southwest Pacific aboard the *U.S.S. Cole* (CVE-13), arriving in Espiritu Santo in March. The long voyage across the Pacific Ocean gave VF-12 additional "work-up" time, especially in aircraft carrier takeoffs and landings. It was not a pretty picture. The squadron's F4U-1s were equipped with the extended tailwheel strut and pneumatic tires. The longer strut was a big improvement, but the pneumatic tires were prone to frequent failures. Some fourteen pilots of VF-12 were killed in training accidents by the time the *Cole* arrived at Espiritu Santa in the New Hebrides. The problems extended far beyond the bad tires. Landing on the smaller escort carrier required an approach that allowed little marginal for error, even in smooth air. In addition to the nasty stall characteristics, the lack of harmony of the primary flight controls and very poor forward visibility exceeded the capabilities of many new pilots. The number of close calls was undoubtedly much higher, since the Corsair's departure from controlled flight at slow approach and landing speeds could be sudden. Even takeoffs posed significant risks if a pilot applied excessive elevator and/or aileron inputs, as might occur if the pilot turned away from the ship's forward path too abruptly. The very poor safety record and high loss of life contributed to VF-12's almost immediate retirement of the F4U. After it arrived in the combat theater, the squadron replaced its Corsairs with the much more pilot-friendly Grumman F6F Hellcat. The Corsair was already establishing its reputation as an "Ensign Eliminator" with the fleet. With more than a little disdain, VF-12 pilots dubbed it the "Hog."

Developing the Gull-Winged F4U Corsair - And Taking It To Sea

CHANCE VOUGHT AIRCRAFT

Corsair Builders Overcome Severe Production Problems To Win "E"

CHEERS echoed through the Chance Vought plant at Stratford on Navy Day when the employees, gathered to hear five Marine fighter pilots tell of the Corsair in action, learned that the division was to receive the Army-Navy "E" award for production achievement. The announcement by General Manager Rex B. Beisel came soon after an appeal from the Navy for still more Corsairs for the fighting fronts.

James Forrestal, Under Secretary of the Navy, expressed "full confidence that your present high achievement is indicative of what you will do in the future" in the letter of notification.

Won Despite Handicaps

The award has been won despite tremendous engineering and manufacturing problems encountered in the course of changeover from the Kingfisher scouting plane, in quantity production for the Navy at the time of Pearl Harbor, to the Corsair, a full-fledged fighting craft designed to break the Japanese hold on air superiority in the Pacific.

Doubling in Brass

At one time Kingfishers and Corsairs were coming down the Vought assembly line together and it was not until the Kingfisher contract was completed that the division could devote its entire effort to attainment of a high Corsair production rate.

A rapid increase in personnel, thousands of whom had to be trained for the precision work required in aircraft production, was effected despite the inroads of the Selective Service system. Women, who previously had never done any mechanical work, were employed and proved in a short time their ability to match the performance of men in many production phases.

First Corsair Completed

The first Corsair rolled from the assembly line late in June, 1942, and in response to an exacting schedule set by the Navy, production rose to the point where Corsairs are now being turned out at a rate considered impossible a few months ago.

Improved manufacturing methods and a moving conveyor line system, together with continuing plant expansion and the "farming out" of sub-assembly and other parts work, are all combining to assure the bettering of today's— and tomorrow's—production rates.

R. I. State College Honors Igor Sikorsky

The honorary degree of Doctor of Science has been conferred on Igor I. Sikorsky, Engineering Manager of Sikorsky Aircraft division of United Aircraft Corporation.

The award was made September 19 at the 51st commencement of Rhode Island State College, where for nine years the helicopter inventor and airplane designer has been a faculty consultant and lecturer on aeronautics.

Corsairs are shown in procession as they taxi down the steel mat runway on Henderson Field, Guadalcanal, to take off against the enemy.

PAGE TWENTY-TWO　　　　　THE BEE-HIVE

U.S. Marine Corps F4U Corsairs taxi out at Henderson Field on Guadalcanal Island in the Solomons. The F4U could beat the highly maneuverable Japanese 'Zero' fighter, but were often outnumbered. The Corsair was a big improvement over the Grumman F4F Wildcat. Image source/credit: Courtesy of the Igor I. Sikorsky Historical Archives, Inc.

146

Because of the transition of VF-12 into Grumman F6F Hellcats, it was VF-17 that initially took the F4U into combat for the U.S. Navy. Under the command of Lt. Cdr. "Tommy" Blackburn, VF-17 was known as the "Jolly Rogers" and became one of the Navy's premier F4U squadrons. Like the Marine Corps squadrons, VF-17 and other Navy units operated from land bases during 1943. At this time the U.S. Navy still considered the Corsair unsuitable for shipboard operations, and would for some time to come. Even while restricted to land bases, the F4U remained a problematic aircraft with a nasty and sudden stall, very poor forward visibility and a host of other problems (e.g., the poorly-pressurized ignition harnesses) that needed to be worked out. Yet the aircraft's deficiencies and the operational restrictions did not hinder the F4U's success, and may have enhanced its usefulness as a multi-role fighter. The early Marine Corps and Navy F4U squadrons, relieved of the burdens of shipboard operations, were developing the tactics that would minimize the Corsair's limitations in a dogfight while exploiting the many weaknesses of its enemies. These tactics, along with skill and an abundance of aggressiveness, led to successful missions and increased kills by both Marine Corps and Navy pilots. As Allied forces began the northward movement against Japanese positions, it was the F4U's superiority – in performance, range, load carrying capability, survivability, and multi-role capabilities – that increasingly drew attention of Allied planners. So it was in 1943 that the full potential of the F4U as a weapon system began to be realized.

Along with the aircraft's inherent capabilities, much of Corsair's early success in combat derived from the skill and tenacity of its Navy and Marine Corps pilots. One example was Marine First Lt. Kenneth A. Walsh, a one-time enlisted pilot who served with VMF-124 during its initial deployment. An aggressive flight leader, Walsh scored his first three aerial victories during a mission on 1 April 1943. This action was one of the many engagements that followed the activation of Admiral Isoroku Yamamoto's *I-Plan*, in which the Imperial Japanese Navy (IJM) planned to stop any Allied advance beyond the Solomon Islands. Walsh's first victories included two A6M Zero fighters and one "Val" dive bomber. On his next engagement on 13 May, he scored two more kills, thereby becoming the first F4U Corsair ace of the war. Walsh participated in the numerous fighter sweeps and escort missions of VMF-124, and was awarded the Medal of Honor for additional victories during aerial engagements of 15 August over Vella Lavella and 30 August over Bougainville. These engagements occurred during the Allied assault on New Georgia, during which Walsh repeatedly dove into overwhelming enemy forces while bringing his total number of aerial victories to twenty. In racking up his impressive number of victories, Walsh had to ditch or force land disabled aircraft on more than one occasion, and was finally shot down after scoring his twentieth victory. Walsh would receive his Medal of Honor in early 1944 from President Roosevelt at the White House.

Walsh's exploits have been well documented, and are an important part of Marine Corps history. Significantly, the missions of VMF-124 show that besides operating over enemy controlled territory, its pilots often engaged numerically superior enemy forces. Along with the units many successes came many losses, one of them being their commanding officer. On 13 May (the day Walsh became the first Corsair ace), Maj. William Gise was killed in action while leading VMF-124 against an overwhelming force of enemy fighters near New Georgia, by September, VMF-124 completed its combat tour and was rotated to stateside duty.

As the air war in the Pacific continued during first half of 1943, Allied forces consolidated their gains. By June, the Grumman F6F Hellcat was joining the U.S. Navy's carriers, greatly improving both offensive and defensive capabilities of the fleet. In addition, three fast fleet carriers – *Essex*, *Lexington* and *Yorktown* – joined the fleet, along with six fast light carriers. With increased numbers of F4Us arriving, the Allies were ready to move beyond the Solomon-Bismark Sea frontier and attack Japanese possessions farther north. On 1 September, Marcus Island was attacked by carrier-based aircraft. On 18 and 19 September, the Gilbert Islands were attacked by aircraft from the carriers *Lexington*, *Princeton* and *Belleau Wood*. On 5 and 6 October, a force of six American carriers attacked Wake Island. It was during this engagement that the F6F scored its first aerial victory. These attacks softened up the Japanese targets, and put Japanese forces further on the defensive. Then, on 27 October, VF-17 arrived in the theater and established its base at Onodono, on New Georgia. The U.S. Navy F4U Corsairs were ready to fight.

VF-17's base at Onodongo placed the unit about halfway up the Solomon Island chain, and northwest of Guadalcanal. When the unit arrived, the Allied invasion of Bougainville was imminent. On 1 November U.S. Marines 3rd Division began a large amphibious assault at Cape Torokina, near Empress Augusta Bay on the west side of the island. VF-17 was tasked with providing top cover, and it was there that the "Jolly Rogers" first drew blood. Lt. Cdr. John "Tommy" Blackburn, VF-17 commanding officer, shot down two aircraft as the rest of the squadron downed three more. It was a most impressive outcome in the unit's first combat engagement. On 8 November, six VF-17 aircraft attacked a formation of fifteen "Val" dive bombers and twenty-four A6M Zeros escorts, shooting down three enemy fighters and damaging four others; there were no American losses.

As a squadron commanding officer, Lt. Cdr. Tommy Blackburn favored aggressive and often innovative tactics to combat the enemy. By 1943 the Japanese Zero was no longer a dominating, superior aircraft, but it still existed in substantial numbers and remained a potent adversary. Moreover, many of the IJN Zeros were land-based, which afforded them another advantage as they often operated near their home bases. But using the superior airspeed, acceleration, firepower and ruggedness of the Corsair, VF-17 quickly established a reputation as a premier F4U fighter squadron. Blackburn's unit also excelled at harassing the enemy with unexpected strafing attacks on enemy installations. Like the Marine Corps F4U pilots in the Solomon Islands, VF-17 pilots established the Corsair as a very versatile multi-role fighter, in which air intercepts, air superiority and fighter escort missions were just some of the repertoire.

The air support of the November landings on Bougainville were tactically important, but the strategic importance of those landings should be appreciated if one is to keep the Pacific war in perspective. As the largest island in the Solomon chain, Bougainville had been occupied by Japanese forces since 1942. After establishing a stronghold on the former Australian territory, the Japanese built airfields on the north, east and southern shores. By attacking the western part of the island and then building Allied airstrips, the Japanese air threat could be substantially contained. Bougainville would not be liberated until after the Japanese surrender on 2 September 1945, but the landings near

Empress Augusta Bay became a prelude for the Allied attack on Rabaul on 11 November. The Rabaul attack was spearhead by five American fast carriers, but land-based fighters augmented the fighter cover. Bougainville was roughly two-thirds of the way of the Solomon chain towards Rabaul, and momentum was clearly on the side of the Allies. Then, without stopping, the U.S. Navy attacked again. On 20 November American marines and soldiers invaded the Gilbert Islands, well to the northeast of the Solomons.

Battle damage was not the only risk that American pilots faced in the Solomons. This F4U from the VF-17 'Jolly Rogers" made an emergency landing on Nissan Island in the Green Island Group. Image source/credit: Courtesy of the Emil Buehler Library Collections of the National Museum of Naval Aviation, from the Robert L. Lawson Photograph Collection, Accession Number 1996.253.7144.033.

The Navy and Marine Corps portion of the Gilbert Island invasion was named Operation Galvanic. The strategic importance was to remove an enemy force that could threaten supply and communications between Hawaii and the southeast Pacific, as well as attacks in the central Pacific region. So Operation Galvanic, planned as a two-pronged attack against two strategically important atolls, and sailed out of Hawaii on 10 November as Task Force 52. The Order of Battle on the American side included six fleet carriers and five escort carriers under the command Rear Admiral Richmond K. Turner (commanding the northern flank) and Rear Admiral Harry Hill (southern flank). Maj. Gen. Holland M. Smith, USMC, commanded the V Amphibious Corp (i.e., the 2nd Marine Division and the Army's 27th Infantry Division); his troops would attack and capture Makin Atoll and Tarawa Atoll. Japan had no more than fifty serviceable aircraft to face roughly seven hundred American fighters and naval bombers. Between 20-23 November, after some of the most gruesome fighting of the Pacific campaign, the Japanese fortifications and airbases on the Gilbert Islands had been captured. The Allied forces had finally advanced in the central Pacific region.

On 4 December the Navy executed its last major offensive of 1943, and it was in the central Pacific Ocean. This time the target was Kwajalein, a strategically important atoll in the Marshall Islands. The U.S. Navy force included six aircraft carriers and nine cruisers, evidence of how rapidly the U.S. fleet had grown within the past year. The raid was a prelude to the invasion that would occur during 1944, but it established the effectiveness of the U.S. Navy's fast carriers. By this time the carriers operated with large numbers of F6F Hellcats, and with Curtiss SB2C-1 Helldivers often replacing the Douglas Dauntless as the principal dive bomber. This was a Navy operation, but no matter. By the end of the year, Marine Corps pilots flying F4Us had shot down an astonishing 584 enemy aircraft and had become well accustomed to their top fighter. So ended the war in the Pacific during 1943. Yet the F4U Corsair, its combat effectiveness then well established and substantially debugged, was still a year away from aircraft carrier duty.

Condition of F4Us in Squadron Service, late-1943

The main problems that were correctable had been identified by late-1943, and this was reflected in operational units in the Pacific. Raising the pilot seat and eliminating the "birdcage" canopy improved visibility, although it was still considered poor while in a three-point landing attitude. The elimination of the movable cowl flaps in front of the pilot eliminated the problem of hydraulic fluid leaking onto the windshield. The extended tailwheel strut had proven its value; directional control on landings improved and the three-point attitude was much improved. The problem with failing pneumatic tailwheels that so plagued VF-12 early in the year had been corrected. One of the most important fixes, and one that would be especially important during carrier landings, was the improved main landing gear oleos. Eliminating bounces on landings would benefit both land- and sea-based pilots, and it made a critical difference. If an F4U pilot did not lose control during the slow approach to a carrier, or take off power too soon at the "cut" he would be able to land during most sea conditions.

The Pratt & Whitney R-2800-8W provided both more "dry" power and the all-important War Emergency Power. The two-stage, two-speed supercharger proved to be reliable and adequate, not prone to the service difficulties of either water-cooled Allison engines or turbocharged versions of the R-2800. For dive bombing, Vought effectively developed the necessary modifications that permitted high-angle bombing with the main gear down and the tailwheel retracted. Unlike many air superiority fighters and interceptors, the F4U was proving its worth at strafing and bombing. The F4U-2 night fighters, although limited in numbers, were establishing the value of nighttime intercepts that were radar guided.

Of course, the Achilles heel of the F4U remained its low speed handling and stall characteristics. The addition of a roughly six-inch long spoiler on the leading edge of the right outboard wing noticeably improved the wing-dropping tendency at the stall, but it did nothing to lower the stalling speed. Although improved, the low-speed characteristics in critical approach, landing and takeoff speeds were still poor. As Capt. Eric M. Brown noted in his *Duels In The Sky: World War II Naval Aircraft In Combat*: "The Corsair was a mixture of the good, the mediocre and the bad." Yet experienced squadron pilots were to a large extent learning to compensate for the aircraft's inherent weaknesses. Like any great combat aircraft, the F4U has to be judged by the record of what it accomplished in operational service. To many pilots on missions over the Pacific, sometimes facing overwhelming odds, the F4U was often the only fighter that could prevail in battle, get the job done and still bring him safely home.

Naval Air War in the Pacific, 1944

The progress in providing necessary assets and personnel would be the major factor in the naval war during 1944. Along with the dramatically increased number of aircraft, American shipyards radically increased the production of fast carriers (CVs and CVLs), escort carriers (CVEs) and other types of surface combatants. It is a point that cannot be over emphasized.

At its low point during November 1942, just three months into the Guadalcanal Campaign, the U.S. Navy had only two operational aircraft carriers in the entire Pacific Ocean. But by mid-1943, the Navy's aggressive shipbuilding had reversed the situation, a trend that continued into 1944. Fourteen of the large, Essex class of fleet carriers saw service during the war, and seven of these – i.e., the *Franklin* (CV-13), *Ticonderoga* (CV-14), *Randolph* (CV-15), *Hancock* (CV-19), *Bennington* (CV-20), *Bon Homme Richard* (CV-31) and *Shangri-La* (CV-38) – entered service during 1944. This was in addition to the nine light, fast carriers (CVLs) of the Independence class that were completed during 1943. The Independence class carriers were usually light cruisers that were modified into light carriers during construction, so although they were smaller they were capable of steaming at over 30 knots. By far the largest numbers of aircraft carriers were the small escort carriers (CVEs). Although much smaller, slower and less heavily armed, their sheer numbers ensured that additional fighter protection could be afforded to convoys of tankers and transports. The numbers tell the story.

During the Second World War, American shipyards produced 151 aircraft carriers, of which 122 were CVEs, also known as jeep carriers. Many CVEs did not see operational service, and others were commissioned but had not yet joined the fleet by the end of the war. Concurrent with the massive production of ships and aircraft, the naval services experienced a burgeoning increase in enlisted ratings, especially mechanics, radiomen and armament specialists. These sailors and marines, along with pilots and other aircrew members, ensured that ships would have adequate crews, and squadrons would be fully staffed. Japan would not be able to withstand the overwhelming American and

Allied forces that would liberate its occupied territory and defeat its extended military. But as 1944 began, that victory was a long way away.

With increased military assets and personnel moving into the Pacific theater and its staging areas, the island hopping naval campaign that begun at the end of 1943 rapidly gained momentum. But the advances beyond Tarawa and the Gilbert Islands did not involve the Corsair. The Grumman F6F Hellcat was a superior fighter with excellent handling characteristics; it, not the F4U, would be the Navy's shipboard fighter for almost the entire year.

Operation Cartwheel, as the island hopping campaign was formally known, did not eliminate the need for land-based fighters, as there remained strong Japanese opposition from bypassed areas. That there remained a considerable amount of air combat for land-based F4Us in the Solomon-Bismark Sea area was brought home on 3 January 1944. On that date Maj. Gregory "Pappy" Boyington, Commanding Officer of VMF-214 and often regarded as the Marine Corps leading ace, was shot down and captured after an engagement near Raubal. Exactly one month later, 1Lt. Robert M. Hanson from VMF-215 was killed in action after downing twenty-five enemy aircraft. But it was not an enemy fighter pilot that downed Hanson. Returning from a fighter sweep, Hanson went down low to attack a lighthouse on Cape St. George, on the island of New Ireland. Lying to the north of Bougainville, the waters surrounding the cape had been the site of the Battle of Cape St. George on 25 November 1943. That destroyer battle, a U.S. Navy victory, was the last surface ship engagement of the Solomon Islands Campaign. But Japan still controlled important parts of Bougainville, New Guinea and the nearby Admiralty Islands, and that threat had to at least be neutralized. Recognizing the lighthouse as an important observation post and flak tower, Hanson came in low in a horizontal attack with guns blazing, but was hit by enemy return fire. His fatal crash into the sea occurred the day before Hanson's twenty-fourth birthday. Boyington and Hanson were the leading Marine F4U aces of the war; each was awarded the Medal of Honor.

In following the F4Us operational history, it is interesting to note the wartime record of its pilots. A high percentage of aerial kills with the F4U occurred during 1943 and the very early part of 1944. Then on 19 February, the Japanese put up their last major air resistance over

Rabaul. VF-17 had its last dogfight with enemy Zeros that day, shooting down sixteen aircraft on that mission, bringing the squadron total to 154 kills. Before ending its combat deployment, thirteen VF-17 pilots – including its CO Lt. Cdr. "Tommy" Blackburn – were aces. But as the Japanese forces pulled back from Rabaul, the focus of the war effort shifted to the central Pacific and then the Philippine Sea, with the Corsair largely operating in the shadow of the highly successful F6F Hellcat.

There were consequences in not having the Corsair as a frontline fighter, and that was evident by the time of the attack on Tarawa. Lt. Gen. Holland M. Smith was the Marine Corps officer in command of amphibious operations, and his views of the tactics and strategy were often out of sync with his superiors. After the war, Smith – the father of modern amphibious warfare, and later the commander of the assault force at Iwo Jima – revealed his candid thoughts about the gruesome attack on Tarawa. Lamenting the high loss of life, Gen. Smith opined:

> *Was Tarawa worth it? My answer is unqualified: No. . . . We could have kept it neutralized from our bases on Baker Island, to the east, and the Ellice and Phoenix Islands, a short distance to the southeast.*

General Smith was also a strong supporter of using Marine Corps fighting squadrons for close air support at the beachhead, as well as farther inland. Unfortunately, the U.S. Navy was resolute in its effort to keep the F4U off the aircraft carriers. So for much of 1944, Navy and Marine Corp squadrons had bifurcated missions. Some duties involved the protection of hard-won Allied turf in the southwest Pacific; this included the interception a greatly diminished number of aircraft, performing reconnaissance and attacking what Japanese shipping was left. In addition, land-based F4Us – many of which were part of Marine fighting squadrons – had to eliminate, or at least neutralize, Japanese air and ground threats on islands that Operation Cartwheel bypassed. Many of these were purely bombing missions. Japanese ground forces were well entrenched, often retaining considerable AAA-assets. There were few frontline Japanese fighters left, and those aircraft that did exist could often be destroyed on the ground. So as the F4Us advanced into the central Pacific Ocean, their use as pure fighters was often limited to escorting Curtis Helldivers and/or North American PBJ-1 Mitchells (the latter often boasting a nose-mounted 75-mm cannon).

If F4U squadrons failed to get to the tip of the spear, they took every opportunity to get into a fight. The problem was the fact that Grumman F6Fs and the various dive bombers on the fast carriers were devastating, completely overwhelming Japanese air opposition with superior aircraft and pilots, plus a lopsided numerical advantage. For Navy and Marine Corps pilots who wanted to get in on the fight, the sad fact was that after the first three months of the year air-to-air combat was limited. When it did occur, Marine Corps and Navy pilots demonstrated their well-earned reputations. Then on 28 March, VMF-213 escorted a group of B-25 Mitchell bombers on an attack on Ponape atoll in the Caroline Islands. The squadron's six F4Us shot down eight of the twelve enemy fighters; it would be the last air-to-air engagement between fighters in the central Pacific Ocean. But while the Japanese air threat in the Caroline Islands was over, there were missions to fly. From its new base on Roi-Namur on Kwajalein Atoll in the Marshall Islands, Marine Air Group-31 was within striking distance of Japanese bases on Wotje, Ponape, Jaluit, Mille, Nauro and Kusale. MAG-31 could handle any unexpected future enemy air threats, such as IJN seaplanes. Other Corsair units faced similar circumstances.

As the war in the Pacific continued, other events unfolded that would eventually get the F4U back into frontline duty. Leading the list was technology. On 25 January, Vought received a letter of intent from the Navy's Bureau of Aeronautics regarding the development of the F4U-4. This would prove to be the ultimate high performance naval fighter when it entered the war. Along with much more power, the F4U-4 would have a much more efficient four-bladed propeller and many engine modifications. Some of these "improvements" would not always be well received by pilots, like the automatic control for the intercooler and oil cooler. The redesigned cockpit was generally well received, especially the raised rudder pedals. In March, the F4U established its dive bombing capabilities in combat operations with VMF-111. Based on the island of Makin, the VMF-111 Corsairs dropped 1,000 lb bombs on Japanese positions on Mille. The Corsair, despite the need to avoid excessive trim changes, was found suitable in dives that approached the vertical. The following month, the F4U-1D began rolling off the Vought production line; it included two center section pylons, each of which could carry a 1,000 lb. The F4U now had an additional capability that would be very useful in the Pacific.

Another use of technology to make the F4U even more lethal was radar. Already in use on U.S. Navy surface warships, radar was one of the major advantages than American warships enjoyed over the Japanese. With radar, American warships could detect approaching Japanese aircraft and naval forces before the enemy was aware of their presence. As the carriers advanced past the Gilbert and Marshall Islands and towards the Philippine Sea, the island hopping doctrine of Operation Cartwheel came into play. It was accepted that with each American victory and subsequent advance, some Japanese bases would remain intact on bypassed atolls. The lingering threats on these bypassed islands and atolls meant that some radar capabilities had to be provided for newly captured island bases. So as the pure fighter activities diminished during 1944, the F4U-2 night fighter began to operate from shore bases and at sea.

VMF(N)-532, commanded by Maj. Everett H. Vaught and operating with twelve radar-equipped Corsairs, was the Marine Corps first single-engine night fighting squadron. VMF(N)-532 began operating on Tarawa, then moved on to Roi-Namur and eventually to Saipan. On 14 April 1944, while operating near Engebi, squadron pilots made their first kills on a night intercept. Using their high-resolution radar, they maneuvered into attack positions and shot down two attacking bombers, with a third attacker listed as a "probable."

The U.S. Navy's first F4U night fighter squadron, VF(N)-75, was land-based. Commanded by Lt. Cdr. William J. "Gus" Widhelm, the squadron initially operated at Munda in the Solomons. While it typically took some time to develop proficiency at using airborne radar for making night intercepts, VF(N)-75 had plenty of practice; the Japanese had been making nighttime harassment raids at Munda. On 16 January 1944, Lt. Cdr. Richard E. Harmer, Commanding Officer of VF(N)-101, took his unit and four radar-equipped aircraft aboard the *U.S.S. Enterprise*. For the naval fighter that in 1940 pushed performance and technology to unforeseeable levels, it was perhaps most fitting that the first U.S. Navy Corsairs to go to war on a carrier would be an F4U-2 equipped with an APS-4 radar, an autopilot and a early radar altimeter.

The technical advances in the ever-maturing F4U were real pluses, but the restriction on aircraft carrier duty remained a big problem. Aside from patrol planes, heavy bombers, seaplanes and transports, naval aircraft were and are expected to operate from carriers, or at least be carrier capable. Although experienced squadron pilots were adapting to the nuances of the F4U, accidents continued to plague young naval pilots receiving operational training. The month of March 1944 finally brought some of the low-speed handling issues to a head. So many low-speed training accidents were occurring (many fatal) that the admiral in command of operational training at NAS Jacksonville was preparing a scathing letter about the dismal record of the Corsair. That letter could have had a serious, detrimental affect on the future of the F4U for Navy squadrons.

Vought, very sensitive to the severity of the high accident rate problem, sent a test pilot and another engineering rep to the training command. Vought had to correct the worst of the issues, one of the last of which involved the introduction of the improved main gear. Vought's Herculean effort paid off, as the letter was never sent. In April, the improved main landing gear struts finally entered production. The new design was immediately dubbed the "de-bouncing gear" because it substantially reduced the likelihood of a bad bounce while landing on the deck of an aircraft carrier. Also during April, the U.S. Navy retested the F4U landing traits aboard the *U.S.S. Gambier Bay*, subjecting the aircraft to 113 landings. The results paid off. What had been a very skeptical naval aviation hierarchy finally approved the F4U for aircraft carrier operations.

As the F4U moved towards aircraft carrier duty, the tempo of the Allied offense in the Pacific Ocean increased. In April, General of the Army Douglas MacArthur began his return to the Philippine Islands, which he realized in October. The Grumman F6F Hellcat remained the Navy's frontline fighter, serving aboard the aircraft carriers and racking up a tremendous kill ratio against enemy aircraft, eventually reaching 19:1. Still, as the F4U moved beyond the Solomon Islands it remained highly effective. On 17 April, Allied forces began an amphibious assault in the Malabang-Parang area of Mindanao Island, with Marine Corps F4Us providing support. By this time the highly effective record of the Corsair in combat, coupled with the series of improvements has made to the aircraft, have provided convincing evidence that the F4U's role should be expanded. On 16 May, the long-awaited decision was rendered. The Navy Evaluation Board that reviewed the Corsair determined that the F4U-1D was the best multi-role fighter for Navy and Marine Corps squadrons. But the Board went even farther; it determined that the F4U was suitable for carrier operations and that existing squadrons should convert from the F6F to the F4U. That was followed by another decision in August. Meeting at Pearl Harbor, senior Navy and Marine Corps officials agreed that Marine fighting squadrons would serve aboard the small escort carriers. Given the very large number of CVEs in the fleet, that one decision would pave the way for the widespread deployment of the F4U at sea.

The tactical advantages afforded by the increased role of the F4U fitted nicely with the overall strategy in the Pacific. During the war, General of the Army Douglas MacArthur was the Supreme Allied Commander, Southwest Pacific Area. MacArthur's naval counterpart was Fleet Admiral Chester Nimitz. For political as well as military reasons, these two powerful leaders controlled separate geographic areas of operation. The F4U, as a naval fighter, largely operated outside of Gen. MacArthur's geographic area until mid-1944. By that time, the bifurcated advance of MacArthur's land forces and Nimitz's naval forces resulted in a geographic proximity near the Philippines. By August F4Us were stationed on Guam after that island was recaptured. The next month, VMF-114 provided close air support during the invasion of Peleliu. By October, VMF-114 was joined on Peleiu by Corsairs of VMF-122 and VMF-121. By that time, Gen. MacArthur made his famous return to the Philippines. The advance towards the Japanese homeland was getting closer and closer to the end game. By then, an increasingly desperate Japan turned to its most desperate weapon to date, the kamikaze.

The appearance of the kamikaze – the suicide aircraft that were tasked with diving into American warships with a bomb – marked a radical change in the naval war. After the American fleet pushed through the Marianas Islands, the Japanese carrier war was over. Japan was losing the war; its defeat was inevitable. But the near and intermediate term threat to Allied naval vessels was real. For the first time, the U.S. Navy authorized Marine Corps F4U fighter squadrons to deploy aboard aircraft carriers. Facing a shortage of carrier-qualified pilots, ten Marine Corps squadrons were ordered to complete carrier qualification training. In November, the percentage of fighter aircraft among the shipboard mix of fighters, dive- and torpedo bombers was also increased to seventy-three percent at Navy conference in San Francisco. By early December, Vice Admiral George D. Murray, the ComAirPac, personally appealed to the chief of naval operations to expedite the deployment of Marine Corps F4U squadrons to the fleet carriers. That the air defense need was critical due to the unexpected threat of the kamikazes was recognized by Admiral King (the CNO) in Washington, D.C. So three years after the attack on Pearl Harbor and just ten months before the surrender ceremony, the F4U was finally headed to war aboard U.S. Navy aircraft carriers.

By mid-December, a prelude of what the coming would be like occurred over the Philippines and surrounding waters. On 11 December, thirty Marine Corps F4Us joined Army Air Force P-40s in a coordinated attack of a Japanese convoy off the west coast of Leyte. The aircraft belonged to VMF-115, VMF-211, VMF-218 and VMF-313. The marine Corsairs repeated their attack the following day and, on 13 December, some thirty-five F4Us of MAG-12 provided cover for the amphibious assault on Mindoro Island. Mindoro, the seventh largest of the Philippine Islands, was critical to retaking the Philippines. West of the main island of Luzon, Mindoro was strategically situated at the boundary of the South China Sea to the north and the Sulu Sea to the south. Japanese forces retaliated, and on 15 December Corsairs of VMF-211 joined other F6Fs from VMF(N)-541 (plus some AAF aircraft) in defending the beachhead from kamikaze attacks.

On 28 December 1944 the Navy's plan to send the F4U Corsair to sea was finally realized – but in Marine Corps colors. VMF-124 and VMF-213 joined the fleet carrier *U.S.S. Essex* at Ulithi. On 30 December *Essex* sortied from Ulithi, headed towards Okinawa. The Marine Corsairs were ready for action, but not completely ready for sea duty. Three were quickly lost in landing accidents, and ten more would be lost in other operational accidents in the coming days. But despite the need for greater acclimation to carrier operations, the Marine pilots were ready to fight.

The Lone Eagle's Quiet Mission

One of the more interesting sidebars to the F4U's history involves Charles A. Lindbergh, the "Lone Eagle" who achieved fame by completing the first solo, non-stop flight across the Atlantic Ocean.

After touring Germany several times between 1936-8, Lindbergh had come to admire the Messerschmitt Bf-109 and other aircraft of the Luftwaffe. After receiving a medal from Luftwaffe commander Hermann Goring, Lindbergh had become an isolationist, and by 1940 was very active in the America First movement. After testifying before Congress in opposition to President Roosevelt's Lend-Lease Act in early 1941, the president publicly criticized Lindbergh as a "defeatist and appeaser." Three days later, on 18 April 1941, Lindbergh responded with a letter to FDR in which he resigned his commission as a reserve colonel in the Army Air Corps. That Lindbergh was considered a *persona non grata* by the president was well understood.

After America entered the war, Lindbergh's opinions on aircraft and systems were sought by a number of aircraft companies, including Hartford-based United Aircraft Corporation (UAC). UAC had a lot at stake in the F4U, which used an engine from its Pratt & Whitney division and a propeller from its Hamilton Standard division in its Vought subsidiary's unique airframe. Lindberg was quietly recruited as an outside consultant, and quickly became very familiar with the F4U project. On 6 January 1943 he made his first flight in the Corsair at Bridgeport Airport, showing no reluctance in making a "three-point" landing. Lindbergh had already flown the Republic P-47 Thunderbolt, and was familiar with the R-2800 Double-Wasp engine (albeit the turbocharged version). By the spring of 1943, Lindbergh was approved for travel to the Pacific theater as a UAC technical representative (although he would evaluate other aircraft types as well). Once in the theater, his assignment was to gather operational information from squadron pilots and mechanics; disseminate current information from the factory and Vought flight test, and render assistance wherever possible. Lindbergh was allowed to fly squadron aircraft, and he did so. Some obvious concerns were raised about the Lone Eagle piloting a military combat aircraft on combat missions, but officers within the theater looked the other way.

Developing the Gull-Winged F4U Corsair - And Taking It To Sea

By any measure, Lindbergh was able to demonstrate greatly improved mission capabilities. During May and June, Lucky Lindy flew missions from the islands of Green and Emira. When not flying he met with countless pilots, including leading aces such as Maj. Joe Foss and Maj. Marion Carl. Besides helping to resolve some maintenance issues, Lindbergh did yeoman duty in increasing the F4U bomb load. This was important, since Marine Corps squadrons were mostly bombing or strafing during mid-1944. Arriving on Roi during September, Lindy went to work with Marine Air Group 31. By that time Marine pilots were regularly carrying two 1,000 lb bombs on under-wing pylons. One Corsair was carrying what two Douglas SBD Dauntless dive bombers could carry, while still retaining the ability to engage enemy aircraft. Working with MAG-31 personnel, Lindberg increased the bomb load to 4,000 lbs: i.e., a center-section pylon carrying a 2,000 lb bomb, with two 1,000 lb bombs slug under the wing. That ultra-heavy load was two-thirds of what a B-17 Flying Fortress could carry! On his last mission with MAG-31, Lindbergh used the 4,000 lb bomb load and destroyed a hidden Japanese shore battery on Wotje.

Lindbergh's success with the F4U was as important to United Aircraft Corporation as it was to the Navy and Marine Corps. Vought's F4U development had been protracted, and the aircraft missed carrier service for most of the war. Time and again the F4U program risked curtailment or outright cancellation because of development delays and operational problems. By October 1944 it was clear that the F4U was a superior fighter, close-support aircraft and a great dive bomber. The F4U's greatness, and the future of the Vought F4U program, was assured.

Naval Air War in the Pacific, 1945

By 1945, as more and more F4Us went to sea on aircraft carriers, it was becoming increasingly clear that Japan was losing the war. As in the European Theater of Operations (ETO), the fighting would continue for some time. The refusal to surrender even as the outcome came into focus was marked with increasingly ferocious attacks on Allied naval vessels. That ferocity was also demonstrated in the island warfare as amphibious assaults advanced towards Honshu, Japan's main island. The Vought F4U Corsair, the premier naval fighter over the Solomon

Islands by mid-1943, had finally worked its way into the same status aboard American carriers. And by 1945, the ultimate wartime version of the Corsair – the F4U-4 – was entering squadron service.

On 2 January 1945, Corsairs from MAG-14 and MAG-12 began arriving at Samar, in the Philippine Islands. The following day Marine Corps Corsairs on the *U.S.S. Essex* escorted bombers on a mission to Okinawa, claiming their first aerial victory. The tempo of the Allied offense was increasing and, just three days into the New Year, the decision to move Corsairs onto carriers had been vindicated.

On 6 January, Vice Admiral Jesse B. Oldendorf began a three-day preparatory bombardment of Lingayen, on the Philippines main island of Luzon. Oldendorf commanded the U.S. Navy's Battleship Squadron 1, a position he received after defeating the Japanese Southern Force in the Battle of Surigao Strait (24 October 1944). A rear admiral at the time, Oldendorf commanded Task Group 77.2, which he deployed in a battle line at the northern portion of the Surigao Strait. Oldendorf successfully used this tactic to "cross the T" of Vice Admiral Shoji Nishimura's Force C, an advancing line of two battleships, one heavy cruiser and five destroyers. In addition to outmaneuvering Nishimura, Oldendorf's six battleships were highly effective at placing their radar-controlled gunfire on the enemy ships. Occurring during the Battle of Leyte Gulf, the action at Surigao Strait earned Oldendorf a Navy Cross and a promotion. It was also the last time battleships had engaged other battleships, and the last time in naval warfare that a surface warfare group "crossed the T" of an opponent.

At Lingayen, Oldendorf's task group of battleships, cruisers and destroyers faced a new threat – significant numbers of Japanese kamikaze aircraft. Although the invasion was a success, the cost at sea was very high. Between 4 and 12 January, Oldendorf lost twenty-four ships, including the older battleships *U.S.S. Mississippi* and *U.S.S. Colorado*, plus the heavy cruiser *HMAS Australia*. The support vessels in the Allied supply train were the most vulnerable to kamikaze attacks, lacking anti-aircraft firepower. So Lingayen made clear that the fleet needed more F4Us in a hurry. But those Corsairs that were available were making a difference. Fifteen F4Us from MAG-12 were among the land-based Corsairs that contributed to the pre-invasion ground attacks at Lingayen.

The Allied forces continued their advance. On 12 January *Essex* was part of a task group with ten other carriers that staged a raid on Saigon, in Indo-China (later Vietnam). The F4Us were used to escort TBMs on the mission. The missions and their targets off the Tonkin Gulf and South China Sea point to the breadth of the Allied advance. The operation of American aircraft carriers in the South China Sea was concurrent with Royal Navy and Fleet Air Arm strikes against the oil-rich areas of Sumatra.

Corsairs continued to arrive on American and British carriers, and the Allied advance moved northward. On 16 February, three days before the amphibious assault began at Iwo Jima, Marine Corps Corsairs with Vice Admiral Marc Mitscher's Task force 58 joined other carrier-based aircraft in attacking targets in the Tokyo area. It was the first carrier-based attack on the Japanese homeland, and occurred almost six months before the first atomic bomb would be dropped on Hiroshima. And once again the F4U displayed its multi-role versatility.

The attacks on the Tokyo area were diversionary raids; they were intended to distract the enemy immediately before the assault on Iwo Jima. In addition, the attacks on the Tokyo area would reduce enemy air opposition through the destruction of enemy aircraft in the air and on the ground. A third object was to inflict damage on aircraft and engine factories in the area. *Enterprise* and *Saratoga* operated together as the main element of Task Group 58.5; this was the first time during the war that the fast fleet carriers operated together. From 10 to 15 February, Task Force 58 loitered in the ocean northwest of the Mariana Islands. TF58 then maneuvered east of Guam, and sailed between the Nampo Shoto Islands and Marcus Island. During the night of 15 February, a high-speed run-in towards the Tokyo area commenced. Early on 16 February, TF 58 had arrived undetected in the waters south of Tokyo, closing to within 60 miles of the coast. Thus began the first carrier-borne air attacks on the Tokyo and Hamamatsu areas by some 800 fighters, bombers and torpedo bombers. By the time TF58 retired from the area on the afternoon of 17 February, Corsairs had claimed twenty-one aerial victories with another sixty aircraft destroyed on the ground. Several Corsairs were lost in these high-risk attacks.

Marine Corps F4U Corsairs escorting PBJ-1 Mitchell bombers over the Philippines. The mission was a surprise attack on the 100th Division Headquarters of the Japanese Army. Pictured inside the lead bomber is the Japanese prisoner who provided information to the air strike coordinator, Maj. Mortimer H. Jordan. Sergeant Charles T. Imai was the Marine Corps interpreter, who relayed information to Maj. Jordan and the pilots. Note that the PBJ-1 was the Navy and Marine Corps version of the North American B-25 medium bomber. Defense Dept. Photo 130977 (Marine Corps) was part of a 1945 press release. Image courtesy of the Emil Buehler Library Collections of the National Museum of Naval Aviation, Accession Number 2011.003.155.006.

On 19 February, TF58 arrived off Iwo Jima. Known as "Sulfur Island" and one of the three Volcano Islands of the Bonin Islands chain, Iwo Jima lies northwest of the Mariana Islands and roughly 750 miles (1,200 km) south of Tokyo. Administratively part of one of the eight villages of Tokyo, Iwo Jima was strategically important because of its three military airfields, early warning radar installation and location along the route taken by American bombers headed for Japan. The island presented a threat to aircraft and could provide the Japanese mainland an early warning of impending bomber attacks, and was considered necessary as a possible emergency landing location for B-29 bombers that would in time be carrying nuclear weapons to bomb Japan. For the plethora of reasons that were considered, an amphibious assault to capture the island was planned. This was known as Operation Detachment, and involved the U.S. Marines V Amphibious Corps (i.e., the Marines' 3rd, 4th and 5th Divisions) and approximately 450 Allied warships.

Iwo Jima was an extremely bloody battle, and the enormous casualty figures created considerable controversy as to whether the volcanic island should have been bypassed. From a tactical air standpoint, American close support aircraft – including the F4U – were highly effective. But kamikaze attacks, while limited, did inflict considerable damage. The *U.S.S. Bismarck Sea* (CVE-95) was sunk, while *Enterprise* was damaged and temporarily immobilized, and *Saratoga* was damaged so badly that she was unable to return to service for the duration of the war. Eight squadrons of Corsairs were involved in the assault, and were primarily used for ground attack missions. That was fine with the mud marines.

In fighting the entrenched enemy, the marines found that the intricate system of tunnels meant that when all enemy soldiers in a pillbox or machine gun nest were killed, other soldiers could mysteriously appear. Many marines lost their lives from these isolated snipers. The Japanese defenders also had artillery pieces hidden and protected; close in air support was a crucial element in what many regard as the bloodiest battle of the Pacific war. One third of all Marine Corps casualties during World War Two occurred on Iwo Jima, where the enemy could and did appear from the earth at any time and direction, and where time to live was often measured not in days or even hours, but sometimes in seconds. The Marine Corps, Navy and Army together suffered 26,038 casualties (6,821 killed, and 19,217 wounded), the overwhelming majority of which were marines. Iwo Jima was also the only battle where, despite its victory, Marine Corps losses exceeded those of the enemy. Japanese casualties totaled 21,570.

Even before Iwo Jima was secure, Task Force 58 made a return to the Tokyo area. Attacks were launched on 25 February in weather so cold that operational effectiveness was hampered. Some Corsairs encountered frozen guns that would not function. But the raids established that in addition to strategic bombing by General Curtiss LeMay's B-29s, naval tactical aircraft would be an additional threat. During the Doolittle B-25 raid in April 1942, *Enterprise* accompanied the *U.S.S. Hornet* as the latter launched the attacking bombers. Nearly three years later the *Hornet* was gone, but not *Enterprise* and the ships of TF58. For the remainder of the war, the raids on Japan's home island of Honshu would become increasingly common.

The Battle of Iwo Jima generated tremendous attention and controversy in America due to the enormous loss of life. Iwo Jima overshadowed the Tokyo raids and other offensive missions of the F4U during the first three months of 1945. Yet both operations were significant to the war effort, and exemplify the multi-role use of the Corsair in the final months of the war. And the number of Corsairs on board ship continued to increase. TF 58 had thirteen Navy and Marine Corps squadrons embarked when it attacked Okinawa on the 1st of March. By that time U.S. Navy use of the Corsair was significantly increasing; of the thirteen squadrons, seven were Navy units.

March was a month with considerable action and, while Corsairs destroyed numerous aircraft and targets, their losses ran high. During the 1 March Okinawa attack, VMF-124 and VMF-213 on *U.S.S. Bennington* scored twenty-three aerial victories and destroyed another twenty-four aircraft on the ground. This was measured against the loss of twenty-three Corsairs. That was quite typical. When VMF-216 and VMF-217 completed more than a month of combat aboard the *U.S.S. Wasp* (CV-18) in early March, it claimed four aerial victories and another fifteen enemy aircraft destroyed on the ground, and also claimed an enemy destroyer having been sunk. Against this was the loss of nine Corsairs. Many of the losses were from aggressive tactics, and some losses were operational. The superiority of the F4U as a fighter could not negate the high risk of ground attack missions over enemy territory. And even with much higher levels of experience, shipboard accidents remained a problem.

On 18 March, TF58 began what was to be three days of air attacks on Japan near Kagoshima and Izumi. Operating within 50 miles of the coast, the ships were attacked by Japanese bombers and thirty-nine kamikazes. The aircraft carriers *U.S.S. Franklin* (CV-13), *Wasp* and *Essex* were heavily damaged, with the worst being inflicted on the *Franklin*. Despite the loss of 804 officers and men, valiant firefighting and damage control managed to save the *Franklin*, although its wartime duty was over. The Japanese counter-attack also reduced the availability of Corsairs, but failed to do more than blunt the American drive into Japanese home waters. With no major naval elements capable of engaging the American fleet, F4Us would thereafter be pressed most often into ground attack missions and air intercepts of kamikazes.

Japanese Yokosuka P1Y1 'Frances' being shot down, possibly near Okinawa, in April 1945. The 'Frances' was damaged by an F4U and finished off from the AA fire from American warships. Image courtesy of the Emil Buehler Library Collections of the National Museum of Naval Aviation, Robert L. Lawson Photograph Collection. Accession Number 1996.488.161.019.

By April, much of the total Corsair air activity centered on Okinawa. Given its position roughly 350 miles from Japan's main island of Honshu, Okinawa was strategically important to both the Empire of Japan and the Allies. The island would be the perfect land base for conducting air attacks on Honshu, and as a staging area for land and naval operations. Even before Okinawa was invaded, Japan's military leaders understood that the war could not be won. However, there was a strong determination to either prevent an invasion of their homeland or, in the alternative, to fight to the death. In the very near term, the military imperative was to slow the Allied advance, and make it as costly as possible.

On 1 April 1945, Easter Sunday, the U.S. Tenth Army (a composite force of Army and Marine Corps units) began the invasion of Okinawa. Code-named Operation Iceberg, the order of battle included 1,570 Allied vessels and over a half-million men who landed at Hagushi Bay, on the southwest side of the island. The Battle of Okinawa became the largest amphibious assault of World War Two (far larger than the D-Day invasion of France in 1944), and the first time that Allied forces would fight on Japanese soil. Like Iwo Jima, the battle would result in a huge loss of life that was unusual even in time of war. Included among the casualties were the two highest ranking military commanders to die in battle during the war: i.e., Lt. General Simon B. Buckner, commanding the Tenth Army, and General Mitsuri Ushijima, commanding the defensive forces of the Imperial Japanese Army. In an interesting and important part of Marine Corps history, Lt. General Roy Geiger – a World War One naval aviator, former commander of the Cactus Air Force at Guadalcanal and then Marine Corps director of aviation – had returned to the field from Washington, D.C. to command the III Amphibious Corps in 1944. General Geiger came ashore in an early wave of the Okinawa landings, which was his fourth amphibious assault. After the death of General Buckner, Gen. Geiger temporarily commanded the Ten Army until Lt. General Joseph W. Stilwell arrived. Thus General Geiger, an aviator and amphibious warfare officer, became the first Marine Corps officer to command an entire field army. As this culminating battle of World War Two began, Corsairs of VMF-221 and VMF-451 from the *U.S.S. Bunker Hill* also made history, by providing fighter cover and conducting strafing missions of the beachhead during the first day of the assault.

In Japan, military leaders were preparing desperate defensive measures. Faced with no effective navy and a limited but still formidable air force, the leadership placed its hope of defending the homeland on kamikaze attacks against American and British Pacific Fleet warships. For this it would rely on hundreds of land-based tactical aircraft of Japan's Fifth Air Fleet. The Fifth Air Fleet was under the operational command of Admiral Matome Ugaki, a one time aide to the late Admiral Isoruko Yamamoto and former commanding officer of the IJN's Battleship Division One. Ugaki's mandate was simple, but the tactics and methodologies were not. Unable to field piloted rocket bombs, the 'Divine Wind' missions would fight the Allied fleet around Okinawa with a series of large air attacks called kikusuis. Flown by young volunteers who were not fully qualified aviators, the kamikaze pilots used an assortment of obsolete fighters and dive bombers. Most kamikaze flights failed, but especially during kikusui missions, even the small percentage that hit their naval targets was deadly.

Unlike the British carriers, the American aircraft carriers lacked armored flight decks. As a result, American carriers were far more vulnerable to damage from kamikazes. Destroyers, being much smaller, could easily be sunk if a kamikaze scored a direct hit. Because of the severity of the kamikaze threat, the sheer size of the combined Allied fleet and the limited effective range of contemporary search radar, an outer screen of early warning destroyers was deployed. Perhaps ironically, these U.S. Navy destroyers – rather than the much larger and offensively powerful aircraft carriers – often became the naval targets of the very young and inexperienced kamikaze pilots. So the speed, range, firepower and maneuverability of the F4U, combined with Grumman F6F night fighters and destroyer early warning alerts, provided a critical combination of detection and interception capabilities. This was the combat environment into which the F4U was thrust at Okinawa. And to meet the new threat of kamikazes, there were many new faces. At this late stage of the war, Corsairs in operational squadrons were often flown by young and newly qualified fighter pilots ("Tail End Charlies").

Beginning on 3 April, the huge combined Allied fleet was met with the largest kamikaze attacks since the Japanese began the suicidal practice at Leyte Gulf. The Marine Corps Corsairs operating off the *Bunker Hill* shot down eleven of the attackers.

On 6 April, Kikusui No. 1 was launched just at the U.S. Tenth Army advanced to the Imperial Army's defensive position at Kakazu Ridge. A large morning attack included Japanese bombers, fighter-bombers and a fighter escort to engage the American fighter CAP. The combination of the intercepting fighters and intense AAA fire from the American fleet destroyed almost the entire attacking Japanese force. But a second wave during the afternoon was more successful and, despite heavy losses, numerous kamikazes were able to hit American surface combatants and ships of the supply train. F4Us from the *Bunker Hill* and the *U.S.S. Bennington* intercepted scores of kamikazes, shooting down seventeen. The following day, when American fighters were involved in providing top cover during an attack on the battleship *Yamato*, a final wave of kamikaze attacks arrived over the American fleet. This was the conclusion of Kikusui No. 1, and more damage was inflicted.

The attack on the *Yamato* was itself important. On the same day that Kikusui No. 1 began, Japan's super-battleship *Yamato*, steamed toward Okinawa as part of the suicidal Operation Ten-Go. Operation Ten-Go resulted from Emperor Hirohito's criticism that the Imperial Japanese Navy needed to be actively involved in the defense of Okinawa. To comply with the emperor's wishes, *Yamato* sortied from her base at Tokuyama on the afternoon of 6 April with the light cruiser *Yahagi* and a screen of eight destroyers. The plan was to have the world's most powerful battleship fight its way to the shore of Okinawa, beach itself and use its massive eighteen-inch gun batteries in a suicidal fight with American warships. Admiral Mitscher ordered Task Groups 58.1 and 58.3 to deploy from TF58 and intercept the *Yamato*. With that order, the Corsair became involved in the war's last naval battle involving a capital warship, providing fighter cover for the operation.

TG58.1 included the fleet carriers *Hornet* (CV-12, not the original carrier of the same name), *U.S.S. Bennington* (CV-20), and light carriers *Belleau Wood* and *San Jacinto* (the latter the carrier on which future president George H. W. Bush served as a pilot). TG 58.3 included the fleet carriers *Essex*, *Bunker Hill* and *U.S.S. Hancock* (CV-19), along with the light carrier *U.S.S. Bataan*. *Yamato* was intercepted and engaged by more than three hundred American aircraft north of the Ryukyu Islands at about 12:30 local time. Two hours later, and after enduring waves of bomb and torpedo attacks, the badly damaged *Yamato* was dead in the water, on fire and listing. The battleship capsized roughly 120 miles south of Kagoshima, Japan.

The sinking of the *Yamato* removed the last significant naval threat, but it was just the beginning of the Battle of Okinawa. By 9 April, two days after the sinking of *Yamato*, F4U Corsairs of MAG-31 and MAG-33 were arriving on the island in significant numbers. Using both the Kadena and Yontan airfields, along with the carriers of the surrounding naval force, Marine and Navy Corsairs were able to engage in all of the fighter roles that the war's last major battle required. This included close air support of the soldiers and marines during combat that was often as gruesome as Iwo Jima. In fact, the high casualty level and the horror of the Okinawa land battle influenced the decision about dropping atomic bombs on Japan, and would have influenced an decision to invade Japan had the empire not surrendered. In addition to the close air support duties, the F4U's air war during the Battle of Okinawa involved duties flying top cover and the air intercept of kamikazes. And it was the kamikazes, the 'Divine Wind' as Japanese military leaders called them, that unleashed the greatest devastation that American and Allied forces had seen since the attack on Pearl Harbor.

On 12 April, President Roosevelt died in Warm Springs, Georgia; Vice-President Harry S. Truman was sworn in as president by Chief Justice Harlan F. Stone. In the East Latitudes Time Zone, VMF-221 and VMF-451 Corsairs from the *Bunker Hill* and *Bennington* intercepted and destroyed fifty-one attacking kamikazes over the East China Sea, while MAG-31 and MAG-33 Corsairs operating from Kadena and Yontan claimed an additional sixteen enemy aircraft. And so it went.

The Battle of Okinawa was not only the largest amphibious assault of the war; it was marked by extremely high casualties among combatant and civilians alike (including mass suicides among the civilian population). It was the last battle of World War Two, and was extremely protracted. The ground advance was painfully slow due to the very large defending force, the formidable lines of defense, and the geographic constraints of the island. There were serious disagreements between General Buckner and Marine Corps Commandant General Alexander Vandergrift concerning tactics. Vandergrift wanted to expedite the capture of the island with an amphibious assault on the Oroku Peninsula, which eventually occurred. The southward advance was slowed by heavy rains in May, but accelerated in June with improved weather. Concurrently, Task Force 58 maintained around the clock radar watch for kamikazes, with airborne fighter cover most of the day.

During the eighty-two day Battle of Okinawa, a total of ten kikusui attacks were launched, with a success rate of about twenty percent. Despite the effectiveness of the radar picket destroyers, fighter CAPs and AAA fire from surface ships, the damage that kamikazes inflicted was the worst in U.S. Navy history. Thirty-six ships were sunk and 368 were damaged, many severely. The list of badly damaged ships included carriers. Typical was the 11 May attack on the *Bunker Hill* which, despite being badly damaged by fires, remained afloat. Some 264 sailors lost their lives and *Bunker Hill*, sometimes referred to as the most damaged ship to ever return to the Puget Sound Navy Yard, was out of the war. Three days later, *Enterprise* – the most highly decorated Navy warship of World War Two – was hit by a bomb blast so severe that her forward elevator was blown hundreds of feet into the air.

F4Us were important to the fleet defense at Okinawa, and contributed substantially to the critical close air support needs of soldiers and marines on the ground. The Corsair was an excellent platform for delivering napalm and Tiny Tim rockets, often providing accurate attacks very close to friendly troops. In the air, F4U pilots were effective interceptors, and had a number of standout days during the battle. On 16 April, land-based Corsairs operating out of Kadena and Yontan recorded thirty-eight aerial victories against kamikazes. On the same day, carrier-based Corsairs on fighter CAP missions engaged and destroyed an additional twenty-nine kamikazes, seven of which were destroyed by Navy Ensign Alfred Lerch. On 22 April, the Kadena and Yontan-based Corsairs shot down another thirty-three attackers, and on 27-28 April, they destroyed another thirty-five kamikazes. The kamikaze threat remained throughout the battle, but with additional Corsairs on newly arriving escort carriers (including brand-new F4U-4s), the outcome of the deadly air component of the battle was never in doubt. On 21 June 1945, Okinawa was finally declared secure. The F4U Corsairs, undisputedly the best naval fighters of the battle, had achieved 436 aerial victories. But the victory at Okinawa came at a extremely high price. American casualties totaled some 62,000, of which 12,500 were killed. It was a sobering thought for the nation's civilian and military leaders, as a invasion of the Japanese homeland was planned for 1 November.

With Okinawa secure, F4Us continued raids on Japan. At this point Japan had lost the war, but the fighting was not over. There was considerable discussion among civilian leaders within the federal government, the Truman administration, and the nation's military leaders concerning the best method for persuading the Empire of Japan to surrender. The term 'unconditional surrender' was preferred, but much of the discussion focused on whether that suggested overly harsh conditions. A surrender would have been vastly better than an invasion of southern Japan on 1 November. In particular, the willingness of Japanese troops to fight to the death without surrender on Iwo Jima and Okinawa was a significant concern; the American public was not pleased with the high American death toll that resulted from those battles. The specter of mass suicides if the Japanese people expected to lose their emperor-god in defeat was also disquieting.

As the internal debate continued in Washington, D.C., the U.S. Navy Third Fleet approached the Japanese mainland and coastal islands. General LeMay's B-29s continued their massive bombing of Japan, including incendiary bombing of Japanese cities and industrial centers. President Truman had made no decision regarding surrender terms, and expected to defer that until his attendance at the coming Potsdam Conference between himself, Prime Minister Winston Churchill and Secretary Josef Stalin of Russia. The conference was to begin outside the captured city of Berlin on 17 July and, as the president prepared to leave, Secretary Forrestal made secret plans to be present. On 10 July, Admiral Halsey's fleet, described as "the greatest mass of sea power ever assembled" commenced air and naval artillery attacks on coastal industrial centers and military installations. Concurrently, F4Us based on Okinawa began to escort B-25 Mitchell bombers on attacks against targets in the southern parts of Japan.

At this late point in the war, the Corsair's ability to carry a significant bomb load from a carrier was critical to the tactical air campaign.

So to were its capabilities as a pure fighter, as both the fleet and the slower Avenger and Helldiver bombers needed protection. Then, on 26 July, the Potsdam Declaration was issued, which included an ultimatum: "We call upon the government of Japan to proclaim now the unconditional surrender of all Japanese armed forces, and to provide proper and adequate assurances of their good faith in such action. The alternative for Japan is prompt and utter destruction." By this time, Corsairs of the British Pacific Fleet had joined the Third Fleet in attacking targets on the main island of Honshu. It was ten days after the United States had successfully detonated its first atomic device in New Mexico,

The naval air attacks continued in southern Japan, and included military targets in the plains of Tokyo, and naval installations at various points. Japan sought help from Stalin, as it had a non-aggression pact with Russia, but the communist leader had other plans. Japan rejected the Potsdam ultimatum, and President Truman authorized the use of atomic weapons. Events then proceeded quickly. Naval air attacks by the Third Fleet on the Kure Naval Arsenal began on 24 July, even before the surrender ultimatum was issued at Potsdam. The attacks continued on 25 and 28 July, with a high loss of aircraft. However, the IJM lost several large warships, including the aircraft carrier *Amagi* and the cruiser *Oyodo*, with numerous cruisers and battleships being heavily damaged and settling to the bottom of the shallow anchorage.

The almost total destruction of Japan's offensive naval and air power still did not result in its acceptance of the surrender ultimatum. Despite the inevitability of defeat, Japan's prime minister and war cabinet continued to seek diplomatic assistance from Russia, Meanwhile, on 26 July – the day that the Potsdam surrender ultimatum was issued, and while Admiral Halsey's Third Fleet aircraft were attacking the Kure Naval Arsenal – the *U.S.S. Indianapolis* (CA-35) delivered America's first atomic bomb to the air base at Tinian. Preparations for the atomic attack proceeded and, with no acceptance of the surrender terms, the B-29 *Enola Gay* dropped the first atomic bomb on Hiroshima. It was 6 August 1945.

The devastation in Hiroshima did not cause an immediate response from Tokyo. President Truman declared:

> *We are now prepared to obliterate more rapidly and completely every productive enterprise the Japanese have above ground in any city. We shall destroy their docks, their factories, and their communications. Let there be no mistake; we shall completely destroy Japan's power to make war. It was to spare the Japanese people from utter destruction that the ultimatum of July 26 was issued at Potsdam. Their leaders promptly rejected that ultimatum. If they do not now accept our terms they may expect a rain of ruin from the air, the like of which has never been seen on this earth.*

Three days later, on 9 August, the B-29 *Bock's Car* dropped the second atomic bomb on its secondary target, Nagasaki. By this time there were fewer doubts about the ability of the United States to destroy Japan with atomic weapons, as resident Truman made very clear. In addition, Japan learned that Russia was entering the war against Japan. Retired Admiral Kantaro Suzuki, who had replaced Prime Minister Kuniaki Koiso after the defeat at the Battle of Okinawa, sought to develop a consensus on accepting the surrender within the divided Imperial Council. After personally meeting with Emperor Hirohito, the emperor publicly announced his acceptance of the surrender terms. A group of rebellious military officers attempted a coup at the Imperial Palace on 14-15 August; this included the attempted assassination of Prime Minister Suzuki. Despite much bitterness the rebellion quickly failed, and the surrender plans went forward.

On 2 September 1945, surrender ceremonies were held aboard the *U.S.S. Missouri* in Tokyo Bay. Japan's Foreign Minister Mamoru Shigemitsu signed the Instrument of Surrender on behalf on Emperor Hirohito and the Empire of Japan. General Yoshijiro Umezu, Chief of the Army General Staff, signed on behalf of the Japanese Imperial Army. General of the Army Douglas MacArthur, Supreme Commander for the Allied Powers, and Fleet Admiral Chester Nimitz, for the United States of America, also signed the document, as did representatives of other attending nations. Some two hundred Allied warships surrounded the Missouri under the cloudy, grey skies over Tokyo Bay. General MacArthur opened the ceremony:

We are gathered here, representatives of the major warring powers, to conclude a solemn agreement whereby peace may be restored...It is my earnest hope, indeed the hope of all mankind, that from this solemn occasion a better world shall emerge out of the blood and carnage from the past, a world founded upon faith and understanding, a world dedicated to the dignity of man and the fulfillment of his most cherished wish for freedom, tolerance and justice.

MacArthur then invited the representatives from the Empire of Japan to sign the Instrument of Surrender. One by one, they were followed by representatives of the other attending nations, now officially at peace. The signing took less than thirty minutes, after which General MacArthur closed the ceremony. While all of the dignitaries and journalists were still present on the *Missouri*, one thousand American warplanes flew overhead in an orderly and impressive formation. Among all of the aircraft, the most easily recognized fighters were the gull-winged F4U Corsairs.

THE MIGHTY BUCKET

Chapter Seven

Corsairs of the Fleet Air Arm and the Royal New Zealand Air Force

. . Now we have emerged from one deadly struggle-a terrible foe has been cast on the ground and awaits our judgment and our mercy. But there is another foe who occupies large portions of the British Empire, a foe stained with cruelty and greed – the Japanese.

– From Prime Minister Winston Churchill, speaking to victory crowds in London on Victory in Europe Day, 8 May 1945.

It is with gratitude in the past, and with confidence in the future, that we range ourselves without fear beside Britain. Where she goes, we go! Where she stands, we stand!

– New Zealand Prime Minister Michael Joseph Savage, speaking to his nation after New Zealand declared war on Germany on 3 September 1939.

Royal Navy Fleet Air Arm (FAA) pilots flying the Vought F4U contributed much to the successful transition of the Corsair to a carrier-based fighter. In doing this, they were roughly nine months ahead of the United States Navy. But in addition to this leadership, their unique contributions served both the United Kingdom and the Allied cause well. In particular, the deployment of Fleet Air Arm squadrons in 1944-5 were especially important to naval operations in the Indian Ocean, the Pacific Ocean – and during the final attacks on Japan in 1945. Another group of Commonwealth pilots flew the F4U Corsair, and their service also deserves recognition. Of particular interest are those New Zealanders who flew and maintained F4Us of the Royal New Zealand Air Force (RNZAF) in the Pacific theater. But here, some notes are in order to ensure that historical credit is properly allocated.

Because New Zealand had a small military during the interwar period, many New Zealand pilots, mechanics and armorers served in Royal Air Force (RAF) units. For many New Zealanders, that was the quickest way to get into the fight after World War Two began on 1 September 1939. But by then it was clear that the United Kingdom would need many thousands of pilots, navigators, bomb aimers, gunners, wireless operators and other trained personnel. They would also be needed quickly, a result that would only be possible with a training scheme that would provide a continuous flow of graduates. Great Britain, itself at risk of invasion, was not a suitable location to conduct this training. So Great Britain, Canada, Australia and New Zealand sent representatives to Ottawa in late 1939 to devise a plan for what would become the world's largest training program for pilots, aircrew and support personnel.

The result of the Ottawa discussions was known as the Riverdale Agreement, since Lord Riverdale (i.e., Sir Arthur Balfour, 1st Baron Riverdale) was instrumental in developing the plan. The final document became known as the British Commonwealth Air Training Plan (BCATP), also referred to as the Empire Air Training Scheme (EATS) in some of the Dominions. Of the 50,000 aircrew members that were scheduled to be trained each year, fewer than seven percent would come from New Zealand. Training would take place in Canada, although in colonies and Dominions some initial and intermediate training would take place. The curricula were designed to follow that of the RAF, and many graduates would be assigned to RAF squadrons that would retain affiliation of the parent nation.

So much for training the pilots. But the Fleet Air Arm also needed naval fighters that were designed for aircraft carrier operation. Many FAA aircraft that served in the fighter role early in the war had significant limitations. Much of this derived from outdated concepts of what a naval fighter's mission would be within the Royal Navy. In the 1930s and even as late as 1940, the intent was to protect the Royal Navy from low-level threats such as enemy scout floatplanes. Naval anti-aircraft fire from fast, maneuvering surface warships was thought to be an adequate deterrent against air attacks. As a result, aircraft such as the Fairey Fulmar, the Blackburn Skua and its stepchild (the Roc) were developed as naval fighters. And the Gloster Sea Gladiator biplane was already operational with the fleet. But early in the war it was becoming apparent that the Royal Navy would be facing more than low-level air threats.

As the reality of the FAA's fighter deficiency came to be recognized, land-based fighters like the Hawker Hurricane and Supermarine Spitfire were modified for naval duty. But even these great fighters were stopgap measures, with the Hurricane lacking speed and range, and the Spitfire lacking range for anything much beyond air intercepts. And the landing traits of the Seafire, the navalized version of the Spitfire, were hindered by poor forward visibility and a very narrow main landing gear. So the FAA obtained the durable Grumman F4F Wildcat (which it initially called the Martlet), the Grumman F6F Hellcat and the Vought F4U Corsair (including some of the Brewster versions). In total, the FAA received 2,012 Lend-Lease Corsairs, while the RNZAF received 421. But when the F4Us were delivered to the first FAA squadrons in late 1943, the Corsair was still considered too risky for aircraft carrier operations by the U.S. Navy. Within just a matter of months, the Fleet Air Arm would demonstrate otherwise.

Corsairs of the Royal Navy Fleet Air Arm

The Corsair's arrival with the Fleet Air Arm followed the much earlier introduction of the Grumman F4F, and was roughly concurrent with the July 1943 arrival of the Grumman F6F. The F4F was an important step up for the FAA, since it replaced Gloster Sea Gladiator biplane fighters on Royal Navy carriers. Unlike the modified Hurricane and Spitfires, the rugged F4F was designed to operate from carriers. The Martlet (Wildcat) had a rugged landing gear and afforded the pilot a very good chance of survival after a ditching in the ocean. The later introduction of the F6F (then named the Gannet 1, but later renamed the Hellcat) in 1943 meant that Royal Navy carriers would have not just an improved fighter, but a first-rate one. The Grumman F6F had the ruggedness of the F4F but with more speed and climb performance. The F6F also had more range, payload capacity and firepower. In the

Indian Ocean and the Pacific, FAA F6Fs could defeat Japanese Zeros and other fighters, and they could carry ordnance for ground attack missions. And like the F4F, the F6F was well suited for takeoffs and landings aboard a carrier. Then came the Corsair.

The Vought F4U was a big step beyond even the Grumman F6F in terms of performance, but at the time of the first Lend-Lease deliveries the Corsair had only been used as a land-based fighter. Details of providing the aircraft, parts and support and training facilities all had to be worked out. In support of the acquisition of aircraft under the Lend-Lease program, the Royal Navy established an administrative and financial affairs base in Washington, D.C. The Corsairs would be "leased" to Britain for use by the FAA, and then returned at the end of wartime service. Training bases were established at Naval Air Station (NAS) Quonset Point, NAS Brunswick (completed in March 1943) and a Naval Air Auxiliary Field (NAAF) in Lewiston, Maine. The initial ninety-five Lend-Lease aircraft would be Vought F4U1s, which the FAA designated as the Corsair I.

The first FAA Corsair units were Nos. 1830 and 1833 Squadrons, which were commissioned during June and July 1943, respectively. The timing very is interesting. Just after No. 1830 Squadron was commissioned on 1 June, the newly built *U.S.S. Bunker Hill* left the Quincy, Massachusetts shipyard for the first time. The U.S. Navy's VF-17, commanded by Lt. Cmdr. J. "Tommy" Blackburn, was aboard the *Bunker Hill*. "Fighting-17" would be the first U.S. Navy fighter squadron to deploy with the F4U, but by the time the *Bunker Hill* arrived in Hawaii the Navy decided that the Corsair would just be a land-based fighter; operational problems and logistical issues precluded shipboard duty at that time. Meanwhile, as FAA training of its first F4U pilots got underway, there was little doubt that they would be going to sea.

In accordance with the BCATP, FAA operational training began using the RAF's curriculum. Under that plan, Corsair fighter squadrons would take rated pilots and "work up" to operational status in the United States, including initial carrier qualification. After that, each FAA squadron would be transported to the United Kingdom aboard an escort carrier, ultimately arriving at its assigned carrier or embarkation point. Both Nos. 1830 and 1833 Squadrons were formed at Naval Air Station (NAS) Quonset Point, which was located on the shore of Narragansett Bay in Rhode Island. The home of the U.S. Navy construction battalions (Seabees), NAS Quonset Point was conveniently located less than one hundred miles east of the Vought plant in Stratford, Connecticut. There was also plenty of free airspace for training nearby, including gunnery. So the operational work up of Corsair squadrons continued in earnest, with a basic airplane checkout, aerobatics, formation flying, night and instrument flying, simulated deck landings, tactics and gunnery all included.

FAA training quickly expanded to its training bases in Maine, which also had lots of free airspace. New England was noted for the sudden weather changes common to coastal areas, but it was certainly no worse than training in or near Great Britain. While surviving training records are sparse, Corsair training appears to have proceeded smoothly. Available records of military aircraft accidents in Maine show no Corsair accidents prior to 23 August 1943. Most accidents were in or near the airport traffic pattern, and most were not fatal. But while training fighter pilots in an accelerated wartime schedule, there were exceptions. One of the first bad accidents occurred on 3 October, when two Corsairs from No. 1837 Squadron collided in midair near Royal River, Maine. Both pilots were lost. Many of the accidents and incidents that did occur resulted from poor landings, something to be expected from a big fighter with a long nose.

Once simulated deck landings with a qualified Deck Landing Control Officer (DLCO) were completed at land bases, the young squadrons were able to carrier qualify on an escort carrier (usually in Chesapeake Bay) before shipping out. In October, No. 1830 Squadron (Lt. Cmdr. B. M. Fiddes, RN, commanding) embarked on the *H.M.S. Stinger* with its ten Corsair IIs and sailed for Belfast. In December, the squadron joined the 15th Naval Fighter Wing aboard the *H.M.S. Illustrious*; the following month *Illustrious* sailed to Ceylon (now known as Sri Lanka). No. 1833 Squadron, commanded by Lt. Cmdr. H. A. Monk, RN, also departed the United States in October. The squadron sailed to Belfast aboard *H.M.S. Trumpeter*, subsequently joining its sister No. 1830 Squadron aboard the *Illustrious* as part of the 15th Naval Fighter Wing. The Royal Navy was about to reappear in the Indian Ocean in force, and would do so with Vought F4U Corsairs.

The ability to operate Corsairs successfully from Royal Navy aircraft carriers was not assured, but several factors enabled the transition to a ship-borne fighter to work. Much like VF-17's field modifications to its U.S. Navy Corsairs, the FAA would not accept the Corsair "as-is." The cumulative effect of changes that were made either at the factory or in the field was significant, as previously discussed. But the FAA, already used to operating somewhat imperfect aircraft from its carriers, was able to use the aircraft that it accepted with the gentle, curved approach with success. As the number of squadrons grew, the Corsairs tended to be used in stateside work up of squadrons, with most of the aircraft being deployed on Royal Navy carriers being later variants for all manufacturers.

The use of the FAA Corsairs in 1944 neatly matched the tempo of the war. In the North Sea and Atlantic Ocean, most Royal Navy surface activity involved convoy escort, anti-submarine warfare (ASW) duties, and patrol. There would be no major surface engagements with the German Navy (Kriegsmarine). But the Royal Navy would return with substantial force to the Indian and Pacific Oceans, and that is where FAA Corsairs would see most of their combat operations. But not all.

The Fleet Air Arm Corsair's baptism under fire occurred far to the north, where the German Kriegsmarine kept the battleship *Tirpitz* in protected Norwegian fjords. The dreadnaught was armed with eight 15-in (38 cm) guns, an impressive secondary gun battery, four Arado floatplanes for scouting, and state-of-the-art radar. Underway in open water, the *Tirpitz* could make a very respectable 30 knots. But despite its impressive capabilities, the *Tirpitz* was also vulnerable. In the arctic waters where it might intercept convoys to Russia, *Tirpitz* had no fighter protection and limited escorts. It would be vulnerable to Allied submarines, possible air attack and surface engagement by the British Home Fleet if it sortied. As a result, *Tirpitz* only engaged the enemy once, during an 8 September 1943 attack on a lightly defended weather station on Spitzbergen Island, at the western end of Norway's Svalbard archipelago.

By 1944 German military planners (including Hitler) were determined to protect this strategic asset, which had suffered considerable damage from British midget submarines during 1943. The war was not going well for Nazi Germany in the spring of 1944, yet despite its vulnerabilities *Tirpitz* remained a formidable threat to Allied convoys that entered the North Sea west of Norway. As a result the battleship tied up the Royal Navy's Home Fleet, which could not afford to have *Tirpitz* dash into the North Sea on patrol. But the threat of this fleet in waiting required more than a defensive strategy, so the Royal Navy, including the Fleet Air Arm, were ordered to conduct large-scale air attacks against *Tirpitz*. The first such attack was code-named Operation Tungsten.

At the time of the attack *Tirpitz* was securely moored in Kafjord, a side branch of the roughly 24 mile (38 km) long Altafjord inlet. The Kriegsmarine naval base at Kafjord was well suited for protecting the *Tirpitz*, although it had failed to stop a midget submarine attack during the previous year. The Royal Navy knew that a repeat attack by submarine was out of the question, so Operation Tungsten would have to come from the air. The operation was carefully planned. Since the mooring at Kafjord was surrounded by cliffs, anti-aircraft batteries and camouflage, the FAA knew that *Tirpitz* would not be an easy target. But there was time to get ready. It took the German repair ship *Neumark* several months to repair the badly damaged main turret 'D,' along with ruptured steam lines and damaged turbogenerators.

The departure of *Neumark* in early March indicated that *Tirpitz* was close to being operational, yet the operation had to be delayed due to ongoing repairs to H.M.S. *Victorious*. When the attack finally commenced on 3 April, *Victorious* was joined by the fleet carrier H.M.S. *Furious*, plus four escort carriers. FAA Corsairs from Nos. 1834 and 1836 were aboard the *Victorious* as part of No. 47 Naval Fighter Wing, and flew top cover during the attack. No opposition from the Luftwaffe was encountered, but the FAA Corsair pilots had a double reason to celebrate. The *Tirpitz* was again badly damaged, and the Fleet Air Arm had been the first service to take the F4U into combat from aboard ship. Perhaps just as telling, the Vought hot-rod was not carrying ordnance; it was used in its element as a fighter.

After Operation Tungsten, the threat posed by the *Tirpitz* did not completely go away. A frantic effort was mounted to repair the battleship, but it would take almost three months before *Tirpitz* could even be tested. During the summer, FAA Corsairs participated in follow up attacks during Operation Mascot (July) and Operation Goodwood (a series of attacks beginning in August). After the summer, responsibility for destroying the *Tirpitz* was transferred to the RAF, which was able to render the ship unseaworthy with heavier ordnance. The F4U would not engage any Luftwaffe fighters, but its continued presence onboard carriers was assured.

The initial use of FAA Corsairs in European Theater of Operations (ETO), while historic, was something of an anomaly. Operation Tungsten was carried out at Kafjord, which, at northern latitude of roughly 78 degrees, was well north of the Arctic Circle. Fighting over arctic waters was a far cry from tropical Guadalcanal, or from the Indian Ocean – where the FAA Corsairs would next see action. Indian Ocean operations would be a prelude to operating in the Pacific Ocean, where the Allies were advancing towards the Philippine Islands and Japan. The advance in the Pacific would also include the liberation of captured British territories, which Britain believed should be accomplished by Commonwealth forces. There would be significant political turmoil over how British forces would operate in that theater. But despite the politics, the Royal Navy, and it Corsairs, would be moving eastward.

Britain's re-entry into the Indian Ocean in force was itself long awaited. Since 1942, the Royal Navy had been largely absent from the region, except for the waters around Ceylon and the African coast. That pullback was due to the superiority of the Imperial Japanese Navy, a threat that no longer existed. The 1944 return to Indian Ocean began as part of a training mission, in which the Royal Navy warships would practice refueling at sea using American methods. After underway replenishing drills, the ships would rendezvous with elements of the U.S. Navy and begin joint Indian Ocean operations. The exercise was codenamed Operation Diplomat.

H.M.S. Illustrious was the first fleet carrier assigned to the Indian Ocean operation. *Illustrious* had embarked No. 15 Naval Fighter Wing, including Nos. 1830 and 1833 Squadrons with their Corsair IIs. The refueling tankers were escorted by *HNLMS Tromp*, a light cruiser of the Royal Netherlands Navy. The U.S. Navy element was Task Force 58.5, comprised of the *U.S.S. Saratoga* with an escort of three destroyers. On 31 March, the combined force arrived at the port of Trincomalee for intensive training. Located on the northeastern coast of Ceylon (Sri Lanka), Trincomalee was the deep-water harbor used by the Royal Navy for anchoring and refueling in the northern Indian Ocean. The RAF also had a permanent airfield, RAF China Bay. In April, before the eastward sweep across the Indian Ocean, it was at RAF China Bay that a tragic accident occurred. Cdr. Richard J. Cork, the famous ace who commanded No. 15 Naval Fighter Wing, was killed when he landed his F4U into an opposite direction aircraft in a freak pre-dawn runway collision.

Once the joint training was completed at Ceylon, *Illustrious* and *Saratoga* began their patrol, searching for commerce raiders as they proceeded eastward. *Saratoga* carried VF-12 – famous for having been the U.S. Navy's first Corsair squadron until it relinquished its Corsairs for Grumman F6F Hellcats. That a Royal Navy fleet carrier was operating with F4U Corsairs while the accompanying U.S. Navy carrier operated with F6F Hellcats was not lost on the American naval establishment. No surface raiders were encountered on the Indian Ocean transit, but more important matters were soon at hand. On 18 April, the combined task group arrived undetected off the western entrance to the Strait of Malacca.

The Strait of Malacca connects the Indian and Pacific Oceans. The waterway was strategically important in the Second World War as an ocean passage, and the surrounding islands were strategically important due to their oil wells and refineries. By 1944, Japan's reduced oil production was constraining its military operations. But the Dutch East Indies (Indonesian since 1945) oil fields of Sumatra, Java and Borneo (now Kalimantan) still held extensive reserves. Before the war Royal Dutch Shell had sizable operations in that area, and both Texaco and Chevron made significant discoveries in the central part of Sumatra. Any attacks that disrupted oil production and transportation would exacerbate Japan's serious supply problems, especially in Burma. In addition, an effective raid would provide a timely diversion for Operation Reckless, the American amphibious landings that were to commence near Hollandia, New Guinea on 22 April. So diversionary attacks from *Illustrious* and *Saratoga* were planned, and were code-named Operation Cockpit.

Operation Cockpit began at 0530 hours on 19 April 1944. In addition to *Illustrious* and *Saratoga*, some twenty surface warships from the Royal Australian Navy, Royal New Zealand Navy and the French Navy participated. The ships were divided into Task force 69 and

Task Force 70 (which included the carriers). The main targets were the oil storage and terminal facilities on Sabang Island, off the coast of Sumatra; they would be subjected to a combination of naval shelling and a coordinated air attack. *Illustrious* launched seventeen Barracuda bombers and thirteen F4U Corsairs, while *Saratoga* launched twenty-nine Dauntless and Avenger dive bombers plus twenty-four Grumman F6Fs for the fighter cap. VF-12 recorded three kills, while the Corsairs from *Illustrious* destroyed several aircraft on the ground at the Lho Nga airfield. The raid was a complete success, although FAA pilots were still waiting for their first aerial victory. Yet the FAA was increasing its strength in the eastern Indian Ocean, and its knowledge of American naval procedures. This would be critically important for the joint naval operations would increase in size and scope during the final year of the war.

In July, *H.M.S. Victorious* arrived at Trincomalee. By this time Britain was preparing to provide substantial naval resources to the final Allied push in the Pacific Ocean. Admiral Bruce Fraser, who had commanded the Royal Navy's Home Fleet, was re-assigned to be the commander-in-chief of the Royal Navy's Eastern Fleet; he would officially replace Admiral James Somerville in August. The Eastern Fleet morphed into the British East Indies Fleet and, on 22 November 1944, into the British Pacific Fleet (BPF). Fraser initially raised his flag aboard the gunboat *H.M.S. Tarantula* when he arrived at Trincomalee. By the time Fraser raised his pennant, *Victorious* had already embarked a third F4U unit (No. 1838 Squadron) to augment No. 47 Naval Fighter Squadron. *Illustrious* embarked No. 1837 Squadron, so both fleet carriers were well prepared for aerial combat. That would happen quickly.

On 25 July 1944, just before Somerville's departure, FAA Corsairs provided top cover during the next naval shelling of Sabang Island. It was during this attack on Sabang Island, at the western approach to the Straits of Malacca, that the FAA Corsairs achieved their first air-to-air victories. A total of seven Japanese aircraft, six of which were Zeros, were victims of the Corsair's guns. In his excellent book *Corsair: The F4U in World War II and Korea*, author Barrett Tillman makes the interesting point that on this attack the FAA Corsairs displayed great versatility; in addition to providing a fighter cap, some F4Us were used as artillery spotters for the naval shelling while others were used for photo reconnaissance. Hours after the combined naval force retired from action, the terminals at Sabang burned fiercely.

Strike photo from the attack on a Japanese airfield at Sabang, on the island of Sumatra. Fleet Air Arm Corsair pilots flew off the *H.M.S. Illustrious*, pictured in the lead image to this chapter. Image source/credit: Courtesy of the Emil Buehler Library Collections of the National Museum of Naval Aviation, Robert L. Lawson Photograph Collection, Accession Number 1996.488.024.026.

On 3 August, Admiral Fraser transferred his flag to the battleship *H.M.S. Howe* when the dreadnaught arrived at Ceylon after a refit. It was an important next step as the Royal Navy prepared for operations in the Pacific. Under Fraser, the BPF would become a true Commonwealth naval force, although the Royal Navy would be the leading contributor. For both military and diplomatic purposes, Fraser would eventually move to a land headquarters in Sydney, Australia. Tactical command at sea would be vested in Vice-Admiral Sir Bernard Rawlings, with Vice-Admiral Sir Philip Vian commanding the Fleet Air Arm component. That reorganization of the fleet was critical. In the vastness of the Pacific Ocean there would be enormous logistical, procedural and tactical issues to resolve. By retaking control of the eastern Indian Ocean, and attacking the mineral rich islands in the Dutch East Indies, the crucial preliminary steps in the eastward movement to the Pacific had been accomplished. More than that, the FAA had shown the U.S. Navy that it could safely use the Corsair aboard its carriers. And as the Royal Navy entered the Straits of Malacca, the Corsair – and not the Seafire or the F6F Hellcat – was establishing itself as the FAA's premier multi-role shipboard fighter. The U.S. Navy was taking notice of that as well.

The eastward advance continued. By late-1944, the Royal Navy and its Fleet Air Arm component had shown that they could work effectively in joint operations with the U.S. Navy. There would now be more independent British operations. In October, Operation Millet was launched. This was another diversionary attack, and was designed to divert attention from General MacArthur's amphibious landings at Leyte. *Victorious* was joined by *H.M.S. Indomitable* (which carried Grumman F6F Hellcats) and was tasked with attacking military airfields in the Nicobar Islands. The islands were located between the Bay of Bengal (off the east coast of India) and the adjoining waters of the Andaman Sea (west of Thailand and the Malay peninsula, and immediately north of the western end of the Strait of Malacca). The operation began on 17 October when airfields on Car Nicobar, the northernmost island of the group, were attacked. Some 100 miles (160 km) to the south, attacks were made oo vessels in Nancowry harbor, a protected harbor that was useful as a staging area for ships. Weather intervened, and caused a one-day delay in further attacks.

On 19 October the attacks on Car Nicobar airfields and Nancowry harbor shipping resumed, a rerun of the prior mission. Whereas the main threat on the first attack came from AAA fire, this time fighter opposition appeared. It came from land-based Nakajima Ki-43 "Oscars," very maneuverable fighters that bore a close resemblance to the Mitsubishi A6M "Zero." The Corsairs acquitted themselves well, shooting down seven Oscars in dogfights with a loss of just two. This was the last major FAA engagement of 1944, but it roughly coincided with three other fateful events that would impact the remainder of the war.

The first such event also occurred on 19 October. Vice Admiral Takijiro Ohnisi, the new commander of the Imperial Japanese Navy's First Air Fleet, proposed that suicide aerial bombing attacks be unleashed against Allied warships. This tactic would become known as the kamikaze, and it would cause enormous losses to the rapidly advancing American fleet. The next day, 20 October, General Douglas MacArthur began the amphibious landings on Leyte in the Philippines. On 24 October, the Battle of Leyte Gulf began in the adjacent waters. In what would be the largest sea battle ever, the Allies would deliver a devastating defeat to the IJN. Japan was losing the war, and its military leaders knew it, but they would not stop fighting. With the arrival of the kamikaze attacks, the already approved assignment of U.S. Navy Corsairs to American carriers proceeded with haste. Meanwhile, the new British Pacific Fleet entered the Pacific Ocean in force.

The BPF's first battle of 1945 was Operation Lentil, a major attack on the Sumatran oil facilities at Pangkalan Brandan. The attack occurred on 4 January when the carriers *Victorious*, *Indomitable*, and *H.M.S. Indefatigable*, supported by a screen of cruisers and destroyers, unleashed its new TBM Avengers. The group operated as Task Force 63, with *Victorious* retaining No. 47 Naval fighter Wing and its F4Us, while *Indomitable* and *Indefatigable* utilized wings with F6Fs and Seafires for fighter duties. The Avengers proved to be far superior to the Barracuda bombers that they replaced, and the destruction that they inflicted on the oil facilities was considerable. Once again, the Corsair had proven to be the superior fighter, this time engaging mostly Oscars. After action reports noted these results, along with the well-known operational deficiencies of the sweet-flying Seafire.

On 24 January, Admiral Sir Philip Vian commenced Operation Meridian One against oil refineries at Pladjoe, Sumatra (north of Palembang). Four BPF carriers were involved: i.e., *Victorious*, *Illustrious*, *Indomitable*, and *Indefatigable*, along the battleship *H.M.S. King George V*, three cruisers (for anti-aircraft protection) and an outer screen of destroyers. In this period of transition, three replenishment tankers sailed under escort from Trincomalee as Task Force 69 of the British Eastern fleet; the underway replenishment was accomplished with some difficulty, in part because of rough seas. The attack was delayed for three days because of poor weather, so TF63 and TF69 loitered away from the target area near Enggano Island. By the morning of the 24th the weather had improved, so despite the calm wind, the attack was launched.

Meridian One accomplished its operational objective, but at great cost. Some forty-two TBM Avengers and twelve rocket-armed Firefly bombers launched, accompanied by the TF63 Corsairs, Hellcats and Seafires. Heavy damage was inflicted despite the presence of barrage balloons and heavy flak near the targets. The fighter cap also had lots of activity, as scores of Oscars and Tojos appeared. Once again, the F4U acquitted itself well as both a bomber escort and in top cover, although the total loss of thirty-two aircraft was high. At the end of the raid, the top cover F4Us destroyed eight enemy fighters against the loss of one Corsair, a daily record that would not be exceeded.

Meridian Two commenced on 29 January after two days of difficulty with underway refueling. This time Vian sent TF63 to attack a refinery at Soengei Gerong (also on Sumatra). Once again, TF63 accomplished its mission, but at a very high cost. Sixteen TF63 aircraft were lost, measured against claims of thirty aircraft destroyed on the ground and another thirty claimed in air engagements. Some questions have been raised about the totals, but there was no question about one pilot's result. Major R. C. Hay was one of eighteen Royal Marines who commanded either a Fleet Air Arm squadron or naval fighter wing between 1939-45. During Meridian One/Two, Hay was the commanding office of No. 47 Naval Fighter Squadron, embarked on *Victorious*. On 29 January, Hay became the only Fleet Air Arm Royal Marine ace of the war when he claimed his fifth aerial victory at Soengei Gerong.

With Operation Meridian Two completed, TF69 returned to Trincomalee, while TF63 continued on to Fremantle, Australia, arriving on 4 February 1945. On 9 February TF63 arrived at Sydney, becoming part of the BPF detachment to the U.S. Navy. Thereafter it would operate as TF57 in joint operations. At this point the war against Japan was entering its final stages, but was becoming ever more deadly with the presence of kamikaze aircraft in the vicinity of the Japanese home islands. With their armored flight decks, the Royal Navy carriers would be able to withstand attacks that the unprotected American carriers could not.

The BPF carriers next sailed from Ulithi as part of operation Iceberg, the support of amphibious landings at Okinawa. The carriers operated with a high percentage of Corsairs, which by the Okinawa landings was the shipboard fighter of choice for both the FAA and the U.S. Navy. The BPF was tasked with attacking installations in the Sakashina Islands, a sparsely inhabited group at the southern end of the Japanese archipelago. The F4U performed well in its strike role, and incoming kamikaze aircraft provided plenty of intercept practice. By early April BPF carriers proved they could withstand considerable punishment. On 1 April 1945 *Indomitable* suffered a hit from a kamikaze that damaged its island and started several fires on the flight deck. But the three-inch thick deck armor did its job, with the island receiving most of the damage and the flight deck being cleared within roughly one hour. On 6 April *Illustrious* was hit by a kamikaze but the damage was minor. The BPF carriers would remain on station until the end of May, with constant threats but only occasional hits. On 9 May *H.M.S. Formidable* suffered a kamikaze hit and *H.M.S. Victorious* was hit twice, but in each case damage to the ship was contained. Maneuvering at sea under these conditions could still be risky, as the destroyer *H.M.S. Quilliam* found out when it collided with *Indomitable* off the Sakashimas. *Quilliam* was seriously damaged but remained afloat.

By early June 1945 the BPF carriers had returned to Sydney for a refit. By that time the FAA had a new ace, and the only Corsair ace of the war. Lt. D. J. Sheppard, a Canadian member of the Royal Canadian Naval Volunteer Reserve (RCNVR), served with the FAA aboard *Victorious*. He was credited with his fifth kill on 4 May. There would be some more battle honors for FAA F4U squadrons and pilots, but the war was rapidly drawing to an end. By mid-July the BPF carriers were on station off the main Japanese island of Honshu, typically running attacks on enemy airfields. The Imperial Japanese Navy of the early war years was gone, with just isolated warships remaining. There was still plenty of flak over Japan, but no significant air opposition. Japan had been defeated, but the war would continue for a few weeks.

On 6 August the first atomic bomb exploded over Hiroshima, but there was still no surrender. Attacks on the Japanese installations continued. One of those missions was on 9 August 1945, the day that the first plutonium bomb was dropped on Nagasaki. Lt. Robert Hampton "Hammy" Gray, RCN, leading a flight of No. 1841 Squadron F4Us off the *Formidable*, was on a mission over the northeast part of Honshu. At the coastal inlet at Anagawa Wan, Gray spotted the sloop *Amakusa*, a small naval escort vessel. Gray commenced an attack, quickly finding that while the warship was small it was well protected. Gray continued his attack on the vessel even after his Corsair was hit by AA fire, releasing his ordnance at very close range. The *Amakusa* was destroyed in the explosion, but continuing the attack cost the courageous Canadian pilot his life. "Hammy" Gray was posthumously awarded the Victoria Cross for his actions.

The end of the war quickly brought an end to the British Pacific Fleet. Assets that were not assigned to the British Commonwealth Occupation Force (BCOF) reverted back to the Royal Navy and the other national navies that contributed to the force. None of the FAA Corsairs remained during the post-war occupation. By September 1945 the U.S. Navy had more than enough fighters; it did not want to take back any Lend-Lease aircraft. The United Kingdom, itself in a delicate financial position after six years of war, did not want to retain unneeded aircraft that it would then have to pay for. So with few exceptions, the unneeded Corsairs were pushed over the side off Australia. Once the Fleet Air Arm's greatest shipboard fighter, they became the final casualties of the war.

Corsairs of the Royal New Zealand Air Force

That New Zealand would need long-range, multi-role fighters, maritime patrol bombers and other modern military assets was understood when it entered the war on 3 September 1939. Being a small island nation in the South Pacific, New Zealand's status as a Commonwealth nation was critical to its national defense. But the Commonwealth nations were spread across the globe, whereas New Zealand's military threats during World War Two were nearby. So began the circuitous route that led to use of F4U Corsairs by the Royal New Zealand Air Force (RNZAF).

By the late-1930s, Japan controlled a significant amount of territory in the Pacific Ocean and the eastern part of Asia. Japan had been an ally against the Central Powers during the First World War, and that enabled it to acquire island territories as a result of the Treaty of Versailles and League of Nations mandates. But Japan in the 1930s had more than a large footprint in the South Pacific; it was increasingly belligerent and militarily robust. New Zealand and its territories were militarily exposed, yet it relied on the Royal Navy – then the greatest in the world – for protection. Complicating any defense of those island territories was their location; they occupied a large swath in the central and southern Pacific. First there was Western Samoa. Beginning in 1920, New Zealand administered Western Samoa under a post-war League of Nations Class C Mandate. This Polynesian territory was southwest of the American Samoa Islands, and was strategically located in the central Pacific. Then there were the Cook Islands. Beginning in 1888, the Cook Islands were a protectorate of Great Britain. But in 1901, administration was transferred to New Zealand (which retained it until 1965). Northeast of New Zealand, south of Hawaii and below the Equator, this territory included fifteen islands that lie between French Polynesia and Western Samoa. Divided into the Northern and Southern Cook Islands, it was another important area at the periphery of the Pacific war. Since New Zealand lacked a large military, and there was no way that it could defend that strategically important area.

By early 1940, Great Britain was not only at war; it was taxed to its limits. The Battle of the Atlantic was underway, and German U-boats were starving Great Britain with torpedo attacks on eastbound convoys headed to England. After the fall of France, the Luftwaffe began its relentless bombardment of English cities and military bases. And as the Battle of Britain began in July 1940, the threat of a German invasion was real. Great Britain, and with it the rest of the United Kingdom, might not survive. So in June, shortly before the fall of France and a month before the Battle of Britain, Winston Churchill – the United Kingdom's new prime minister – was compelled to warn New Zealand that the Royal Navy could not be counted on for defense. Exposed and alone New Zealand turned to its own strong-willed citizens, and friends like the United States, for help.

In November 1941 New Zealand sent Walter Nash, its former minister of finance, to Washington, D.C. as a diplomat. It was the first diplomatic mission that New Zealand established outside of the Commonwealth, and it was timely. New Zealand became a beneficiary of America's 1941 Lend-Lease Act; this led to its receipt of numerous "leased" aircraft, including F4Us during 1944. In time the RNZAF would operate thirteen F4U squadrons. But even in a global war, politics would play a major role in the allocation of men and equipment, as well as military strategy. On 12 December 1941 – just five days after the attack on Pearl Harbor – the Imperial Japanese Navy sank the Royal Navy's *H.M.S. Repulse* and *H.M.S. Prince of Wales*. Two months later, on 15 February 1942, Singapore surrendered to Japan. The United States did send an infantry division to New Zealand the next month, but its defense needs were not a major concern of the United States or Britain. The biggest concerns of America and Britain were always those of protecting Britain, and defeating Germany, Italy and Japan. So when President Franklin D. Roosevelt and Prime Minister Winston Churchill met to develop their global war strategy at Placentia Bay, Newfoundland (in August 1941), neither Australia nor New Zealand was consulted. That practice would not change during the war.

Despite the lack of consultation, the RNZAF assisted in the defense of Guadalcanal and the Solomons. Beginning in 1943, it deployed six squadrons of P-40s for interception, escort and ground attack duties. New Zealand's air war also involved maritime patrols by its Lockheed Hudsons, Sunderland flying boats and Consolidated PBY Catalinas. With its fighter and maritime air campaign, along with ground actions in support of General MacArthur, New Zealand was doing its part in the Pacific war. But its complete exclusion from decisions about the Pacific theater remained troubling. Aware of their subordinate positions when it came to planning war strategies for the Pacific theater, Australia and New Zealand began discussions in 1943. The talks between Australia and New Zealand were not in any way meant to inhibit the Allied war effort; they focused on common diplomatic interests, territorial and military needs. And to prove that they were good sports, the two countries did this without consulting with the United States or Britain. The outcome of this collaboration was the January 1944 Canberra Pact between Australia and New Zealand. Britain was none too pleased with this unexpected development, and Washington was livid. U.S. Secretary of State Cordell Hull severely (but privately) directed his criticism at New Zealand's ambassador, after which New Zealand was excluded from many Pacific Ocean operations. Yet it was at precisely this stage of the war that the RNZAF began receiving its F4Us. So much for the consistency of wartime policies.

The Lend-Lease F4U-1 Corsairs added a significant offensive punch to the RNZAF squadrons, and a big improvement over the Curtiss P-40s and Grumman F4Fs. It also reflected the large and rapid growth of New Zealand's armed forces, in which roughly 140,000 of its citizens served. At the beginning of the war in 1939, the RNZAF had fewer than one hundred regular officers and no front-line fighters. As a Commonwealth nation, many New Zealanders volunteered for duty in the Royal Air Force. In the frugal 1930s, many New Zealanders accepted short service (i.e., temporary) commissions, as did many pilots from England, Wales and Scotland. In the RAF, many New Zealanders became aces, or otherwise distinguished themselves during wartime service. The RAF was diligent about trying to keep nationals together, so New Zealanders tended to be grouped with one of seven RAF squadrons. But even with many young men going to to RAF, the buildup of the RNZAF proceeded.

The first RNZAF Corsairs to see operational service within the combat theater was No. 20 Squadron. The unit transitioned out of its Grumman F4F Wildcats in early 1944; by May it was operating its new F4U-1As from Bougainville. By the time all deliveries had been received, a total of thirteen RNZAF units flew the Corsair operationally. But just as the U.S. Navy was delayed in getting their Corsairs assigned to shipboard duty, the "Kiwi Corsairs" were deployed too late to see much air-to-air combat. However, the RNZAF did perform escort duty, and the Corsairs flew a significant number of strike missions. Highly regarded as aggressive fighter pilots, the RNZAF squadrons ranged across the Solomons and beyond. Under Lend Lease, New Zealand received a sizable number of Corsairs. The actually number is in dispute; some sources give it as 370, while others state that a total of 421 Corsairs were delivered. Except for FG-1D Corsairs from Goodyear, the aircraft were F4U-1A aircraft built in Connecticut by Chance Vought. Over a third of the RNZAF F4Us were lost, mostly from operational accidents on missions in the Solomon Islands. Even with most Japanese aircraft gone, the Solomons and adjacent Pacific operating areas were challenging. Weather, along with aggressive tactics by RNZAF pilots on low-level missions, were apparently the major factors.

By the end of the war, all thirteen RNZAF F4U squadrons were slated for transition to the North American P-51 Mustang; Japan's surrender forestalled those plans. But even with Japan's surrender wartime duty was not immediately over for some of the pilots and ground crews. No. 14 Squadron, the RNZAF's first homegrown fighter squadron, was assigned to occupation duty on Japan. The squadron arrived in March 1946 and remained there until late-1948. Of the British Commonwealth Occupation Force's air contingent (BCAIR), only No. 14 Squadron operated the Corsair.

Looking back in time, the contributions of the RNZAF Corsair squadrons are as important as those of other RNZAF squadrons, and of the nation itself. It is helpful to remember that New Zealand could not control when it received its first F4U Corsairs. Yet in the dark early days of the war, the nation pressed on with Brewster Buffalos and other aircraft that were decidedly inferior to the enemy aircraft that it faced. Many New Zealanders distinguished themselves with RAF squadrons and became aces; some served with both the RAF and RNZAF. Colin Falkland Gray and Alan Christopher Deere were among the leading New Zealand aces with the RAF. Raymond Brown "Hess" Hesselyn became a leading RNZAF ace, while Evan Dall Mackie and William V. Crawford-Compton were aces were who served in both services. These are just a few of the many names of distinguished New Zealand fighter pilots.

Had the Corsair arrived sooner and had the RNZAF area of operations been moved, New Zealand Corsair pilots were have engaged in the air-to-air combat that they so relished. Most World War Two fighter pilots did not achieve ace status and many did not engage in dogfights, but distinguished themselves in escort, ground attack and air superiority missions. Much more needs to be written about New Zealand's wartime contributions, including its maritime patrols using Lockheed Hudsons, Sunderland flying Boats, and the ubiquitous Consolidated PBY Catalina. And there are too many unwritten stories about its pilots, both in the RAF and the RNZAF. But from the darkest early days of the war until its very end, and regardless of the tactical or strategic situation, New Zealanders and the RNZAF and were an important part of the fight.

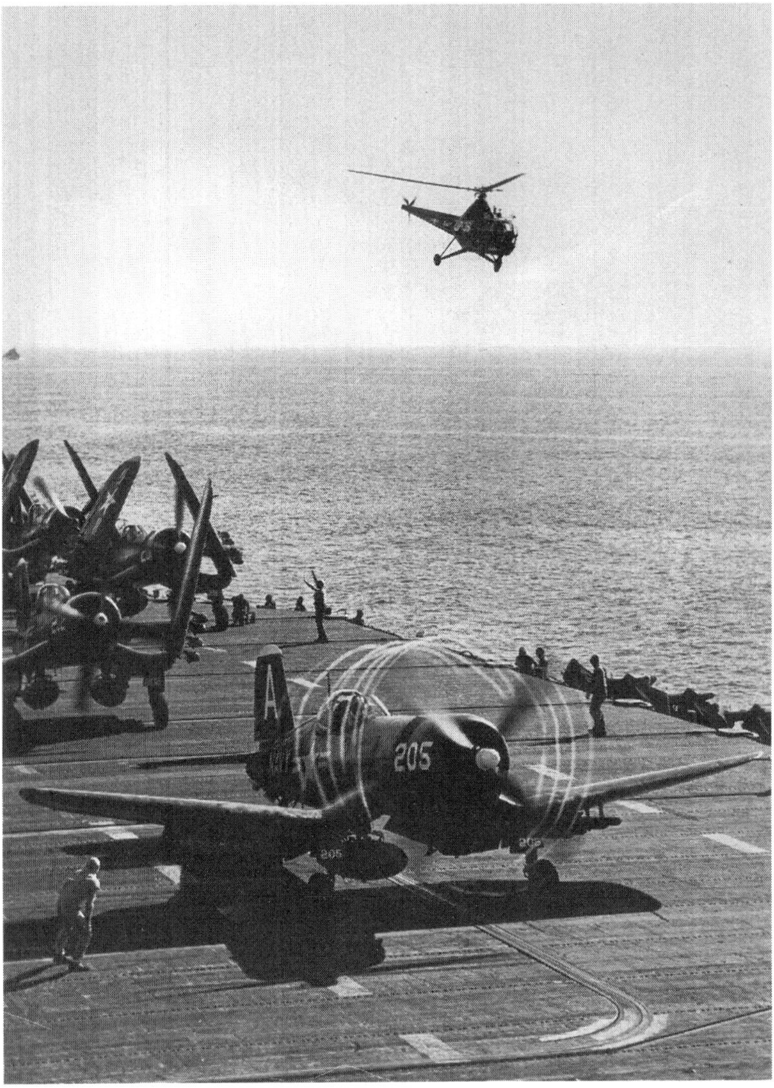
A
205
205

Chapter Eight

Moving To Texas, Then Deploying To Korea

The U.S.S.R. is improving its military position with respect to the United States in such ways, for example, as construction of air bases in northeastern Siberia from which the United States can be attacked, and the construction of large numbers of submarines for commerce raiding.

– From a Top Secret report to President Harry S. Truman by Special Counsel Clark M. Clifford entitled 'American Relations With The Soviet Union.'

It is right for us to be in Korea now. It was right last June. It is right today.

– President Harry S. Truman, speaking to the American people about the Communist attack on the Republic of Korea, broadcast from the White House on 11 April 1951.

The continued production of the Vought F4U after the end of World War Two derived from some very basic facts. First, at the end of the war the Corsair remained America's most capable naval fighter, with proven multi-role and shipboard capabilities. Second, America had an immediate need to provide adequate naval force projection, with carrier-based aircraft available for the fleet needs and those of the Marine Corps. Third, jet-powered fighters, although very promising, were still unproven. Turbine powerplants had relatively low thrust, and the progression from (e.g.) centrifugal-flow to axial-flow compressor technology was still in its infancy. How capable would these new aircraft be in meeting the needs of air superiority, interception, close support or other strike missions? It would take the Navy years to find out. And fourth, advanced versions of the F4U were immediately available, and at a very reasonable cost. During the post-war demobilization period, defense budgets were very tight and almost all of the developmental costs of the F4U had been absorbed in earlier fiscal years. But after that, things got complicated.

At Chance Vought's Stratford plant, F4U production continued while the experimental, jet-powered F6U Pirate was designed and built. While only thirty F6Us would make it into Navy inventory, the aircraft was both the company's first jet and a prodigy of the future. The F5U, a full-scale prototype of the propeller-driven V-173, had also been built but would never fly. The Navy would use jet aircraft like the F6U Pirate rather than a radical, flying saucer shaped aircraft to break the 500 m.p.h. barrier. Meanwhile, early work on the tailless, twin-jet V-346 project (which would become the V7U Cutlass) was underway. Yet as Chance-Vought entered the jet age, its 1.7 million square foot facility in Stratford remained a hodge-podge of buildings spread out over more than seventy acres. Across the street, the Bridgeport Airport's runways – the longest being only 4,761 feet – were not designed for testing new jet aircraft. Unlike the Corsair, both the F6U Pirate and the F7U Cutlass would receive most of their flight-testing at Muroc Field, California, later to be known as Edwards Air Force Base. If Chance Vought's future rested with the F4U and nothing else, and if there were no compelling national interests that dictated a move, then the Stratford plant would have been more than adequate. But that was not the case.

That there were compelling national interests was becoming apparent by 1946. The Navy was very conscious of the fact that an extremely large percentage of military aircraft were designed, developed and produced along the East Coast and the West Coast of the United States. Within just several minutes, an aircraft could fly from the Chance Vought plant in Stratford, Connecticut to the Republic Aircraft plant in Farmingdale, Long Island. A couple of minutes flying time to the west of Farmingdale was the Grumman main plant in Bethpage. That the Navy's two most important manufacturers of fighters and attack aircraft were only a short distance apart created a vulnerability that the post-Pearl Harbor naval establishment did not want. And on the West Coast, Boeing, Consolidated Vultee (Convair), Lockheed,

North American Aviation and Douglas Aircraft Corporation were all easy coastal targets. As if all that weren't bad enough, the relatively small state of Connecticut was home to United Aircraft Corporation's Chance Vought Aircraft, Sikorsky Aircraft, Pratt & Whitney and Hamilton Standard divisions. General Electrical and many other important defense contractors, including submarine manufacturer Electric Boat, also had a major presence in the Nutmeg State.

With these strategic vulnerabilities came new strategic threats, primarily from the Soviet Union. In a top-secret report to President Truman dated 24 Sept 1946, Special Counsel Clark M. Clifford stated:

> *The most obvious Soviet threat to American security is the growing ability of the U.S.S.R. to wage an offensive war against the United States. This has not hitherto been possible, in the absence of Soviet long-range strategic air power and an almost total lack of sea power. Now, however, the U.S.S.R. is rapidly developing elements of her military strength, which she hitherto lacked and which will give the Soviet Union great offensive capabilities. Stalin has declared his intention of sparing no effort to build up the military strength of the Soviet Union. Development of atomic weapons, guided missiles, materials for biological warfare, a strategic air force, submarines of great cruising range, naval mines and minecraft, to name the most important, are extending the effective range of Soviet military power well into areas which the United States regards as vital to its security.*

While many of the most immediate threats to Soviet aggression were the territories in Eastern and Western Europe, the strategic risks to America's defense infrastructure were real. This was aptly demonstrated by Soviet espionage within the United States in the immediate post war period. Noted Clifford:

> *In addition to building up its own military strength and undermining U.S. influence wherever possible, the Soviet Government is actively directing espionage and subversive*

movements in the United States. . . . An example of a group of Soviet specialists who have entered the United States for an exhaustive survey of considerable espionage value is the case of ten engineers who are touring the principal cities of the United States at the present time.

Clifford's investigation occurred during a major re-alignment of the U.S. defense establishment. During World War Two, the United States Armed Forces were part of either the Department of War or the Department of the Navy. Throughout the war, the well-known and highly respected Henry L. Stimson was the secretary of war, in charge of the Army and Army Air Force. Prior to that Stimson was the secretary of state under President Herbert Hoover and, prior to that, served as the secretary of war under President William H. Taft (1911-13) During his five-year wartime tenure that ended in September 1945, Stimson was a strong advocate for industrial mobilization and a robust military. In addition, Stimson's preferences concerning the use of atomic weapons were affirmed by President Harry S. Truman, sometimes over the objections of military planners. One such decision was to spare the city of Kyoto from a nuclear attack; Nagasaki replaced it as the second atomic target. But the powerful and respected Stimson retired three weeks after the Japanese surrender, to be replaced by Judge Robert P. Patterson and, two years later, by retired-Brig. General Kenneth C. Royall. Royall served just a month before the position of secretary of war was eliminated; he then became the first secretary of the Army.

Then there were the naval forces. The U.S. Navy and the U.S. Marine Corps came under the jurisdiction of the Department of the Navy during the war (as did the Coast Guard, albeit temporarily). Completely separate and distinct from the Department of War, the department was headed by Secretary of the Navy William Franklin "Frank" Knox, a Republican who President Franklin D. Roosevelt appointed in July 1940. Although he was a staunch internationalist and succeeded in building the Navy into a massive armed service, Knox enjoyed less political power than did Stimson, his counterpart at the Department of War. Chief of Naval Operations Admiral Ernest J. King ran naval operations, and was a tough political infighter. In reality, Assistant Secretary James V. Forrestal ran most of the department's affairs, relieving substantial burdens from Knox's shoulders. When Knox suffered a fatal heart attack on 28 April 1944, Forrestal was the person best qualified to take over the department. President Roosevelt appointed Forrestal in recognition of that fact, a decision that would have a major impact of the remainder of the war, and the post-War era.

James V. Forrestal was a one-time newspaper reporter who attended Princeton University, where he served as an editor of *The Daily Princetonian* and was voted "Most Likely To Succeed" by his classmates. Forrestal left Princeton a few credits shy of graduating, becoming a bond salesman at the firm that later became known as Dillon Reed. During World War One, Forrestal enlisted in the U.S. Navy, where he became Naval Aviator # 154 in the fledgling naval air service. Assigned to Washington, D.C., Forrestal did not see combat and was discharged as a lieutenant (junior grade) when the war ended. Forrestal then returned to Wall Street, and by 1938 had risen to the presidency of Dillon Reed. Forrestal had become a rich man, but his patriotism and willingness to serve best defined him. In May 1940 responded to calls to serve and joined the Roosevelt administration, initially in minor administrative roles. That quickly changed; on 22 August 1940 he began his service as under-secretary of the Navy. It was an assignment for which the former naval officer was well suited. Forrestal was intimately involved in resolving naval procurement issues, including those of the Navy's Bureau of Aeronautics.

Forrestal's involvement with procurement matters never stopped, but his sudden elevation to Navy secretary in 1944 provided far more responsibility. An activist leader, Forrester toured the Pacific combat theaters just as the tri-powers Yalta Conference ended. And Forrestal wanted to get to the tip of the spear. At 0600 hours East Longitude time on 19 February 1945, Secretary James Forrestal viewed Iwo Jima from the *U.S.S. Eldorado* as the amphibious assault began. On 23 February, Forrestal transferred to a shallow-draft patrol craft sweeper, and then to a small Higgins boat, which took him ashore at Iwo Jima's Red Beach. Forrestal landed roughly an hour after the beach had been shelled, and followed marines as they fought near the beachhead. Among his more memorable recollections was the sight of marines raising the American flag atop Mount Suribachi as he approached the beach and, later that day, the sight of marines removing bodies of Japanese soldiers from enemy pillboxes. It was the first time that a civilian Navy secretary had been physically present during an amphibious combat assault. After experiencing the beachhead at Iwo Jima firsthand, Forrestal continued his tour. The remainder of his itinerary included at meeting with Admiral Nimitz on Guam, after which he flew to Leyte, in the Philippine Islands. There, on 28 February, Forrestal met with General MacArthur in the recently liberated capital of Manila (just five days after the fighting stopped). This was James Forrestal, not just an administrative leader, but a man whose active, fully engaged *modus operandi* continued throughout the war, and into the immediate post-war period.

By the time of Clark Clifford's top-secret report, Forrestal was dealing with the multiple problems of maintaining military preparedness. This was aggravated by a very rapid demobilization; the introduction of jet aircraft into the naval inventory, and the establishment of a new cabinet-level department to administer the Army, Navy and the soon-to-be U.S. Air Force. The political maneuvering behind the reorganization was complicated and protracted, but it culminated in the passage of the National Security Act of 1947. The Act created a new position entitled Secretary of Defense and a new service, the U.S. Air Force. Unfortunately, the Act did not create a new Department of Defense. Instead, a convoluted organization named the National Military Establishment emerged, becoming effective of 18 September 1947. This *sui generis* creation of Congress used the unfortunate acronym NME, which sounded like "enemy" when spoken. Under the law, Forrestal became the first 'Secretary of Defense' the previous day.

Despite these political machinations inside Washington, D.C., F4U production continued at Vought's Stratford plant. The nation had demobilized too rapidly and the U.S. Navy, stretched thin due its global commitments and increased risks from the Soviet Union and communists in China, realized that it could not completely rely on the newly developed jet fighters. Into this environment, on 5 March 1948, tensions with the Soviet Union dramatically increased. U.S. Army General Lucius D. Clay, the military governor of the American sectors of Germany, sent a top secret war warning from Berlin to Lt. Gen. Stephen J. Chamberlin, the chief of military intelligence to the Army General Staff in Washington. The Soviets were about to establish restrictions on air travel and supply trains in and out of Berlin, and a shooting match between Russian and American troops could easily arise. It was less than three months before hostile acts by Soviet troops would precipitate the Berlin Airlift.

Armed with a strong consensus about vulnerabilities in the nation's defense manufacturing infrastructure, and very aware of the recent war warning from Gen. Clay, the NME and the Navy decided to act. On 6 April 1948, Secretary Forrestal personally notified Chairman Frederick B. Rentschler of United Aircraft Corporation of the Navy's plans. In particular, the Navy selected Chance Vought as the preferred tenant to take over Plant B at what came to be known as the Dallas Naval Weapons Industrial Reserve Plant. This was the factory that North American Aviation used during the war for the production of P-51 Mustang fighters, SNJ Texan trainers for the Navy, and the licensed production of Consolidated B-24 Liberator heavy bombers. The adjacent Naval Air Station at Dallas provided suitable runways for first-flights and other flight test work, and the favorable year-round weather was also conducive for test flying. But best of all for the U.S. Navy, its two main aircraft manufacturers – Chance Vought and Grumman – would now be 1,700 miles apart, and far less vulnerable to military attack.

There were important supporters for agreeing to the Navy's request in 1948, one of them being Chance Vought's general manager Rex Beisel. The move to Dallas would not only provide a geographical separation between the Chance Vought division and United Aircraft corporate headquarters in Hartford; it would also provide for a greater degree of autonomy. Unknown at the time, what was then still a division of United Aircraft Corporation would in six years achieve full autonomy again. On 1 July 1954, amid anti-trust concerns, Chance Vought would be spun-off from United Aircraft Corporation. But in 1948, after Secretary Forrestal's message to UAC, the immediate concerns focused on the cost and logistical considerations of the move.

It so happened that with much lower F4U production rates and limited needs of the new F6U program, what was often regarded as the largest corporate relocation up to that time went smoothly. Chance Vought moved approximately 1,500 workers to the Dallas, Texas area between April 1948 and July 1949. During that period, it was able to synchronize production activities an keep F4U production moving despite the fact that riggers and movers had to remove, transport and the reinstall in a completely different factory roughly 25,000 tons of jigs, fixtures, cranes, conveyors and machinery. The situation with the ill-fated F6U was not so fortunate.

After building the F6U airframes in Stratford, the fuselage, wing and tail assemblies were trucked to Dallas. But after installing the engines and running ground tests, it was decided that NAS Dallas was not adequate for testing the underpowered Pirate. The completed F6Us were again disassembled, and then trucked to an airpark in Oklahoma for acceptance testing. By late October 1950, after thirty-three aircraft were completed, the Navy terminated the F6U Pirate program. At about the same time, the abandoned Stratford factory complex became a U.S. Army engine plant. In the post-Chance Vought years, the Stratford complex became well known as the Army engine plant that produced engines for the Bell UH-1 helicopter, and later the AGT-1500 turbines for the Army's M1A1 Abrams tank. Textron-Lycoming, the long time tenant, also developed the ALF-502 fanjet engine at the plant before it finally shut down in the 1990s.

Chance Vought's move to Dallas, which began before the present day Department of Defense even existed, also happened as the F4U was upgraded with several post-war improvements. World War Two ended with the F4U-4, the ultimate wartime version, rolling off the Chance Vought assembly line in Stratford. The F4U-4 would continue to be produced until 1947, the year before the move. What had promised to be the ultimate Corsair in terms of performance was actually built in Ohio by Goodyear. Featuring a huge 3,000 h.p. Pratt & Whitney R-4360 powerplant, the FG2 series (including -1 and -2 variants) would have had a top speed in the range of 480 m.p.h. But developmental problems with the huge engine resulted in only ten copies being built before the program was canceled, and it never saw active service. The most successful postwar improvement of the F4U was the F4U-5, conceived during the waning months of the war and first flown on 3 July 1946 by Vought test pilot Bill Horan.

In addition to offering different mission-specific versions (e.g., the F4U-5N night fighter; the F4U-5P photo reconnaissance version, and the F4U-5NL winterized version), the basic F4U-5 had the very large Pratt & Whitney R-2800-32(E) powerplant. Rated at 2,850 h.p. and incorporating a two-stage supercharger, this engine would produce almost as much level flight speed as the Goodyear FG2 test versions, but with far less complexity. Some of the changes on the F4U-5 were incremental, as when metal replaced fabric and wood on the outboard wing trailing edges, ailerons and elevators. This reflected the ease in using aluminum, which had been very scarce during the war. This change substantially reduced drag, adding 20 knots to the level flight top speed. A two-degree reduction in the cowl angle was accomplished; it offered an incremental but important improvement in forward visibility. Spring tabs for the rudder and elevators were included, along with an improved cockpit layout.

Not all of the changes in the F4U-5 were universally liked by pilots. Generally not liked were the automatic blower controls and the new intercooler doors; these changes were good in theory but often problematic. Yet overall, the F4U-5 and its variants were very successful aircraft. Even with the reduced postwar production levels some 223 copies were produced. But despite the maturity of the basic F4U design, the risks involved in flight-testing design changes remained. On 8 July 1946 test pilot Dick Burroughs was killed while attempting to land at the Tweed New Haven Airport following an engine failure in the XF4U-5. Later that year, project pilot Bill Horan survived a risky bail out of an F4U-5 following an engine failure during a high altitude dive test over Long Island Sound.

The F4U-5 would be the last Corsair variant to be developed in Stratford. Chance Vought's 1948-9 move to Texas followed the firm's initial 1940s work on jet fighters at its Stratford, Connecticut plant. But an important design initiative on the venerable F4U Corsair began in Dallas after the move. It has largely escaped notice, even though as an attack aircraft it was and is historically important. That was Chance Vought's XF4U-6, which was later redesignated as the AU-1 Corsair once it entered production.

Starting with the basic F4U-5 design, Chance Vought sacrificed speed, performance and maneuverability – the attributes that are most important to a fighter aircraft – to produce the ultimate close air support airplane. Although almost indistinguishable in photos from earlier Corsairs, the AU-1 incorporated significant internal changes to meet the needs of the soldiers and "mud marines" that it would support, plus the safety of the pilot. A considerable amount of armor protection was added around the cockpit and the underside of the engine, important changes that improved survivability but substantially increased the empty weight. Air intakes were moved into the wing root for greater protection from enemy ground fire, and the R-2800-93W had just a single-stage supercharger. In addition to the center section pylons, the outboard wing housed four 20 mm cannon and had ten under-wing pylons. The AU-1 could alternatively be armed with bombs or rockets on the outer wing pylons, depending on the mission. Fully loaded with ordnance, the aircraft would weigh in at approximately 19,400 lbs, far more than the F4U-4 or F4U-5, and even heavier than the larger Douglas A-1 Skyraider. This was essentially what the French Navy would receive; those Corsairs were designated as F4U-7s. The F4U-7 would be the last of the F4U Corsairs, and would serve in the French navy until 1964. The very last one rolled off the Dallas production line in January 1953.

Although it has often been the subject of derogatory remarks because of its anemic performance, the AU-1 Corsair was conceptually way ahead of its time. It is true that at high operational combat weights and with the considerable extra drag from ordnance and drop tanks, a fully loaded AU-1 was slow; cruising speeds of roughly 200 m.p.h. were common. Loaded with fuel, bombs and/or rockets, the AU-1 would operate almost exclusively below 10,000 feet; there was no need for high-altitude performance. And the aircraft also suffered some poor flight characteristics. Its biggest deficits were poor directional control in low-speed, and high drag powered approaches to short runways (in which the pilot could run out of right rudder authority), and wing rocking during dive bomb attacks. But except for survivability, the AU-1 version of the Corsair was never designed to be a pilot's airplane. It was designed to carry a lot of ordinance, and deliver it very close to friendly troops at lower speeds, but with greater accuracy than would be expected from any jet fighter. Just 111 copies were produced, and by the time the AU-1 was deployed the three year long Korean War was half finished. It would not be until the A-10 entered USAF service in 1977 that the superiority of a highly armed, well armored, and slow attack aircraft would be established.

Moving To Texas, Then Deploying To Korea

In moving to Texas, Chance Vought turned a page in its corporate history, but the relocation also preceded big changes in manufacturing and aircraft technologies. For example, the company's move occurred just as the numerical control (NC) of machines began to appear in aircraft factories. As with many technological advances, government fingerprints could be found behind the scenes. One major NC breakthrough occurred in 1949 as a result of a U.S. Air Force research project. In this instance, scientists at the Massachusetts Institute of Technology's (MIT) Servomechanism Laboratory developed a numerically controlled milling machine. Besides being servo-controlled, MIT's experimental machine used instructions that were embedded in paper tape. This was still in the pre-electronics age when servo-controlled machinery, often using cams or equivalent mechanisms, began to utilize instructions that were encoded on punch cards or paper tape. The greater integration of programmable instructions with more accurate and precise control mechanisms heralded the arrival of the NC age in manufacturing. By the time that the F8U (later redesignated as the F8) Crusader entered production in 1957, automated NC machining for complex wing and fuselage shapes were being practiced by Chance Vought and other aircraft manufacturers.

As NC technology advanced during the 1950s, so did computer technology and metallurgy. It is helpful to remember that as the F4U production line entered its final years, the UNIVAC represented state-of-the-art computer technology. Computer Numerical Control (CNC) and computer workstations were still decades away, but big advances in machine control, automation and computers had arrived.

Powerplant technology was also moving rapidly. The F6U Pirate was powered by a Westinghouse J34 single-spool turbojet that produced 3,400 lbs of thrust. But as early as 1947, the Navy understood that in order to operate jet aircraft from its carriers, turbojets would need considerably more thrust. The Navy prodded Pratt & Whitney to obtain a license to produce the Rolls-Royce Nene powerplant, which appeared in the USA as Pratt & Whitney's J48. The J48 was used successfully in the Grumman F9F Panther and the USAF's Lockheed F-94 all-weather interceptor. The J48 was a big improvement, but it still retained centrifugal-flow technology. Then in 1952, while the Korean War raged and Chance Vought was producing AU-1s and F4U-7s, Pratt &

Whitney developed its revolutionary J57 turbojet. A twin-spool, axial-flow engine, the J-57 had sixteen compressor stages, a single-stage high-pressure turbine and a two-stage turbine on the low-pressure spool. This was the powerful engine that would push jet fighters well beyond the speed of sound, including the F8 Crusader.

Another watershed leap in technology developed with the arrival of electronics. On 30 June 1949, the development of the transistor was announced by Bell Laboratories – just after Chance Vought's move to Dallas had been completed. This announcement foretold the enormous advances that would follow in offensive and defensive avionics, flight control systems (including multi-channel autopilots) and air-to-air missiles. Although defense research languished in the immediate postwar period, by the 1950s there was a sudden reversal. After existing unofficially for five years at what was then known as the Naval Ordnance Test Station, an experimental heat-seeking, air-to-air missile finally appeared as a recognized program in 1951. That missile became the AIM-9 Sidewinder, the most successful air-to-air missile of all time. But aside from its contributions to air warfare, the Sidewinder serves as a benchmark of the rapid changes that were occurring in technology. Sidewinder development started in 1946, two years before Chance Vought's relocation was started, and became a funded Department of the Navy program just two years after Chance Vought arrived in Texas. The F8 Crusader would be a direct beneficiary of this research when it was equipped with the Sidewinder 1B. This was the first air-to-air missile with semi-active radar homing, and was offered as an improvement over standard infrared-based guidance. Without knowing it, acceding to the Navy's relocation request helped to neatly position Chance Vought for its next major success, the supersonic F8 Crusader.

Along with the benefits of new technologies, a smaller product line eased Vought's post-move burdens and prepared it for Cold War defense needs. The bold but unusable F6U Pirate was scrapped by the Navy, while F4U production continued. The even bolder F7U Cutlass, which did see active service in the U.S. Navy, proved to be short-lived. But even before the demise of the Cutlass, and with the manufacturing operation in Dallas running smoothly, Rex Beisel decided to retire. Fred Detweiler took over when Beisel left, and Chance Vought continued into the jet age. It is significant that even in the early 1950s, the F4U that

Rex Beisel's team began designing in 1938 remained the company's most successful product. So F4U-5s, the limited production run of AU-1s, and then the F4U-7 for the French navy continued to roll off Chance Vought's production line. But in the final years of its production, and even as more and more jet fighters were purchased by the military, the F4U Corsair had another war to fight.

• • • •

At dawn on 25 June 1950, the North Korean People's Army (NKPA) crossed the 38th parallel on the Korean peninsula and invaded the Republic of Korea (i.e., South Korea). The 38th parallel was the line that had been established at the Potsdam Conference in 1945; it divided the Korea peninsula into a northern and southern section that were administered separately under a trustee program. The separate nations known as North Korea and South Korea were created in 1948, with the north controlled by Kim Il-sung's communist dictatorship and the south by a constitutional government led by Syngman Rhee. Both sides preferred a unified Korean nation; the 1950 invasion followed an uneasy truce with numerous border provocations. General Douglas MacArthur, who had spent nearly five years as Japan's postwar military governor, was tasked with commanding American and other United Nations forces in repelling the invasion.

The Korean War service of the Corsair began as USAF jet fighters were becoming operational; their primary function was to establish air superiority. However, not all of the early jets filled the bill. The Lockheed F-80 Shooting Star and early Navy jet fighters such as the McDonnell F2H Banshee and Grumman F9F Panther were soon relegated to a strike fighter role, while the more capable North American F-86 Sabre took over air superiority duties. And in that air-to-air role, the F-86 was very successful against the nimble MiG-15. So the venerable F4U, including the newer F4U-5 and the AU-1 version used by the Marine Corps, were mainly tasked with strike and close support missions. And with its piston-engine attack aircraft, the United States did not worry about its latest jet aircraft technology falling into enemy hands.

The Korean War, often overlooked by students of postwar geopolitics, was also a revealing episode in the operational history of the F4U and other tactical aircraft. By 1950, jet fighters had been around for roughly five years. Turbojets (and their related technologies) were maturing, but the extensive use of jet fighters in a combat environment had yet to occur. Unlike the early jet fighters, the Corsair could provide close in support for ground troops at speeds that permitted accurate placement of ordnance on the target. The Corsair could also loiter at lower altitudes (or at night) for periods that were not possible in turbojet aircraft, which burned fuel at a high rate when down low. And when the heavily protected AU-1 became operational midway through the conflict, the Marine Corps had an aircraft that was not only capable of delivering a formidable amount of ordnance and firepower, but which provided the pilot with unparalleled protection. This was ideal for the old-fashioned ground warfare that occurred on the Korean peninsula. So in Korea, the slow but deadly AU-1 version of the Chance Vought F4U Corsair – and its contemporary, the Douglas A-1 Skyraider – became the operational predecessors of the unmatched Fairchild A-10 attack aircraft that flew in 1972.

Landing Signal Officer (LSO) aboard the *U.S.S. Sicily* (CVE-118), underway off Korea on 4 July 1950. Qualified naval aviators, LSOs provided critical guidance that could sometimes prevent accidents. Image source/credit: Courtesy of the Emil Buehler Library Collections of the National Museum of Naval Aviation, Robert L. Lawson Photograph Collection, Accession Number 1996.488.020.019.

The substantial U.S. naval deployment to Korea involved a number of Navy and Marine Corps F4U squadrons. Including both regular and reserve units, a total of thirty-five Corsair squadrons – seven from the USMC – served in Korea. Unlike World War Two, a significant number of F4U squadrons operated from aircraft carriers. While exploits of USAF F-86 Sabres dogfighting MiG-15s attracted considerable attention, the F4U was not being left behind as it had been in late-1943 and most of 1944. F4Us operated over both North and South Korea, proving their effectiveness as strike fighters and close air support weapons. Some F4U-5s performed night air interdiction of propeller-driven enemy aircraft, with varying degrees of success. However, in June 1953, just before the cease-fire, there was some unexpected good luck. While detached from the *U.S.S. Princeton's* Air Group 15 for TDY with the USAF, Lt. Guy P. Bordelon managed to shoot down five low and slow intruders, becoming the only Corsair ace over Korea. In a chance daytime encounter, Capt. Jesse Folmar of VMF-312 shot down a MiG-15 during a lopsided air-to-air engagement. Although a badly outnumbered Folmar was himself shot down, his "kill" showed that while obsolete as a dogfighter, the F4U could still be lethal. The Korean War quickly became a proxy war, with Communist China and the U.S.S.R. supporting North Korea and the United States and its United Nation's allies supporting South Korea. The great majority of tactical air operations involved close air support and strike missions, but to understand the importance of those missions a general understanding of the course of the war is essential. As with World War Two, America and its allies were caught unprepared.

At the time of the North Korean invasion, the Korean People's Army (KPA) outnumbered the Republic of Korea (ROK) Army by a factor or nearly 2:1. South Korea lacked manpower, artillery and tanks. South Korea lacked tactical aircraft and had no navy. An early American counter-offensive (Task Force Smith) was defeated, and allied forces were pushed backwards far below the 38th parallel. General Douglas MacArthur, who had spent the five years since 1945 as the military governor of Japan, became the supreme allied commander of the allied coalition. He was badly needed. The KPA rapidly advanced south, forcing the Rhee's government to flee from the capital city of Seoul. The retreat continued until the ROK established a defensive perimeter at the Pusan peninsula, in the southeast corner of South Korea. There, during August and September 1950, the Battle of Pusan wore on as MacArthur prepared his offensive plans.

While South Korea was being overrun, the United States was quick to respond. ROK forces at Pusan were resupplied from the U.S. mainland and Japan. Between 15-19 September, MacArthur directed a large bombardment and amphibious assault on the coastal city of Inchon (Operation Chromite). The 75,000 troops included 1st Marine Division, the Army's 7th Infantry Division, other Army units, and ROK Marines. Some 260 naval vessels participated in the bombardment and invasion. On the second day of the battle, an F4U spotted six columns of NKPA T-34 tanks approaching Inchon. VMF-214 quickly responded with an air attack, destroying or badly damaging most of the columns, with only one Corsair being lost. U.S. tanks finished the destruction. On the third day of the battle, the 2nd Battalion, 5th Marines captured the strategically important Kimpo Airfield near Soul. This was the largest airfield on the Korean peninsula, and it permitted allied fighters, bombers and transports to operate from a large land airfield. The landing at Inchon and the battle was brilliantly executed and a decisive allied victory, although the 11-day advance on Seoul was painstakingly slow. By 26 September the Marines had retaken Seoul, but most surviving NPRA troops escaped north across the Yalu River in China.

The course of the largely conventional war after the retaking of Soul involved MacArthur's capture and control of most of the Korean peninsula, followed by tactical withdrawals as reinforced troops spilled southward from China. As MacArthur's forces advanced rapidly into North Korean territory, they were affected by the harsh terrain and cold weather conditions. Because the Taebaek Mountains imposed a physical separation between the western and eastern portions of the peninsula, the ground operation was bifurcated. The U.S. Eighth Army controlled the western frontier while the ROK I Corps and U.S. X Corps (composite) advanced up the eastern frontier. As North Korea lacked an effective air force or navy, it was hoped that a rapid ground advance up the peninsula could result a united Korean nation. With control of

U.S. Navy F4U from the *U.S.S. Philippine Sea* (CV-47) on patrol over Allied invasion fleet at Inchon, South Korea, 15 Sept 1950. Image source/credit: Courtesy of the Emil Buehler Library Collections of the National Museum of Naval Aviation, Robert L. Lawson Photograph Collection, Accession Number 1996.253.7150.037.

By October 1950 Communist China and the Soviet Union became active in supporting the beleaguered NKPA. On 19 October the Chinese Communist's People's Volunteer Army (PVA) secretly crossed the Yalu River and moved south towards the advancing X Corps. A fateful battle occurred at the Chosin Reservoir, after which the UN forces fought their way to the port of Hungnam. This action, known as the breakout, occurred between 6-11 December 1950. After the Battle of Chosin Reservoir and the evacuation at Hangnam, and faced with direct Chinese support of the NKPA, the UN forces quickly retreated back towards the 38th parallel. The retreat included the Eighth Army on the western frontier. The Battle of Chosin Reservoir was a victory for communist forces, but at a very high price. But with Chinese troops augmenting

Developing the Gull-Winged F4U Corsair - And Taking It To Sea

the NKPA and the U.S. unwilling to escalate the war north of the Yalu River, the ground war wore on without any major advances by either side. The action had become a stalemate, and after another two and a half years an armistice was agreed to. The armistice document was signed on 27 July 1953 by Lt. General William K. Harrison and General Nam Il, his North Korean counterpart. So the Korean War never ended, but most hostilities did.

Much of the post-war reporting of the air campaigns has focused on the dogfights between the F-86 and the MiG-15 in "MiG Alley" near the Yalu River. To a lesser extent, the extensive use of helicopters has attracted historical notice. But a high percentage of the F4U/AU-1 missions were accomplished in close proximity to friendly ground troops. In Korea, F4U-5s and AU-1s would carry up to 5,000 lbs of ordnance, eight-five percent of a B-17s bomb payload. Being able to utilize napalm, bombs or rockets, the Corsair was a versatile weapons platform. Unlike the early jet fighters, the F4U also had endurance; it could loiter in a threat area if needed to protect ground troops. But the F4U also operated extensively over hostile areas in North Korea, and it operated from aircraft carriers far more extensively than it did in World War Two.

One of the important air strikes in the north was an attack on the military airfield at Pyongyang early in the war. Because the NKPA advanced so quickly, land airfields in South Korea were not unavailable to the allies. So from the beginning, it was clear that naval aircraft would plan an important role in the war. By 3 July 1950, just over a weak after the North Korea invasion, the carriers *U.S.S. Valley Forge* (CV-45) and the Royal Navy's *H.M.S. Triumph* appeared in the Yellow Sea as Task Force 77. The carriers had an interesting mix of aircraft. The Fleet Air Arm provided piston-engine attack capability with its Fairey Firefly, a slow but capable aircraft. Aboard the *Valley Forge* were Grumman F9F Panthers; these were the straight-wing version of what would evolve into the swept-wing Grumman F9F Cougar. Also aboard the *Valley Forge* were F4Us of VF-53 and VF-54, plus Douglas AD-1 Skyraiders of VF-55. The F9Fs operated as fighters, and managed to strafe prior to returning to the ship. The sixteen piston-engine attack aircraft arrived with rockets (on the F4Us) and bombs (on the AD-1s). The raid, a complete surprise, was a complete success.

From this start, the F4U proved its worth time and again. For one thing, it was available in numbers, especially as naval and marine reserve units deployed. And while air superiority was not its mission, just about everything else was. By 1950, the experience level in most F4U squadrons was high, and that – along with the years of improvements to the Corsair – made carrier requalification, and shipboard operations, far smoother than in the previous war. There were also a number of F4U pilots whose exploits achieved worldwide attention. One F4U pilot, Lt. (j.g.) Thomas Hudner, received the Medal of Honor.

The actions that earned Hudner the Medal of Honor occurred on 4 December 1950. While part of an eight plane patrol with VF-32, Hudner observed Ensign Jesse Brown crash land near the Chosin Reservoir after being hit by ground fire. Ens. Brown, the U.S. Navy's first African-American pilot, survived the crash but was trapped in the cockpit of his smoking aircraft. While awaiting a rescue helicopter, Hudner made a wheels-up landing in the small clearing to try to pull Brown from the wreckage. Despite frantic efforts, the mortally wounded Brown did not survive and died in the wreckage. For his actions in flying armed reconnaissance in support of encircled allied troops, Lt. Brown was posthumously awarded the Distinguished Flying Cross (DFC). On 13 April 1951, in the presence of Brown's widow Daisy, President Harry S. Truman presented Hudner with the Medal of Honor.

By mid-1953, it was clear that the 38th parallel would remain the dividing line between North and South Korea. As the hostilities came to an end, it was clear that the F4U's days of active service with the Navy and Marine Corps were drawing to a close. The F4U in its various versions, and some AU-1s, would continue to serve with other nations, including Egypt, Israel, and especially with the French Aeronavale. Interestingly, French F4U-7s did see action in French Indo-China, and the Douglas A-1 Skyraider saw extensive action with the USAF and U.S. Navy in Vietnam. But not the Corsair. After the Korean War went cold, F4Us were stricken from Navy and Marine Corps inventory, usually replaced by jets. The last copy served in the reserves until 1957, and then it too was gone. So ended the American military service of the Vought F4U Corsair, America's greatest multi-role naval fighter of World War Two and close support workhorse of Korea. It was a quiet but proud ending.

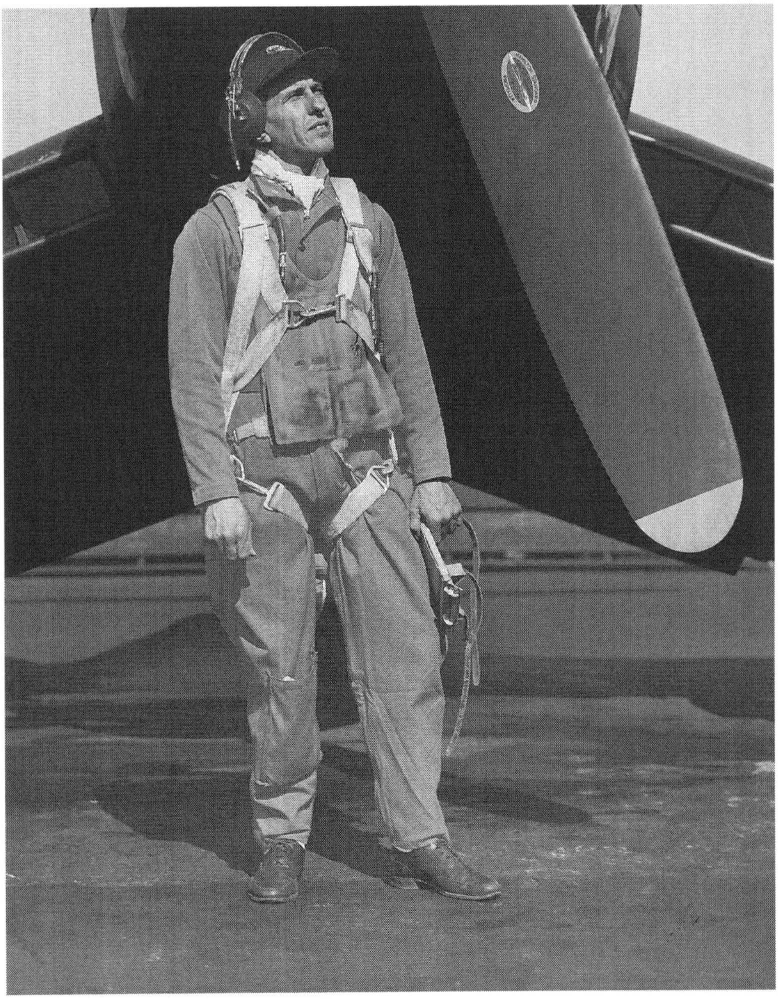

Epilogue

Things do not happen. Things are made to happen.

– John F. Kennedy

None of my inventions came by accident. I see a worthwhile need to be met and I make trial after trial until it comes.

– Thomas A. Edison

Here Men From Planet Earth First Set Foot Upon the Moon, July 1969 A.D. We Came In Peace For All Mankind.

– Plaque left in the Sea of Tranquility on the lunar surface by Apollo 11 Astronauts.

It was the summer of 1969, and the band Three Dog Night's hit song *Easy To Be Hard* was rocking the airwaves. So too was *Aquarius / Let the Sunshine In* by The Fifth Dimension; it was ranked number one among the top 40 in May. The Beatles were still together, but their studio album *Yellow Submarine* failed to top the charts in either the UK or the USA. 1969 was the year that Ford offered the Boss 429 version of its classic Mustang. Chevrolet, constantly improving its Corvette, came out with its new small-block V-8. With that change the displacement of Chevy's venerable engine rose from 327 to 350 cubic inches.

In Hollywood, 1969 was a year in which some of its most epic films would be released. In September, Twentieth Century Fox released *Butch Cassidy and the Sundance Kid*, starring Paul Newman, Robert Redford and Katherine Ross. This film would be the most acclaimed picture of the year, winning four Academy Awards, and would catapult Robert Redford's long and impressive career. United Artists released

Midnight Cowboy just in time for the Memorial Day weekend. Starring Dustin Hoffman and Jon Voight, the film classic would win three Academy Awards. And in July, Columbia released *Easy Rider*, starring Peter Fonda and Dennis Hopper. Nominated for several Academy Awards, this counterculture classic would later be added to the United States National Film Registry.

    1969 was also a year in which baseball history was being made. This would be the first year in which there would be divisional play-offs to determine the Major League Baseball pennant winners. In the National League East, Chicago Cubs fans swarmed to Wrigley Field to watch manager Leo Durocher and his Cubs hold their commanding first place lead. On July 16, Cubs fans had reason to be hopeful as their team faced the New York Mets in the final game of a three game set. The Cubs were not just leading in the NL East; they were due for a World Series win. The Cub's last World Series Championship was in 1908, and its last series appearance was in 1945 – the year that World War Two ended. Besides having stars such as Ernie Banks, Randy Hurley and Billy Williams in the lineup, third baseman Ron Santo made the 1969 All Star team. Pitching that day for Chicago was Ferguson "Fergie" Jenkins, a 6' 5" right-hander who would finish the year with a 21-15 record. Jenkins, a future Hall of Fame pitcher, had won twenty games during his 1967 rookie season, and could be dominating on the mound. Cal Koonce, a former Cub, was the starter for the Mets. Koonce was born on 18 November 1940, the month after the F4U first broke the 400 m.p.h. barrier for a fighter. Koonce had the bad luck of being the losing pitcher on 8 April when the Mets lost to the Montreal Expos (a first), but would end the season with a 6-3 record. With two fine starting pitchers and two great baseball teams, both Cubs and Mets fans expected to watch a thriller of a game.

    Not all Americans were focused on the game between Cubs and the Mets. Hours earlier, television networks broadcast an even greater event as it unfolded at Pad 39A at Cape Canaveral, Florida. For the first time in the history of mankind, humans would travel from the Earth to the Moon, and hopefully land on the lunar surface. It was an enormous event and television provided viewers with an awesome sight. Standing on the launch pad, the Saturn V and the Apollo 11 capsule stood 363 feet high when; that height was greater than the takeoff

Epilogue

distance of an F4U from a small escort carrier. Then, at 9:32 AM, the television cameras broadcast the sounds and images as the three-stage Saturn V booster rocket blasted off with the Apollo 11 capsule and astronauts Neil Armstrong, Edwin "Buzz" Aldrin and Michael Collins. After Apollo 11 cleared the launch tower and soared skyward, initially entering an Earth orbit to complete a post-launch spacecraft checkout. After one and a half revolutions of the Earth, the third-stage rocket was fired and the astronauts began their Trans-Lunar Injection (TLI). The TLI, which required a six-minute burn of the third-stage, would accelerate the spacecraft to 24,000 m.p.h. so it could escape from the Earth's gravitational field.

> *Apollo Eleven, this is Houston at 1 minute. Trajectory and guidance look good, and the stage is good.*

And good it was. Two hours and forty-five minutes after liftoff, Apollo 11 departed its Earth orbit and began the three-day, 235,000 mile journey to the Moon. But as Planet Earth slowly receded into the background, a less dramatic history was being made in Central America. For many years, significant numbers of Salvadorans migrated to neighboring Honduras and went to work on that country's farmland. Honduras was five times as large as El Salvador, but its neighbor to the west had the greater population. Neither country had a strong military, but both still operated F4U Corsairs – the last nations to use them in active service. On 14 July, after relations between the two nations deteriorated, El Salvador commenced land and air attacks on Honduras. It was more than twenty-nine years since the XF4U first flew off Runway 29 at the Bridgeport Airport. But once again, while Apollo 11 was headed toward the Moon, the F4U was going to war.

> *Hello Apollo 11. Houston. We see your middle gimbal angle getting pretty big. Over.*

Apollo 11 was six hours and twenty-one minutes into its mission.

> *Well, it was, Charlie, but in going from one AUTO maneuver to another, we took over control and have gone around gimbal lock; and we're about to give control back to the DAP.*

When he called on America to put astronauts on the Moon before the end of the 1960s decade, President John F. Kennedy knew that the Apollo missions would require a tremendous leap in several technologies. Smart, hard working and bold men and women would drive the enormous technology advances, and put their lives on the line in order to with the "Space Race." Such boldness in aerospace design and capabilities had happened before, as with the F4U Corsair, the North American P-51 Mustang and the Lockheed P-38 Lightning, to cite just some examples. And then there were jet aircraft, with a new and completely different method of propulsion. Neil A. Armstrong, as a young Navy pilot, flew the jet-powered Grumman F9F Panther with VF-51 during the Korean War. Buzz Aldrin flew F86 combat missions in Korea as a USAF pilot, and Michael Collins flew F-86 fighters for the USAF in Germany. Each of these astronauts was a leader in manned space flight, and each had participated in the risky transition from piston-engine fighters to jets. So too had Vought.

Apollo 11's three-day coast out required coordinated systems management with both Mission Control and the astronauts participating; CSM separation from the S-IVB; CSM docking with the LM/S-IVB, and CSM/LM separation from the S-IVB. The flight plan also called for a mid-course correction as the CSM/LM coasted towards its lunar destination. Back on Earth, the Chicago Cubs lost to the Mets 9-5 on Wednesday, and prepared to travel to Philadelphia for a Friday game against the Phillies. But 23 hours and 14 minutes after the Apollo 11 liftoff, the capsule communicator at Mission Control had some not so serious matters to discuss with Mission Commander Neil Armstrong.

> *[Apollo] Eleven, this is Houston. If you're interested in the morning news, I have a summary here from PAO. Over.*
>
> *Okay. We're all listening.*
>
> *Okay. From Jodrell Bank, England, via AP: Britain's big Jodrell Bank radio telescope stopped receiving signals from the Soviet Union's unmanned Moon shot at 5:49 EDT today. A spokesman said that it appeared the Luna 15 spaceship "had gone beyond the Moon." Another Quote: "We*

don't think it has landed," said a spokesman for Sir Bernard Lovell, Director of the Observatory.

Included in the morning news transmission was another surprise for the Apollo 11 crew:

> . . . *Washington UPI: Vice President Spiro T. Agnew has called for putting a man on Mars by the year 2000, but Democratic leaders replied that priority must go to needs on Earth. Agnew, ranking government official at the Apollo ll blastoff Wednesday, apparently was speaking for himself and not necessarily for the Nixon administration when he said, "We should, in my judgment, put a man on Mars by the end of this century."*

If a mission to Mars were to occur in the future, Apollo 11 astronauts – and many others – would first have to demonstrate successful travels to and from the closest celestial body to Planet Earth. Yet the risky Apollo 11 was less than halfway to the Moon when Vice-President Agnew called on a mission to Mars. By this time, news organizations on virtually every nation on Earth were following the progress of Apollo 11. The events over the skies of El Salvador and Honduras were almost completely removed from the public's attention.

17 July 1969 was the second day of the Apollo 11 mission. In the pre-dawn darkness, hours before the astronauts woke up from their overnight rest, three Honduran F4U-5s departed Tegucigalpa and headed for the El Salvador border. There were some good targets just across that border, and the Honduran Air Force was ready to inflict some damage. It did not go exactly as planned. When the guns on the F4U flown by Capt. Francisco Zepeda jammed, he was ordered to detach from the strike package and orbit clear of the target area. But what had started out as a strafing mission quickly changed when Zepeda's Corsair was pounced by two Salvadoran F-51 Mustangs. Capt. Fernando Soto and his wingman, Capt. Edguardo Acosta, quickly pulled away from the target and went to Zepeda's aid. Soto engaged one of the F-51s, turning inside him to deliver a lethal burst with his 20 mm cannon. The F-51 was destroyed; the other fled the area. Later that day, Soto would score two more kills, this time against the Goodyear-built FG-1 version of the Corsair. On 18 July,

the last Honduran Air Force F4U ground support missions of the war were flown.

Houston, Apollo Eleven.

Go ahead, [Apollo] Eleven.

Roger. I've got the world in my window for a change and looking at it through the monocular, it's really something. I wish I could describe it properly. The weather is very good. South America is coming around into view. I can see on the - what appears to me to be upper horizon, a point that must be just about Seattle, Washington, and from there I can see all the way down to the southern tip of Tierra del Fuego and the southern tip of the continent.

Roger. Sounds like you've got a beautiful view up there.

Absolutely fantastic. I hope the pictures come out. We're rotating around where it's going out of view again.

Apollo 11 was proceeding smoothly, but events on Earth reflected the constancy of human nature. On 18 July Massachusetts Senator Edward M. "Ted" Kennedy, returning from a late night party, accidently drove off a narrow bridge that connected Martha's Vineyard to nearby Chappaquiddick Island. His companion, Mary Jo Kopechne, drowned in the accident, and the ensuing events provided one of the leading non-Apollo news stories for weeks. But there was tranquility in space, a peaceful quiet as the ever more distant blue planet named Earth appeared farther and farther away.

The arrival of Apollo 11 in the proximity of the Moon was evidence of more than positional progress; the mission itself was going very smoothly. The bluish Earth was much smaller in the background, but still an absolutely amazing sight. Unknown to the Apollo 11 astronauts or Mission Control, the Soviet Union's Luna 15 unmanned spacecraft had crashed on the lunar surface. Luna was another incredibly bold, high-risk project that had been part of the space race between the U.S.A. and the U.S.S.R.. Apollo 11 would be tasked with making a lunar landing, and subsequent liftoff and return to Earth, safely. But first,

Epilogue

the Apollo 11 mission – which had by then separated from the S-14B third-stage rocket – had to be injected into a lunar orbit. Lunar Orbit Insertion (LOI) was about to start.

> *Apollo Eleven, this is Houston. Over.*
>
> *Roger. Go ahead Houston, Apollo Eleven.*
>
> *[Apollo] Eleven, this is Houston. You are GO for LOI. Over.*
>
> *Roger. GO for LOI.*
>
> *And we're showing about 10 minutes and 30 seconds to LOS. I would like to remind you to enable the BD roll on the AUTO RCS switches. Over.*
>
> *Roger. And confirm you want PCM low going over the hill. Over.*
>
> *That's affirmative, [Apollo] Eleven.*

Apollo 11 would make a total thirty lunar orbits during its mission, and it would afford the astronauts with a close up view of the Moon. On the backside of the Moon, Mission Control and the astronautics would be out of communication with each other. But the Moon was much smaller than the Earth; the orbits would pass quickly. And the first lunar orbit was rapidly approaching.

> *Stand by for a Mark at TIG minus 12.*
>
> *Mark.*
>
> *TIG minus 12.*
>
> *You were right on, Bruce. Thank you.*
>
> *Roger. Out.*
>
> *Two minutes to LOS.*
>
> *Apollo Eleven, this is Houston. All your systems are looking good going around the corner, and we'll see you on the other side. Over.*
>
> *Roger.*

At 1:28PM EDT on 19 July, the Apollo 11 spacecraft entered lunar orbit. There would be a total of fourteen lunar orbits before the LM would begin its powered descent from its lowest point in the orbit, roughly 50,000 feet above the lunar surface. Mission Control was satisfied with all flight and system parameters, and the astronauts began their final pre-landing rest period eighty-six hours into the mission. As the astronauts slept, Mission Control remained alert and active. Flight profile and systems management were nonstop activities on any space flight, and none would receive more attention than the first landing on the Moon. The lunar landing site was one detail that received considerable attention after the Apollo 8 mission. When the LM *Eagle* descended towards the surface, details would matter. The preferred sites were near the lunar equator; that would minimize the fuel burn during descent and ascent, and provide the most time for updating the landing computer with the latest tracking data on the final orbit. Apollo 11's flight path ran east to west over the Moon, so as viewed from Earth's Northern Hemisphere the preferred landing site would be near the equator and towards the right side. After a substantial amount of planning and vetting, the Sea of Tranquility was selected. The time to make the descent to the landing site was fast approaching.

At 1:12PM EST on 20 July, the CSM *Columbia* and the LM *Eagle* separated. Descent preparations continued, with CSM *Columbia* remaining in a high orbit while LM *Eagle* made its descent to the lunar surface.

> *Eagle, Houston. If you read, you're GO for powered descent. Over.*
>
> *Eagle, this is Columbia. They just gave you a GO for powered descent.*
>
> *Columbia, Houston. We've lost them on the high gain again. Would you please - We recommend they yaw right 10 degrees and reacquire.*
>
> *Eagle, this is Columbia. You're GO for PDI and they recommend you yaw right 10 degrees and try the high gain again.*
>
> *Eagle, you read Columbia?*

Epilogue

Roger. We read you.

Okay.

The LM *Eagle* continued the descent. It was on a tight descent profile with little margin for error. Retired Navy Capt. Eugene Cernan, who landed twice on the Moon (and who, as the Apollo 17 mission commander, would be the last man on the lunar surface), once remarked that landing a jet aircraft on an aircraft carrier at night was more difficult than landing a lunar module on the Moon. That opinion is a strong testament to the special skills that uniquely belong to naval aviators. But as CSM Pilot Michael Collins continued his orbits in *Columbia*, Mission Commander Neil Armstrong and LM Pilot Buzz Aldrin encountered some unexpected problems while descending in the *Eagle*. A series of nuisance alarms activated during the descent below 3,000 feet. Armstrong and Aldrin, with immediate responses from Mission Control engineers, where able to override the alarms and safely continue the descent. *Eagle* closed to within 100 feet of the lunar surface. The dialogue between Neil Armstrong, Buzz Aldrin and Mission Control tells the story best.

Okay. 75 feet. There's [sic] looking good. Down a half, 6 forward.

60 seconds.

Lights on ....

Down 2 1/2. Forward. Forward. Good.

40 feet, down 2 1/2. Kicking up some dust.

30 feet, 2 1/2 down. Faint shadow.

4 forward. 4 forward. Drifting to the right a little. Okay. Down a half.

30 seconds.

Forward drift?

Yes.

Okay.

> *Contact Light.*
>
> *Okay. Engine Stop.*
>
> *ACA - Out of Detent.*
>
> *Out of Detent.*
>
> *Mode Control - both AUTO. Descent Engine Command Override – OFF.*
>
> *Engine Arm – OFF.*
>
> *0413 is in.*
>
> *We copy you down, Eagle.*

And then came the historic words that the world was waiting to hear.

> *Houston, Tranquility Base here. The Eagle has landed.*

It was 3:17 PM on 20 July 1969 when the Lunar Module *Eagle* landed on the Moon. At 9:56 PM, Mission Commander Neil A. Armstrong stepped onto the lunar surface from the bottom step of the LM *Eagle* and uttered his now famous words:

> *That's one small step for [a] man, one giant leap for mankind.*

For the first time in human history, a manmade spacecraft had carried astronauts from Planet Earth to the Moon. Around the world, an estimated six hundred million people stopped their activities and monitored the suspenseful descent and landing of the LM *Eagle* on the lunar surface. It was an event that would be followed, but never surpassed. From Tranquility Base, Astronaut Buzz Aldrin implored radio and television listeners:

> *I'd like to take this opportunity to ask every person listening in, whoever and wherever they may be, to pause for a moment and contemplate the events of the past few hours, and to give thanks in his or her own way.*

Epilogue

Astronauts Neil Armstrong and Buzz Aldrin spent 21 hours on the surface of the Moon, securing their lunar module, resting, and engaging in Extra-Vehicle Activities (EVAs) that included experiments, taking photographs, and planting the American flag. The astronauts spoke with President Richard M. Nixon, collected 47 lbs of Moon rocks, and left a plaque on the surface near Tranquility Base. The plaque stated:

Here Men From Planet Earth First Set Foot Upon the Moon,

July 1969 A.D. We Came In Peace For All Mankind.

Apollo 11 landed in the Sea of Tranquility more that twenty-nine years after Lyman Bullard, Jr. first flew the XF4U-1 into the skies over Stratford, Connecticut. The lunar landing also occurred just three days after a Corsair shot down an enemy fighter for the very last time. Although not planned, the plaque in the Sea of Tranquility now serves as another benchmark – a reminder of an important moment in aviation history. Only one fighter aircraft that was born during the biplane era remained operational when space travel to other celestial bodies began. And so it ended. When Apollo 11 landed on the surface of the Moon, the last combat mission of the gull-winged F4U Corsair was over.

Glossary

A-36 Apache: The designation and name given to the original version of North American Aviation's P-51 Mustang fighter.

A6M (also "Zeke" or "Zero"): The designation and name(s) of the famous Japanese 'Zero.' The A6M was officially known as the 'Zeke' but the informal name 'Zero' is more popular, and is used in this book. This lightweight fighter appeared early in the war, and was used by the Imperial Japanese Navy from both land bases and aircraft carriers. Although in many ways superior to the Curtiss P-40s and Grumman F4Fs that it encountered early in the war, it was outclassed by Allied fighters that it encountered during and after 1943.

B-17: Boeing B-17 Flying Fortress was widely used in the European Theater of Operations (ETO), but also saw action in the Pacific and the China-Burma-India (C-B-I) theaters. America's first four-engine bomber, the B-17 was unpressurized but could carry a heavy bomb load and sustain considerable damage and remain aloft.

Boeing (The Boeing Company): The manufacturer of such aircraft as the B-17 Flying Fortress and the B-29 Superfortress.

aileron: Primary flight control attached to the trailing edge of a wing structure, with one on each wing. Used for lateral control by inducing and inhibiting roll motion (i.e., bank). The ailerons on the F4U had to be enlarged and improved with balance tabs in order to achieve the roll rates that the Navy desired.

airspeed-limited: The region of an aircraft's flight envelope in which the maximum velocity is limited by either calibrated airspeed (CAS) or indicated airspeed (IAS). Aircraft are airspeed limited until they reach an altitude/flight level when their velocity is instead limited by mach number, typically at altitudes above 25,000 feet.

air superiority fighter: A fighter aircraft that is capable of entering enemy airspace and dominating it. This term was not used during World War Two, but it is used by the author since F4U Corsairs, while used in multiple tactical roles, were sometimes tasked with dominating enemy airspace.

Allison (The Allison Engine Company): The manufacturer of the liquid-cooled V-1710 powerplant that was used in the Curtiss P-40, the North American P-51A, and the Lockheed P-38 Lightning fighters. Beginning with the P-51B, the Mustang switched to the Packard V-1850 version of the Rolls Royce Merlin engine. The Lockheed P-38 had numerous operational problems using the Allison V-1710 engine in the high-altitudes environment of the European Theater of Operations. However, the same turbosupercharged engine was very successful in the Pacific.

balance tab: Secondary control surface used to increase control effectiveness and reduce pilot effort. Balance tabs move in the direction opposite to the desired movement of the primary control surface to which they are attached. May be found on an aileron, elevator or rudder.

"batsman": See Deck Landing Control Officer.

"Betty": Name given by the Allies (for identification purposes) to the Mitsubishi G4M medium bomber of the Imperial Japanese Navy. This land-based bomber lacked armor protection or self-sealing fuel tanks, making it vulnerable to Allied fighters.

Bf-109: (also Me-109): Messerschmitt single-engine fighter that was used by the German Luftwaffe as an air defense interceptor against Allied bombers, and as an escort for Luftwaffe bombers. The Bf-109 was produced in greater numbers than any other fighter in World War Two.

"bird cage" canopy: The original F4U canopy, which had structural supports that restricted the pilot's view. Replaced by a "bubble" canopy.

Brewster (short for Brewster Aeronautical Corporation): The manufacturer of the Brewster Buffalo fighter (F2A) and a licensed version of the Corsair. The Brewster manufactured Corsairs were designated as F3A.

British Pacific Fleet (BPF): Naval force of British Commonwealth nations that was organized by the Royal Navy on 22 November 1944. The BPF met the political imperative of having British forces liberating British colonies that were captured by Japan, and the military imperative of augmenting Allied naval forces during the final year of World War Two. Based in Sydney, Australia with a forward base at Manus Island.

Buffalo: Name give to a single engine monoplane fighter build by Brewster Aeronautical Corporation, and designated as the F2A. Three versions (-1, -2 and -3) were produced. Widely regarded as the worst fighter of World War Two, it was quickly withdrawn from service and replaced by the Grumman F4F Wildcat. The Buffalo was the first monoplane fighter to be used by the U.S. navy and the Marine Corps.

Bureau of Aeronautics (also referred to as BuAer): The bureau of the United States Navy tasked with evaluating aeronautical needs of the U.S. Navy and U.S. Marine Corps; issuing Requests for Proposals (RFPs); establishing design, manufacturing and performance requirements for naval aircraft; awarding contracts, and managing naval aircraft procurement programs.

BuAer: Acronym for the U.S. Navy Bureau of Aeronautics.

CACTUS: The military code-name given to Guadalcanal Island.

Cactus Air Force: The name given to the various Allied military aircraft, units and personnel that operated from Guadalcanal Island between August and December 1942. In December 1942 until April 1943 the official name of the Cactus Air Force became the Allied Air Forces in the Solomons. In April 1943 the Cactus Air Force was given the designations AirSols (for Air Solomons). On 15 June 1944 the name changed again to AirNorSols, since operational control of much of the forces passed from Fleet Admiral Chester Nimitz, Commander-in-Chief, Pacific Ocean Area, to General of the Armies Douglas MacArthur, Supreme Commander, South West Pacific Area. The term Cactus Air Force continued to be used informally throughout this period. Note that while the center of Cactus air operations was Henderson Field on Guadalcanal, but auxiliary fields existed at various times and locations nearby.

canopy: The acrylic glass enclosure of the pilot at the top of the cockpit.

Ceylon (British Ceylon; Sri Lanka): Island territory and one time British Crown Colony located east of the southern tip of India. It is adjacent to the southwest portion of the Bay of Bengal, northeast of the Laccadive Sea and north of the Indian Ocean. Britain maintained a longstanding naval presence at Ceylon, especially in the vicinity of Trincomalee. It became the Dominion of Ceylon in 1948 and the Free Sovereign and Independent Republic of Sri Lanka in 1970.

Consolidated Aircraft: Manufacturer of military aircraft such as the PBY Catalina, B-24 Liberator and PB4Y Privateer (i.e., the latter the naval version of the B-24).

Consolidated-Vultee (also known as Convair): The successor company that resulted from the 1943 merger of Consolidated Aircraft with Vultee Aircraft, the latter a subsidiary of AVCO Corporation.

CINCPAC (also written as CinCPac): Military acronym. As used during the period covered by this book, CINCPAC referenced the position of Commander-in-Chief, United States Pacific Fleet. In World War Two, the CINCPAC was Fleet Admiral Chester W. Nimitz.

CINCPOA (also written as CinCPOA): Military acronym. As used during the period covered by this book, CINCPOA referenced the position of Commander-in-Chief, Pacific Ocean Area. In World War Two, the CINCPOA's wartime command authority extended to all Allied military units, personnel and operations of land, sea and air forces within the Pacific Ocean Area theater. Held by Fleet Admiral Chester W. Nimitz concurrent with his position as CINCPAC. The POA was separate from the Southwest Pacific Area (SWPA), of which General of the Army Douglas MacArthur was the Supreme Commander. Establishing separate theaters enabled the president and the military chiefs of staff to avoid political problems that might have resulted if either General MacArthur or Admiral Nimitz subordinate to the other.

CO: Acronym for the commanding officer of a military unit, such as a squadron or group.

combat radius: The distance from the base (or ship) that a combat aircraft can fly, engage in combat for a specified amount of time, and then

Glossary

return to the starting point with no less than the minimum required fuel reserve. The combat radius of an aircraft can be increased with the use of external (drop) fuel tanks.

constant-speed propeller: A propeller where increases or decreases in power result in changes in the propeller blade angle, rather than changes in the revolutions per minute (r.p.m.). A constant-speed propeller works with a prop governor. At reduced power settings, the propeller is below the governing speed, so that power changes will change the propeller r.p.m. The alternative is a fixed-pitch propeller, highly impractical for a fighter aircraft.

conventional [landing] **gear**: In a fixed-wing aircraft, a landing gear that is distinguished by two main landing gear and a third gear called a tailwheel, as distinguished from the more modern tricycle landing gear.

cowling: The metal cover that surrounds the sides of the engine. The cowling provides protection, and aids the cooling process by forcing the passing airflow to stay close to the radiating fins on the engine cylinders.

cowl flaps: Adjustable surfaces at the trailing edge of the cowling that can be extended outward (open) ot streamlined (closed). The cowl flaps are normally kept open during ground operations, and as needed in flight, to ensure sufficient airflow around the cylinders for cooling. Cowl flaps are typically adjusted by the pilot.

CSM (nomenclature specific to Apollo 11 mission): Command and service moduke.

"cut": A signal by a Landing Signal Officer (U.S. Navy) or a Deck Landing Control Officer (Royal Navy) to reduce (cut) the power and land aboard the aircraft carrier, as opposed to a signal to "wave off."

CVE: Hull designation for small escort-type of aircraft carrier. CVEs were often converted from tankers and other merchant ships, but as the war progressed they were mass-produced in shipyards. Slower than fleet carriers and lightly armored, they could be built and deployed quickly. CVEs were often called "jeep carriers or "baby flattops" because of there smaller size. The ship number would follow the hull designation: e.g., CVE-21 for the *U.S.S. Block Island*.

CVL: Hull designation for a light carrier. Often built by using an existing cruiser hull, CVLs could operate with fleet carriers due to their comparable speed. Example: CVL-30 for *U.S.S. San Jacinto*.

CV: Hull designation for a fleet carrier. These were the largest aircraft carriers, and were most heavily armed and armored. Example: CV-17 for *U.S.S. Bunker Hill*.

CXAM [radar]: The U.S. Navy's first production radar for use on ships at sea, and developed concurrently with the U.S. Army's SCR-270 radar. CXAM radar typically had large, rectangular antenna and gave U.S. Navy warships a tactical advantage over warships of the Imperial Japanese Navy. CXAM evolved from experimental XAF and CZX. The acronym CXAM derives from the acronyms for the two prior technologies, of which CXAM was a merger.

DAP (nomenclature specific to Apollo 11 mission): Digital autopilot.

Deck Landing Control Officer (DLCO): The officer on a Royal Navy aircraft carrier who provided signals to approaching pilots as to whether they were properly aligned, and/or on a reasonable approach angle. In addition, the DLCO would evaluate the airspeed of the arriving aircraft by checking the attitude and configuration. The DLCO positioned himself on a platform at the left (port) stern of the ship, and was commonly referred to as a "batsman" in the Royal Navy.

dive bomber: A tactical aircraft designed from dropping bombs on a target nears the bottom of a dive. Most dive bombing involved dives at steep angles. Example: Douglas SBD Dauntless.

Douglas: Short version of The Douglas Aircraft Company, later McDonnell Douglas, and later absorbed by Boeing. During World War Two, The Douglas Aircraft Company built aircraft such as the SBD Dauntless dive bomber, the C-47 Skytrain (military version of the DC-3) and the C-54 Skymaster, a four-engine transport that was most famous for its service during the 1948-9 Berlin Airlift.

Dutch East Indies (Netherlands East Indies, now Indonesia): Territory of islands in south Asia where the Indian Ocean meets the Pacific Ocean, and southwest of the Philippine Islands. Rich in oil and minerals, the territory was captured by Japan early in the war as a result of the Japanese Centrifugal Offense. Important areas include Sumatra, Java, Dutch Borneo and Celebes.

elevator: The primary flight control that is hinged to the horizontal stabilizer, and which is used to control the pitch attitude of the aircraft.

empennage: The tail structure of an aircraft. This includes the horizontal and vertical stabilizer structural components, and the elevator and rudder flight controls.

FAA: See Fleet Air Arm. Not to be confused with the Federal Aviation Administration, which is not mentioned in this text.

fighter: A military aircraft designed for tactical missions, of which the primary capability is that of engaging enemy aircraft in flight. Fighters can be further categorized according to mission. Examples: fighter interceptor, air superiority fighter, fighter escort or fighter-bomber. Fighter-bombers are often referred to as strike fighters and, under contemporary protocol, is usually given the designating prefix 'A', as in A-7. In contemporary American naval service, the noun nomenclature 'attack aircraft' is used instead of 'fighter bomber.'

fighter escort: A fighter tasked with escort missions, usually to protect bombers on tactical or strategic bombing missions. Also designates a group of such fighters.

final approach: The final segment of a landing approach. On land-based aircraft, the final approach is usually aligned with the centerline of the runway, unless modified for terrain or other purposes. For landing on a ship, the final approach is aligned with the landing deck close to the ship, but the final approach may include portions of the curved approach while the pilot is under the control of the Landing Signal Officer (LSO, in the U.S. Navy) or Deck Landing Control Office (DCLO, in the Fleet Air Arm). The final approach ends with either a "cut" or a "wave off" during approaches to an aircraft carrier.

final assembly: The portion of the manufacturing process in a factory in which sub-assembly sections are completed and joined together, and remaining production tasks are completed.

flap (also wing flap or trailing edge flap): A structural surfacce that is attached to the trailing edge of the wing, usually the inboard section (with the exception of full-span flaps). Flaps change the shape (camber) of the wing, resulting in a increase of lift and drag. Flaps can be of a single-section hinged type; slotted (multi-section) flaps, and fowler flaps. The latter extend rearward as well as downward, thereby increasing both the camber and wing surface area and shape (planform). Not to be confused with leading edge Krueger flaps.

Fleet Air Arm (FAA): The component of the Royal Navy that is responsible for the operation of aircraft. During the inter-war period, the Fleet Air Arm operated as a component of the Royal Air Force. In 1939, the control of the Fleet Air Arm was transferred to the Royal Navy, where it has remained.

flight envelope: The flight regime of an aircraft, usually depicted graphically, that identifies the minimum and maximum airspeed (or mach number) at which the aircraft can operate for a specified altitude (or flight level). Airspeed boundaries can be calibrated airspeed (CAS) or indicated airspeed (IAS), and typically use the 'knot' as the unit of velocity. One knot equals 1.15 miles-per-hour (m.p.h.). In the past, a considerable amount of data was expressed in m.p.h. Inside the cockpit, airspeed indicators often provided both m.p.h. and knot values, similar to the display of m.p.h. and kilometers-per-hour (km/h) are sometimes displayed on a speedometer. Different formats can be used by manufactures, as the affect of factors such as g-loading can included in a graphic depiction.

flight leader: The leading aircraft in an element or group of military aircraft or, alternatively, the pilot of the lead aircraft.

flight level: The nominal altitude of an aircraft above the average sea level datum plane. Pilots maintain a flight level by reference to the aircraft altimeter(s), which must be set to a standard setting of 29.92 inches Hg (Mercury), or 1,013.2 hPa (hectoPascals). The altimeter setting can be selected by the pilot. The method of altimetry that is used while operating at a flight level is denoted as QNE, as opposed to the QNH method that uses local altimeter settings, which vary with local atmospheric pressure. Flight levels are referenced by the prefix 'FL' which is

Glossary

then followed by the altitude, which is expressed in hundred-foot increments. Example: FL-200 is read as "flight level-two-two-zero" which is an altitude of 20,000 feet above the standard sea-level datum plane. At lower altitudes, the term 'flight level' is not used and the method of altimetry reverts to the QNH method. Using QNH, a local altimeter setting is used so that the altimeter will indicate field elevation when the aircraft is on the runway.

F3A: Military designation for Corsairs that were built under license by Brewster Aeronautical Corporation.

F4F: (Wildcat; known for a while as the 'Marlet' in the Royal Navy's Fleet Air Arm): Manufactured by Grumman, the F4F was the fighter that replaced the disappointing Brewster Buffalo prior to America's entrance into the war.

F6F (Hellcat): Manufactured by Grumman as a replacement to the F4F Wildcat, it entered service in 1943. The F6F was used aboard U.S. Navy aircraft carriers while the F4U was still restricted to land bases by the U.S. Navy and Marine Corps. Slower than the F4U, it had vastly superior low-speed flight characteristics. The F6F ended the war with a 19:1 kill ratio against enemy aircraft, better than the Corsair's impressive 11:1 ratio.

F4U: Military designation for Corsairs that were built by the Vought-Sikorsky division of United Aircraft Corporation or, beginning in January 1943, Chance Vought Aircraft (then a successor division of United Aircraft Corporation). The letter 'F' denotes a fighter aircraft; the number '4' refers to the design serial number, and the letter that follows identifies the manufacturer. In this case, the letter 'U' identifies the manufacturer as Vought (i.e., either Vought-Sikorsky or Chance Vought). Corsairs that were built under license by either Brewster Aeronautical Corporation or Goodyear received different designations. For the convenience of the reader, the author normally refers to the F4U parent design, and refers to the license designations only as needed.

FG1: Designation for Goodyear-built Corsairs.

fuselage: Main structural portion of the airframe, to which the wings and empennage are attached. In most single-engine aircraft, the engine is contained within the fuselage with the cowling forming the outside skin. The cockpit is contained within the fuselage.

gimbal: Ring-shaped mechanical support for a rotating object, as in a gyroscope.

gimbal lock: A condition in which two of the three gyroscope gimbals establish a parallel alignment, thereby resulting in the loss of rotation about one of the three axes. Note that there is no mechanical lock or restraint.

Hamilton Standard: Manufacturer of the Hydromatic propeller that was used on the Corsair. Hamilton Standard was, and is, a division of the current United Technologies Corporation Technologies (UTC). UTC was named United Aircraft Corporation in the 1940s.

Henderson Field: The main military airfield on Guadalcanal Island, and the main objective during the Allied invasion in August 1942. After Allied forces (primarily American) captured Henderson Field and surrounding areas, satellite fields were developed nearby. The Allied aircraft that operated from Henderson Field and its satellite fields were referred to as the 'Cactus Air Force,'

Hydromatic: Name given to Hamilton Standard's A6501-0 constant-speed propeller that was used on the Corsair.

interceptor: A fighter aircraft that is tasked with the interception of unknown or hostile aircraft. Because a fighter interceptor is typically based at or near the area (or ship) that it defends, range is less important than good speed and rate-of-climb capabilities.

"in the groove": An expression that denotes an aircraft on final approach that is positioned within the desired lateral and vertical boundaries as it approaches the touchdown point of the runway (or the ship). The expression would only be used if the properly positioned and aligned aircraft were close to the proper approach speed, properly configured for landing and in the proper attitude. In the U.S. Navy, the determination of whether or not a landing aircraft was "in the groove" as it approached the ship would be made by the Landing Signal Officer (LSO). In the Royal Navy, the equivalent person would be the Deck

Glossary

Landing Control Officer (DLCO), commonly referred to as the "batsman."

"Ironbottom Sound": Informal but widespread name given to Savo Sound by Allied forces during the Guadalcanal Campaign. So named because of the large numbers of Allied and Japanese warships and transports that were destroyed in the water area adjacent to Guadalcanal Island. Located near the southern end of New Georgia Sound (see 'The Slot') and bounded by Guadalcanal, Savo Island and Florida Island. May be indicated by the name Sealark Sound on pre-war charts.

island (on an aircraft carrier): Elevated structure on an aircraft carrier within which the bridge is located, and upon which masts and antenna are located. The island is on the starboard (right hand) side of the ship at the edge of the flight deck.

The ships captain and those officers who supervise flight operations (exclusive of the LSO, and certain officers with similar functions) are stationed in the island while on duty.

Kriegsmarine: German Navy during the Third Reich (1935-45). Not to be confused with the post-war Reichsmarine.

Landing Signal Officer (LSO): U.S. Navy or Marine Corps officer responsible for monitoring the flight path of aircraft as they approached the stern of the aircraft carrier. The LSO would signal corrections for the pilot to take during the approach, and either "wave off" the pilot or provide the "cut" signal to authorize the landing. The U.S. Navy equivalent of the Royal Navy's Deck Landing Control Officer (DLCO). LSOs were almost always rated pilots, but there were a few exceptions during World War Two. After the war, all LSOs were pilots.

lean manufacturing: Term applied to practices that are used to maximize efficiency and minimize waste in the manufacturing process. The term came into common use after 1988, but lean practices existed far earlier. See also Society of Manufacturing Engineers (SME).

LM (nomenclature specific to Apollo 11 mission): Lunar module.

LOI (nomenclature specific to Apollo 11 mission): Lunar Orbit Insertion.

LOS (nomenclature specific to Apollo 11 mission): Loss of Signal or Loss of Site.

Luftwaffe: German Air Force.

mach number: Numeric value that expresses an aircraft's velocity through the air as a percentage of the speed of sound. The speed of sound equals Mach 1.0; Mach 0.70 would be a velocity equal to seventy percent of the speed of sound. The speed of sound varies according to the temperature, decreasing as the ambient temperature decreases. Named in honor of the Austrian physicist Ernst Mach (1838-1916).

mach-limited: Regime of flight in which an aircraft will reach its limiting mach number before reaching its limiting airspeed. Aircraft are airspeed-limited until they climb to their airspeed-mach crossover point, above which they are mach-limited. This crossover point varies with each aircraft, but is often between altitudes of 25-30,000 feet (FL-250 – FL-300).

mach-trim compensator: A safety system that automatically increases the aircraft pitch trim or elevator position to prevent the inadvertent overspeed of aircraft traveling at high subsonic or transonic speeds. System design differs with aircraft, and not all jet aircraft are equipped with this type of system. Designed for use in cruise flight, not for fighters in steep dives. Used in the text only to reference the state of flight control technology that existed during the 1940s.

Marine Corps Air Station (MCAS): U.S. Marine Corps airfield and base.

Marine Air Group (MAG): U.S. Marine Corps organizational unit consisting of multiple squadrons. The number that follows the acronym MAG- is the Group number. A MAG is part of a Marine Air Wing.

Marine Air Wing (MAW): U.S. Marine Corps organizational unit that consists of multiple Marine Air Groups.

Mass production: The practice of producing very large numbers of a standard product quickly, usually with the use of assembly lines also known as production lines). Mass production using assembly-line methods was pioneered by Henry Ford in his Highland Park factory near Detroit, Michigan. This revolutionary factory was built in 1909 to produce the Model T Ford. The Highland Park factory was designed in 1908 by Alfred Kahn, a leading architect who later designed the major wartime additions to the Vought-Sikorsky factory complex. The first assembly line (a magneto line) opened at the Highland Park plant in 1913.

Messerschmitt (Messerschmitt AG): German aircraft manufacturer that produced such aircraft as the Bf-109 and Bf-110 fighters. The firm evolved from Bayerische Flugzeugwerke (Bavarian Aircraft Works, or BFW), which Willy Messerschmitt was able to take over in 1938. The BTW lineage resulted in the Bf- prefix, although the above aircraft are also referred to as the Me-109 and Me-110.

Messerschmitt, Wilhelm "Willy" (1898-1978): German aeronautical engineer, manager and entrepreneur. Messerschmitt studied at Munich Technical College, and began his career designing and building gliders and then light aircraft. His 1933 Messerschmitt M37 sport monoplane (also know as the Bf-108) evolved into the Bf-109 fighter the following year.

miles-per-hour (m.p.h.): Speed measurement that denotes the number of statute miles that an aircraft would fly through the air (airspeed) or travel over the ground (groundspeed) if the speed were maintained for sixty minutes. Not to be confused with 'knots', which refers to nautical miles per hour.

Mitsubishi (Heavy Industries): Japan's largest private company in World War Two, based in Nagasaki. From 1917 to 1934 the firm was named Mitsubishi Shipbuilding & Engineering Company, Ltd. Manufactured the famous A6M "Zero", also referred to by the Allied military code-name "Zeke."

Mustang: Name given to the P-51 fighter manufactured by North American Aviation.

National Advisory Committee for Aeronautics (NACA): Predecessor to National Aeronautics and Space Administration (NASA). Aircraft wing profiles are usually categorized using one of the NACA numbering systems.

Naval Air Station (NAS): U.S. Navy land airfield and base.

North American Aviation (NAA): Manufacturer of the A-36 Apache which morphed into the P-51 Mustang. Also manufactured the AT-6/SNJ advanced military training aircraft, and the B-25 Mitchell bomber. Located at the perimeter of the future Los Angeles International Airport, and adjacent to Northrop Corporation. Evolved into North American Rockwell. Later famous for building the F-86 Sabre, F-100 Super Sabre and the Space Shuttle.

Northrop (Northrop Corporation): Military aircraft manufacturer established by Jack Northrop in 1939 in El Segundo, California. Manufactured the P-61 Black Widow, a large, twin-engine night fighter that appeared late in the war. In 1994 Northrop merged with Grumman and is now known as Northrop Grumman. Famous in the late Twentieth Century as the builder on the B-2 Stealth bomber.

oleo (landing gear strut): Cylinder inside a landing gear strut that acts as a shock absorber. The interior cylinder typically has a piston that separates hydraulic fluid from a nitrogen or air charge.

PAO (nomenclature specific to Apollo 11 mission): [NASA] Public Affairs Office.

PB4Y (Privateer): Manufactured by Consolidated, this was the naval version of the ubiquitous B-24 Liberator four-engine bomber that appeared in 1943. Evolved from the earlier PB4Y-1 Liberator, which were basically B-24 bombers that were delivered to the U.S. Navy and U.S. Coast Guard for use as a naval maritime patrol bomber. With the PB4Y-2 version the aircraft was modified, most notably with a single vertical stabilizer, as opposed to the distinctive twin-tail of the PB4Y-1 and B-24. The shorter notation PB4Y Privateer is often used for the PB4Y-2.

PBY (Catalina): Manufactured by Consolidated, this twin-engine amphibian was a maritime patrol bomber. The slow but rugged PBY had a long range and was extremely versatile. Used extensively by the U.S. Navy, Royal Navy's Fleet Air Arm and Royal New Zealand Air Force.

PCM (nomenclature specific to Apollo 11 mission): Pulse code modulation.

Glossary

P-36 (Hawk): Early monoplane fighter for the U.S. Army Air Corps, manufactured by Curtiss. The P-36 was innovative: besides being a monoplane, it featured metal construction (but fabric-covered controls) and the rotating main landing gear that was later found on the F4U Corsair. The underpowered P-36 morphed into the P-40 Warhawk.

P-38 (Lightning): Manufactured by Lockheed, the radical P-38 was the first fighter capable (in its definitive versions) of exceeding 400 m.p.h. in level flight. The initial (experimental and prototype) versions preceded the F4U, although it appears that the F4U Corsair exceeded the 400 m.p.h. earlier due to the latter's power advantage.

P-39 (Airacobra, also P-400 version): Manufactured by Bell in Buffalo, New York, the innovative P-39 featured an engine that was housed in the fuselage behind the pilot, a tricycle landing gear, and a 37-mm T9 cannon that fired through propeller hub. The P-39 had very poor performance above 12,000 but was extremely effective when used as a ground attack aircraft against armored targets. Despite severe limitations, the P-39 Airacobra was one of the few modern American fighters in production at the beginning of World War Two.

P-400 (Airacobra): Modified P-39D Airacobra that were originally intended for export to the United Kingdom. Britain only used a limited number of these aircraft, but some were diverted to the U.S. Army Air Force where they played a critical role in the defense of Guadalcanal in 1942. Not to be confused with the later Bell P-63 Kingcobra.

P-40 (Warhawk): Manufactured by Curtiss, the P-40 was a much-improved successor to P-36 Hawk. A major difference was the use of a more powerful, liquid-cooled Allison V-1710 powerplant. Most famous for its use by the American Volunteer Group (AVG), better known as the "Flying Tigers." The Curtiss P-40 was the best fighter in the U.S. Army Air Force at the outbreak of World War Two and, along with the Bell P-39/P-400, the only other modern fighter that was in production.

P-47 (Thunderbolt): Manufactured by Republic Aircraft, this Army Air Force fighter was also equipped with the Pratt & Whitney R-2800 radial engine. Because the P-47 used a turbosupercharger instead of a conventional supercharger, its high altitude performance was better than that of the F4U Corsair. Nicknamed the "Jug" because of its large, rounded fuselage, the P-47 was replaced by the North American P-5q Mustang as the Allies primary high-altitude, long-range escort for bombers in the European Theater of Operations. Nonetheless, the P-47 was a formidable fighter and was extremely effective when used in ground attack roles.

P-51 (Mustang): Manufactured by North American Aviation, the P-51 Mustang replaced the P-47 Thunderbolt as the primary fighter in the European Theater of Operations (ETO).

P-61 (Black Widow): Manufactured by Northrop, the P-61 Black Widow was a large, twin-engine, twin-tail night fighter. The size of a light bomber, it had a crew of three that included a radar operator. The P-61 was produced in limited numbers and arrived in the Pacific late in the war.

port (as in port side of a ship): when facing forward towards the bow of a ship, the port side would be the left side. Example: The Landing Signal Officer (LSO) would be positioned on a platform on the port side of the stern.

Pratt & Whitney (The Pratt & Whitney Aircraft Company): Manufacturer of the R-2800 series of radial piston-engines for aircraft. Based in East Hartford, Connecticut, Pratt & Whitney was a division of United Aircraft Corporation (now United Technologies Corporation).

knot(s): Nautical unit of speed. One knot is equal to one mile-per-hour (m.p.h.). Because one nautical mile equals 6,080 feet, one nautical mile equals 1.15 statute miles. Hence, an airspeed of 200 knots equals 230 m.p.h. Performance data for 1940s era aircraft is often expressed in either miles-per-hour or knots.

indicated airspeed (IAS): Airspeed that appears on the airspeed indicator in the cockpit instrument panel. Indicated airspeed is uncorrected for pitot-static system errors. The typical airspeed indicator is calibrated for standard sea level atmospheric conditions. An aircraft flown at sea level with no instrument error would have an indicated airspeed that equals the true (i.e., actual) airspeed. However, atmospheric pressure decreases as altitude increases, resulting in an indicated airspeed that is less than the true airspeed. Example: An airspeed indictor is installed in an aircraft with a pitot-static system that has no instrument or

Glossary

position errors below 20,000 feet. The aircraft is cruising at 15,000 feet in standard atmospheric conditions with an indicated airspeed (IAS) of 200 knots. Under these conditions, it would have a true airspeed of 250 knots (288 m.p.h.).

radar (<u>ra</u>dio <u>d</u>etection <u>a</u>nd <u>r</u>anging system/equipment): System(s) and/or equipment that uses transmitted radio waves and return signals to determine the range, relative bearing and (in some cases) the altitude or height of a target. Radar systems are affected by such factors transmission power; frequency, antenna design and position, and stabilization of the antenna. Of particular interest is the development of airborne-intercept (AI) radar for fighters such as the F4U-2. The name 'radar' was coined by S. M. Tucker and F. R. Furth of the U.S. Navy, which formally adapted the nomenclature in November 1940.

range: The distance that an aircraft can fly unrefueled and land with the minimum required fuel reserve. Also refers to the distance of a radar target from the interrogating radar system.

RCS (nomenclature specific to Apollo 11 mission): Reaction control system.

Republic (short for Republic Aircraft Corporation): Manufacturer of the P-47 Thunderbolt fighter, based in Farmingdale, New York (on Long Island).

Royal Aircraft Establishment (RAE): British aeronautical research organization that evolved from the Royal Aircraft Factory in 1918. Part of the United Kingdom defense establishment, the REA was involved in the flight testing of British and Allied military aircraft of all types, including the F4U Corsair. The REA also performed operational testing the navalized versions of the Hawker Hurricane and Supermarine Spitfire aboard aircraft carriers.. Merged into Britain's Defense Research Agency (DRA) in 1981, and with other United Kingdom defense organizations later on.

Royal Air Force (RAF): The air force of the United Kingdom, established in April 1918. During the inter-war period, the Fleet Air Arm was part of the Royal Air Force until May 1939, at which time the FAA became part of the Royall Navy.

Royal Navy (RN): Navy of the United Kingdom.

Royal New Zealand Air Force (RNZAF): New Zealand's air force. As a Commonwealth nation, many New Zealanders served in the Royal Navy (RN) and Royal Air Force (RAF) after World war One. In 1923 the RNZAF was established as an independent national air force, with most personnel coming from dedicated New Zealand units of the RAF. However, some New Zealanders continued to serve in the much larger Royal Navy and Royal Air Force.

rudder: On aircraft, a primary flight control used to yaw the aircraft about its vertical axis. On a ship, an underwater control surface that I used to turn the vessel to port or starboard.

Savo Island: Island formed by a volcano to the north of Guadalcanal Island, and the site of an important naval battle between the U.S. Navy and the Imperial Japanese Navy during the Guadalcanal Campaign (on 9 August 1942). Savo Island also bounds the northwestern end of the so-called 'Ironbottom Sound.'

SCR-268: World War Two radar system. The 'SCR' prefix denotes '[U.S. Army] Signal Corps Radio' while the '268' denotes the model number. Due to power issues in developing early radar systems, the bulky SCR-268 went into production using ring oscillator technology and operated with a 1.5-meter wavelength. The SCR-268 remained the U.S. Army's standard radar for anti-aircraft artillery (AAA) until 1944. Due to its excellent range, it was rushed to Guadalcanal in 1942 for use as an early warning radar.

SCR-270: The SCR-270 development overlapped that of the slightly earlier SCR-268, but was designed for greater mobility. Instead of using ring oscillator technology, the SCR-270 used Westinghouse laboratory's specially designed WL-530; this was a water-cooled tube that was rated at 100 kilowatts (kW) of power. The SCR-270 operated with a 3.0-meter wavelength, and remained the U.S. Army's principal early warning radar throughout the war. It was also used at Guadalcanal.

Sea of Tranquility: Lunar mare (i.e., basaltic plain) on the surface of the Moon. The unmanned *Ranger 8* spacecraft crashed in this plain in 1965 after photographing the lunar surface. Site of the 1969 Apollo 11 landing.

Glossary

self-sealing fuel tank(s): One of various methods of protecting aircraft fuel tanks from rupturing after being penetrated by enemy fire. In the United States, Goodyear chemist James Merrill developed a method that utilized a double layer of rubber compounds that would automatically expand to seal a breach in a tank. This technology was adapted on the Corsair's fuselage tank, with a weight penalty of nearly 180-pounds.

S-IVB (nomenclature specific to Apollo 11 mission): Manufactured by Douglas, the S-IVB was the third stage of the Saturn V rocket. It had a singe J-2 engine.

service ceiling: Maximum altitude at which an aircraft can sustain level flight at a specified gross weight under standard (ISA, International Standard Atmosphere) conditions. Typically a minimal climb requirement is included to ensure that the altitude can be maintained in banks or turbulence. Not to be confused with absolute altitude, which is a certification value without the foregoing margins, and which is of little practical value.

'Snapper': Name given to radar used for aircraft position monitoring and course guidance in the vicinity of the aircraft carrier on which it was mounted. Radar installation was typically on the port beam. Also used as a call sign for the 'Snapper' control officer, who could communicate with the pilot, the bridge and the LSO using split-phones. The 'Snapper' team would include experienced radar operators stationed near the officer.

Solomon Islands (also known as British Solomon Islands): Group of islands in the southwestern part of the Pacific Ocean that were part of the British Empire. In 1893 the British Solomon Islands Protectorate was established for the southern islands, while Germany retained its interest in the northern Solomons. As a result of The Tripartite Convention of 1899, Britain exchanged its rights and interests in Samoa to Germany in exchange for Germany relinquishing to Britain its rights and interests over the portion of the Solomon Islands east and southeast of the island of Bougainville. However, the islands of Buka and Bougainville remained part of German New Guinea. The Solomon Islands are south of the Equator, and lie east of Papua New Guinea and northeast of Australia. The most familiar of the islands is Guadalcanal, as a result of the protected warfare that existed on and in the vicinity of that island during the war.

slot ('The Slot'): Informal but widespread name given to New Georgia Sound, the water area that runs in a northwest to southeaster direction roughly through the center of the Solomon Islands. The island of Bougainville lies at the western end of the 'Slot' while the island of Guadalcanal lies at the eastern end.

spar, or wing spar: Structural load-carrying member of a wing, designed for high strength and flexibility. There are different spar designs, and a wing (or horizontal stabilizer) may have more than one spar. Spars extend outward from the fuselage towards the wing tip. The spar provides the structural foundation for the wing. If more than one spar is included, the forward spar is usually the 'main spar' and will form the back of the 'torque box.' A smaller and roughly parallel trailing edge spar often forms the trailing edge of the wing, to which devices such as flaps and ailerons may be attached. Loads from a landing gear that is attached to the wing are transmitted into the main spar.

spot welding: Technique for welding metals such as aluminum where the heat from an electrical resistance causes the metal to melt, thereby forming the weld. Spot welding became common during World War Two; collaboration between Vought-Sikorsky and the Naval Aircraft Factory accelerated the development of this technique.

squadron (fighter squadron): Military organizational unit, typically commanded by a lieutenant commander (U.S. Navy), or the equivalent rank of major (U.S. Marine Corps). In either branch the 'V' stands for heavier-than-air vehicle (as opposed to lighter-than-air), while the 'F' portion of the prefix indicates that the unit is a fighter squadron ("Fighting Squadron"). For Marine Corps units, the additional letter 'M' denotes a Marine Corps squadron (e.g., VMF-124), with the numbers indicating the squadron number. Several squadrons would form a 'wing.'

starboard (as in starboard side): when facing forward towards the bow of a ship, the starboard side would be the right side. Example: A turn to the right would be a 'starboard turn.' Applied mainly to vessels; aircraft would turn left or right. However, the terms port and starboard would sometimes be used to denote the left or right wing, respectively.

stall (also aerodynamic stall): A condition of flight in which the lifting surface (usually th wing) passes through the air at too great an angle to effectively produce lift. The angle between the wing and the local airflow (relative wind) is called the 'angle of attack.' A stall (aerodynamic stall) occurs when the wing exceeds its critical angle of attack.

strafe (strafing): Act of attacking ground troops or targets from a low-flying aircraft by use of machine gun or cannon fire. Term does not apply to the firing of rockets or the dropping of bombs or illumination flares.

strut (landing gear strut): Structural component of the landing gear that provides for the multiple functions of connecting to and supporting the wheels; lowering and retracting the wheels; establishing the proper attitude when being operated or stored on the ground, and absorbing the force of touchdown and transmitting it to the associated load-carrying member (typically the main spar of the wing).

supercharger: Mechanical device that increases the density of the air the is inducted into the engine cylinders of a piston engine prior to combustion, thereby providing more power than would otherwise be possible under ambient conditions. Supercharger design varied considerably, but in general these were mechanically-driven compressors that were driven by the engine. The supercharged R-2800 engine on the F4U produced more power than a normally aspirated version of that engine would have provided, but above 20,000 feet it was less powerful than the turbosupercharged version. This is why the P-47 Thunderbolt was faster a higher altitudes.

Supermarine: (Supermarine Aviation Works): Company that manufactured the famous Spitfire and Seafire fighters. Supermarine operated as a mostly autonomous subsidiary of Vickers-Armstrong. Supermarine was based in Southampton, England.

tailhook: Device at the tail of a naval aircraft that would be lowered by the pilot prior to landing, and which would engage one of several cables running across the deck of the aircraft carrier. The tailhook made it possible to "trap" the aircraft so as to accomplish a landing on the short aircraft carrier deck.

Thunderbolt: Name given to the Republic P-47 fighter.

TIG (nomenclature specific to Apollo 11 mission): Time of ignition. Not to be confused with TIG welding.

"Tokyo Express": Informal name given by Allied troops to Imperial Japanese Navy destroyers that would make high-speed night runs to Guadalcanal, acting as armed transports and carrying troop reinforcements.

"Tony": Allied code name given to the Kawasaki Ki-61 Hien (Swallow) fighter of Japan's Army Air Force. Used primarily as a high-altitude interceptor, the "Tony" was a formidable opponent but suffered from a problematic liquid-cooled engine.

top cover: Fighters assigned to provide the highest protective screen for other aircraft on a mission (usually bombers).

Tranquility Base (nomenclature specific to Apollo 11 mission): Name given to the LM *Eagle* when it was stationary on the surface of the Moon, whereupon it became a lunar outpost.

Trans-Lunar Injection (TLI): Maneuver in which a spacecraft in a parking orbit around Planet Earth accelerates as a result of a short engine propulsion, thereby establishing an eccentric orbit. The burn is planned so that the apogee of the eccentric orbit will place the spacecraft at the radius of the lunar orbit.

"trap": Process and/or act of recovering aircraft to an aircraft carrier by trapping it. The trap involves the successful engagement of one of the arresting cables by the aircraft's tailhook. Naval aviators refer to landings aboard an aircraft carrier as traps.

trim-tab: Secondary flight control that consists of a small surface that adjusts the neutral point of the primary flight control to which it is attached. Used tio improve controllability and reduce pilot workload. Most aircraft have adjustable trim tabs that can be adjusted by the pilot during the flight based on (e.g.) desired airspeed, configuration or lateral imbalance.

Glossary

true airspeed (TAS): Actual (true) airspeed of an aircraft through the air. See notes in Glossary on 'indicated airspeed.' Not to be confused with groundspeed, calibrated airspeed or indicated airspeed.

turbosupercharger: Nomenclature common to World War two-era aircraft that utilize turbochargers but no longer used. The turbosupercharger was nothing more than a turbocharger, a system that used hot exhaust gases to spin a centrifugal turbine to compress incoming air for the engine. Because of the increased mass airflow of the incoming air, the engine could produce more power. Differed from a supercharger in that the latter did not extract energy from exhaust gases to spin a turbine-compressor.

United Aircraft Corporation (UAC, now known as United Technologies Corporation); Parent corporation of Chance Vought Aircraft (and Vought-Sikorsky) into Chance Vought was divested in 1954

U.S.S.R.: Abbreviation for Union of Soviet Socialist Republics (the Soviet Union).

War Production Board (WPB): Federal agency that was created by Executive Order 9024 (by President Franklin D. Roosevelt) on 16 January 1942. WPB replaced the earlier Office of Production Management and the Supply Priorities and Allocation Board. Based in Washington, D.C., it operated with twelve regional offices until it was disbanded on November 1945.

wavelength: Measurement of the distance between peaks of a longitudinal radio wave. Early ground- or ship-based radar systems had wavelengths that were measured in meters; these provided adequate range information when used as early warning systems. Airborne-intercept (AI) radar, mounted on aircraft, had to have smaller antennas and needed reduced wavelengths to attain the necessary higher resolution. These wavelengths were measured in centimeters. There is an inverse relationship between wavelength and frequency: i.e., as wavelength decreases, frequency increases.

"wave off": Signal from an aircraft carrier's LSO (U.S. Navy) or DLCO (FAA) to abort the landing attempt and go around.

wheel well: Recessed area within an aircraft wing or fuselage within which a retracted landing gear can be housed.

wingman: An aircraft flying in close formation with another aircraft (the leader) and responsible for providing tactical cover against threat from enemy aircraft while in combat. When not in combat, an aircraft in close formation with a lead aircraft. Also refers to the pilot of said aircraft.

work cell: A group of workers who act as a team and perform specialized production tasks.

"Zeke": Mitsubishi A6M Type 0 fighter, more commonly known as the "Zero." This fighter is referred to as the "Zero" in this text rather than the "Zeke" in deference to the more common name.

Appendix

Appendix A

F4U Models, Designations and Notes

V-166B Internal Chance Vought Aircraft/Vought-Sikorsky Aircraft company designation for the proposed aircraft that became the XF4U-1. Vought also submitted a second proposal for the 1938 design competition; that was designated the V-166A. The V-166A was to be powered by the proven, but less powerful, Pratt & Whitney R-1830 powerplant. Two designs were submitted to increase the odds of receiving a contract. The V-166A only existed on paper; it was never built.

XF4U-1 The single experimental prototype. This was the version that made the first flight, and which set the speed record of being the first naval fighter to surpass 400 m.p.h. in level flight. Numerous reliable sources claim that the XF4U-1 was the first fighter of any service to exceed 400 m.p.h. However, had the earlier Lockheed XP-38/YP-38 been matched with the proper powerplant and propeller combination, been would have achieved 400 m.p.h. first.

Pratt & Whitney R-2800-4 rated at 1,800 h.p.

Gross weight (takeoff): 10,500 lb.

Maximum speed (level flight): 405 m.p.h.

Typical enroute cruise speed: 180-210 m.p.h.

F4U The general designation for the Corsair. Note that the U.S. Navy and Marine Corps used the 'F' designation

Developing the Gull-Winged F4U Corsair - And Taking It To Sea

for 'fighter' during the years that the U.S. Army Air Corps / Army Air Force used the equivalent 'P' designation (for 'pursuit'). The number '4'was the forth fighter designation, and the following letter identified the manufacturer. Hence, the 'U' identified Chance Vought / Vought-Sikorsky. In this book the generic F4U is typically used, since it is not possible to determine when Brewster or Goodyear Corsairs appeared in operational units.

F4U-1   The initial production model that was delivered to operational units. The F4U-1 was initially plagued by the "bird cage" canopy that restricted pilot visibility, and stiff main landing gear struts that had to be modified to reduce bouncing. An improved canopy did appear after production began, but not until the 759th production aircraft. The low tailwheel was also a problem, and was replaced by a longer assembly. To improve forward visibility the pilot seat was raised approximately 8-inches, and the cowl flap gills on the top section were closed, thereby eliminating fluid leaks.

Other important changes included an improved, pressurized ignition harness (for high altitude flight); a stall strip on the right leading edge to improve stall characteristics; modifications to the horizontal stabilizer and improved gun feet to the M2 machine guns. The F4U-1A included most of the improvements. Many F4U-1s received field mods prior to the changes on the production line.

Specifications.

Wingspan: 41 ft 0 in

Length: 33ft 4 in

Gross weight (takeoff): 14,009 lb.

Fuel capacity (internal, fuselage and unprotected wing leading-edge tanks) (F4U-1, -1A & -C): 361 gal

Appendix

Fuel capacity (internal, fuselage tank only) (F4U-1D): 237 gal

Pratt & Whitney R-2800-8 Double Wasp rated at 2,000 h.p. (to s/n 1549)

Pratt & Whitney R-2800-8W Double Wasp (water-injection available for 5-minute use for war emergency power) (s/n 1550 on). Rated at 2,000 h.p. (dry) and 2,135 (water injection, war emergency power at 12,400 ft

Supercharger: two stage, two speed (pilot controlled)

Maximum speed (approx. 17,000 ft.): 425 m.p.h.

Typical enroute cruise speed: 180-210 m.p.h.

Rate of climb (sea level): 3,100 f.p.m.

Service ceiling: 37,000 ft.

Range: 1,015 mi.

Armament: six .50-caliber M2 machine guns (three on each outboard wing, with 400 rounds per gun)

F4U-2   This was the first night fighter version of the F4U. The F$U-2 was basically a modified F4U-1 with an airborne intercept (AI) radar mounted on the right outboard wing; flame retardant exhaust stacks, and the removal of one machine gun and ammunition to maintain good lateral balance. Significant cockpit improvements were introduced in this night fighter: i.e., a radar altimeter; autopilot; new cockpit instrumentation, and an upgraded aircraft electrical system. Most modifications were accomplishing by the Naval Aircraft Factory (NAF) in Philadelphia to avoid production problems at Vought-Sikorsky's factory in Stratford, CT. Only 34 F4U-1s were modified to F4U-2 night fighters, 32 of which were completed at the NAF.

In operational use, the F4U-2 often operated from land bases. The Grumman F6F Hellcat night fighter was much easier to operate a night from aircraft carriers. In addition, the fuel capacity of the F4U-2 was reduced to just 178 gal (internal). Nonetheless, the F4U-2 was a big technological advance.

XF4U-3 The high altitude performance of the F4U was noticeably inferior to another high-speed, R-2800-powered fighter: i.e., the Republic P-47 Thunderbolt. The difference was that the P-47 used a turbosupercharger, which provided more power at higher altitudes than the supercharged version of the R-2800. Three experimental test aircraft were evaluated, using the R-2800-18W powerplant. The effort was abandoned as it turned out that there were significant reliability issues with the more complicated turbosupercharger. However, the high altitude performance issue was of less concern in the Pacific theaters, where combat operations were often conducted at lower altitudes than in the European Theater of operations. The project was abandoned and no F4U-3s were produced.

F4U-4 The ultimate version of the F4U in World War Two. An improved engine, air-induction system and a four-bladed propeller boosted performance noticeably. A redesigned cockpit, including improved armor protection for the pilot, an improved seat and a redesigned instrument panel were significant improvements.

The F4U-4 also saw improved firepower; the six .50-caliber machine guns were replaced by the four 20-mm cannon, the latter being more lethal to enemy aircraft. Under the outer wing section, the F4U-4 had rocket mounts. The wing center section could carry two 1,000 lb. bombs or two 150-gallon drop tanks. The heavily armed F4U-4 was also one of the first fighter-bombers to carry the large "Tiny Tim" bunker busting air-to-ground rocket, which was used at Okinawa.

Appendix

Unfortunately, the F4U-4 did not arrive until April 1945, very late in the war.

<u>Significant Differences.</u>

Fuel capacity (internal, fuselage tank only): 234 gal

Fuel capacity (external, two drop tanks): 300 gal

Pratt & Whitney R-2800-18W Double Wasp, combat power ratings:

2,380 h.p. at sea level

2,080 h.p. at 23,300 ft

Maximum speed (25,000 ft with combat power): 447 m.p.h.

Service ceiling: 41,500 ft

Range: 897 mi

Note: There was a change in power nomenclature during the war. The familiar 'war emergency power' that was used for emergencies was changed to 'combat power' and so reflected in Vought performance plots.

F4U-5   Post-war version of the Corsair. There were some minor changes in the air inlets, and Vought finally replaced the fabric skin of the outer wing surfaces with metal A Pratt & Whitney R-2800-32W Double Wasp engine rated at 2,675 h.p. with a variable-speed, two-stage supercharger was used. The F4U-5 retained the four 20-mm cannon of the F4U-4. An F4U-5N night fighter version was built, which was very similar to the earlier F4U-2, but with improved radar. The F4U-5 used either an AN/APS-6 or an AN/APS-18A, with improved detection range and resolution.

Two other variations of the basic F4U-5 appeared. The F4U-5P photo-reconnaissance version was manufactured, and a winterized F4U-5NL was a radar-equipped night fighter that was plumbed for pneumatic wing and tail de-icer boots, which could be installed for us in cold weather ops (e.g., Korea). It also had de-ice shoes for the four-blade propeller.

<u>Significant Differences</u>.

Maximum speed: 469 m.p.h.

Designed service ceiling: 45,000 ft

Note: The designed ceiling was not practical, and the unpressurized aircraft was never used operationally at very high altitudes.

F4U-6/AU-1 The F4U-6 was developed from the F4U-5 and was redesignated as the AU-1 during the Korea War. Intended solely for the Marine Corps, it relinquished the air-to-air combat role for low altitude close support and other ground attack missions. Performance and maneuverability were readily sacrificed as the AU-1 was heavily armored to protect the pilot and vital systems. A heavy airplane when laden with bombs and/or rockets, the AU-1 was far slower than World War Two fighters. But like the Douglas AD-1 Skyraider, the AU-1 version of the Corsair was a formidable ground attack platform. The 'A' (for attack) was an early use of that designation by the Navy and Marine Corps. Only 111 were produced.

<u>Significant Differences</u>.

Gross weight: 19,398 lbs

Pratt & Whitney R-2800-83W Double Wasp rated at 2,300 h.p.

Supercharger: single-stage (pilot controlled).

Maximum speed (sea level, gross weight): 238 m.p.h.

Initial rate of climb (sea level, gross weight): 920 f.p.m.

Appendix

          Service ceiling: 19,500 ft

          Armament (external): ten 5-inch rockets or 3,000 lb of bombs

F4U-7	The final version of the Corsair, designed as a conventional, multi-role fighter for the French Navy. A total of 97 were delivered, with the last ones being retired in 1964. The F4U-7 served in action in French Indo-China (Vietnam) prior to the United States involvement in that area.
FG-1	Designation for Goodyear-built Corsairs. The FG-1 aircraft were manufactured at the Goodyear factory in Akron, Ohio, and were the equivalent of the Vought F4U-1. The original FG-1 lacked folding wings.
FG-1A	Goodyear-built version of the Vought F4U-1A Corsair; these had folding wings.
FG-1D	Goodyear-built version of the Vought F4U-1D.
F2G-1	Goodyear built Corsair that was designed around the Pratt & Whitney R-4360, 3,000 h.p. engine. This version did not have folding wings. Only 5 were built, and none saw operational service. The aircraft failed to produce a spectacular increase in F4U performance, and the Navy was happy with the new Grumman F8F Bearcat.
F2G-2	Goodyear-built Corsair that was essentially an F2G-1 with folding wings. Only 5 were built, and it did not serve operationally.
F3A-1	Brewster-built Corsairs for the U.S. Navy.
Corsair I	F4U-1 aircraft that were delivered to Britain's Fleet Air Arm under the Lend-Lease program.
Corsair II	F4U-1A aircraft that were delivered to Britain's Fleet Air Arm or the Royal New Zealand Air Force under the Lend-Lease program.

Corsair III	Brewster-built F3A-1 Corsairs that were delivered to Britain's Fleet Air Arm under the Lend-Lease program.
Corsair IV	Goodyear-built FG-1D aircraft that were delivered to Britain's Fleet Air Arm or the Royal New Zealand Air Force under the Lend-Lease program.
Note 1	The designation F4U-1A was used extensively, but was unofficial.
Note 2	During World War Two, a total of 11,426 Corsairs were manufactured. Of these, 6,674 were built by Vought; 4,017 were built by Goodyear, while Brewster produced just 735. F4U production continued until the final F4U-7 was delivered in January 1953, bringing the combined total to 12,571.
Note 3	The Royal Navy's Fleet Air Arm received a total of 2,012 Corsairs. The total delivered to the Royal New Zealand Air Force is cited as either 370 or 421 by various sources. The author was not able to resolve this discrepancy with archived records.

Appendix B
2002 Map of the Inter-Ocean Operational Area(s)

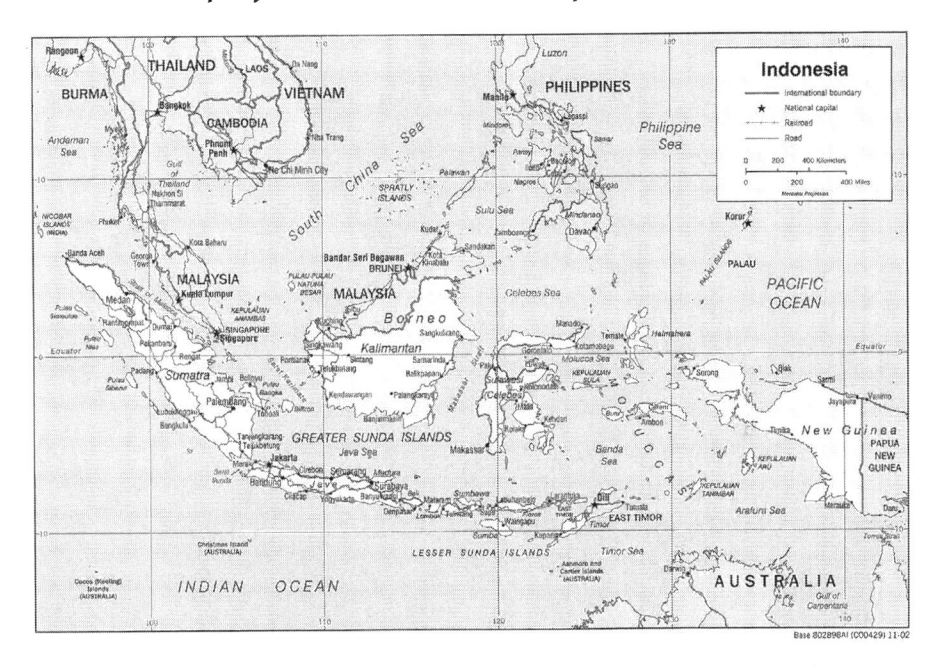

The archipelago that extends from the west of Malaysia towards the ocean area north of Australia is the present-day nation of Indonesia. During World War Two, this area was known as **the Dutch East Indies** and was occupied by Japanese military forces. Within the Dutch East Indies, the oil-rich island of **Sumatra** was targeted by Allied forces. Note the location of the **Strait of Malacca** and **Singapore**, the latter just off the southeastern tip of the **Malay Peninsula**. Singapore was captured by Japanese forces in 1942. The **Java Sea** separated the Dutch East Indies from **Borneo**. In the northern portion of the map is the **South China Sea** and Vietnam, which was known as French Indo-China. French Indo-China was controlled by Japanese forces, and was the target of Allied air attacks (including F4Us) late in the war. Note the proximity of Borneo to the **Philippine Islands** just to the northeast.

Source Notes/Credit: Map created by the U.S. Central Intelligence Agency. Map Indonesia (Political), Central Intelligence Agency 2002. "Base 802899AI (C00429) 11-02." Call Number G8070 2002.US. Repository: Library of Congress, Geography and Map Division, Washington, D.C. 20540-4650 USA. Image also available at: Image:Indonesia 2002 CIA map.jpg. Also available at Wikimedia Commons; see Wikimedia Commons notes on use when using that website. Visit: http://creativecommons.org/licenses/by-sa/3.0/

Selected Bibliography

The following sources are useful for further reading about World War Two fighter aircraft in general, and/or the F4U Corsair in particular.

America's Hundred Thousand: U.S. Production Fighters of World War Two, by Francis H. Dean, © 1997 by Francis H. Dean, Schiffer Publishing, Ltd.

Bent Wings – F4U Corsair Action & Accidents: True Tales of Trial and Terror, by Fred "Crash" Blechman (and others), © 1999 by Fred Blechman, Xlibris Corporation.

Corsair: The F4U in World War II and Korea, by Barrett Tillman, © 1979 by the United States Naval Institute, Naval Institute Press.

Duels In the Sky: World War II Naval Aircraft In Combat, by Capt. Eric M. Brown, RN, © 1988 by the United States Naval Institute, Naval Institute Press.

Fighter Pilot: The Memoirs of Legendary Ace Robin Olds, by Robin Olds, with Christina Olds and Ed Rasimus, © 2010 by Robin Olds with Christina Olds and Ed Rasimus, St. Martins Press.

Fighter Pilot, by Paul Richey, © 2001 by Diana Richey, Cassell Military Paperbacks / Orion Books, Ltd.

The American Aircraft Factory in WWII, by Bill Yenne, © 2006, 2010 by Bill Yenne, Zenith Press / MBI Publishing Company.

The Jolly Rogers: The Story of Tom Blackburn and Navy Fighting Squadron VF-17, by Tom Blackburn, © 1989 by Tom Blackburn and Words To Go, Inc., Orion Books.

They Gave Me A Seafire, by Commander R. "Mike" Crosley, DSC, RN, © 1986 by R. M. "Mike" Crosley, Wrens Park Publishing / W. J. Williams & Son, Ltd.

Spitfire: A Test Pilot's Story, by Jeffrey Quill, © 1983 by Jeffrey Quill, Crécy Publishing Limited.

Whistling Death: The Test Pilot's Story of the F4U Corsair, by Boone T. Guyton, © 1994 by Boone T. Guyton, Schiffer Publishing, Ltd.

Wings On My Sleeve, by Capt. Eric 'Winkle' Brown, CBE, DSC, MA, Hon FRAeS, RN, © 2006 by Eric Brown, Phoenix / Orion Books.

The following sources are useful for further reading about history that pertains to World War Two, including political developments and the development of technology.

A Radar History of World War Two: Technical and Military Imperatives, by Louis Brown, © 1999 by IOP Publishing, Ltd, Institute of Physic Publishing.

Documentation of the Stratford Army Engine Plant (Final Report), by Edward G. Salo, PhD, Brockington & Associates, Inc., for the U.S. Army Corps of Engineers, Mobile District, contract number W91278-07-D-0111 (2010).

The Appeasers, by Martin Gilbert and Richard Gott, © 1963 by Martin Gilbert and Richard Gott, Orion Press.

Henry J. Kaiser, A Western Colossus: An Insiders View, by Albert P. Heiner, © 1991 by Halo Books, San Francisco, Halo Books.

The Forrestal Diaries edited by Walter Millis with collaboration E. S. Duffield, © 1951 by New York Herald Tribune, Viking Press.

Tuxedo Park: A Wall Street Tycoon and the Secret Place of Science That Changed the Course of World War Two, by Jennet Conant, © 2002 by Jennet Conan, Simon & Schuster.

Notes on Images and Credits

In addition to the source notes and credits contained within this text, the author hereby extends the following acknowledgement, credit and thanks.

The cover image depicts an F4U coming aboard the *U.S.S. Wolverine* (TX-64), which was underway in the Great Lakes. This training flight occurred over Lake Michigan during 1943. Courtesy of the Emil Buehler Library Collections of the National Museum of Naval Aviation, Accession Number 1996.488.019.011.

The image of the Vought-Sikorsky F4U production line at the Stratford, Connecticut factory ahead of the Prologue was provided courtesy of the Igor I. Sikorsky Historical Archives, Inc. in Stratford, CT.

The side view image of the XF4U-1 that appears ahead of Chapter One was made available courtesy of the National Aeronautics and Space Administration (NASA), which acquired the 1940 image from the predecessor National Advisory Committee on Aeronautics.

The inflight image of the XF4U-1 that precedes Chapter Two and the factory image that precedes Chapter Three were also provided courtesy of the Igor I. Sikorsky Historical Archives, Inc. in Stratford, CT.

The image that precedes Chapter Four is from a photograph of Vought test pilot Charlie Sharpe, and was made available courtesy of Sue French and the Connecticut Air and Space Center in Stratford, CT.

The image of the F4U that precedes Chapter Five is part of a series of images of a crash sequence. While it is generally well known that many F4U Corsairs crashed while trying to come aboard their carrier, take-offs could be just as risky. The undated accident that is depicted was apparently the result of a bad launch of a Corsair from VMF-211 off the *U.S.S. Saipan* (CVL-48). Courtesy of the Emil Buehler Library Collec-

Developing the Gull-Winged F4U Corsair - And Taking It To Sea

tions of the National Museum of Naval Aviation, Accession Number 2001.283.001, titled 'F4U Corsair accident sequence.'

The image that precedes Chapter Six was selected to convey a sense of what some of the fighter strips in the Solomon Islands area were like during the war. This particular image shows F4U-1 Corsairs of VMF-123 and -124, along with Grumman F6F Hellcats, Douglas SBD Dauntless dive bombers and Curtiss P-40 Warhawks, at Vella Lavella in the Solomon Islands. The object description in the archived collection notes that the aircraft were used in support of Allied landings in the Treasury islands and at Cape Torokina. Photograph taken on 10 December 1943. Courtesy of the Emil Buehler Library Collections of the National Museum of Naval Aviation, Robert L. Lawson Photograph Collection, Accession Number 1996.253.7152.012, titled 'F4U Corsairs Ready For Action.'

Taking the F4U Corsair to sea involved the often overlooked efforts of the Royal Navy, including its Fleet Air Arm. Readers will be very familiar with the image of the F4U, but may not be as aware of the Royal Navy's aircraft carriers. Shown in this image ahead of Chapter Seven is the *H.M.S. Illustrious*, plowing through the seas of the Indian Ocean. *Illustrious* played an important role during the attacks on Sumatra, and in later operations of the British Pacific Fleet. Courtesy of the Emil Buehler Library Collections of the National Museum of Naval Aviation, Commander Joseph C. Clifton Photograph Album, Accession Number 1977.031.085.071. Complied by Rear Admiral Joseph C. Clifton.

The image ahead of Chapter Eight shows F4Us preparing to launch on a strike over Korea. In Korea, as in every other subsequent use of American airpower, being able to accurately deliver ordnance was been a critical part of tactical aviation. In Korea, the Corsair often did what faster jet fighters could not accomplish. Courtesy of the Igor I. Sikorsky Historical Archives, Inc., in Stratford, CT.

The image ahead of the Epilogue shows Vought production test pilot John R. French in front of an F4U-4 on the flight line at Bridgeport Airport. Courtesy of Sue French and the Connecticut Air and Space Center, in Stratford, CT.

2002 Map of the Inter-Ocean Operational Area(s)

The image on the rear cover of the shows an F4U-4 of VF-713 coming aboard the *U.S.S. Antietam* (CVA-36), underway of Korea circa 1951. Per caption notes, VF-713 was a Naval Air Reserve fighting squadron that was activated during the Koran War; its pilots flew combat missions off the *Antietam* from September 1951 until May 1952. Creator AOM2c Dick Bayley. Courtesy of the Emil Buehler Library Collections of the National Museum of Naval Aviation, Robert L. Lawson Photograph Collection, Accession Number 1996.489.021.

The author appreciates the assistance and permissions that the above parties provided in making these images available for publication, and apologizes for any errors or omissions. Proper citation and credit are always a top priority.

About the Author

Ralph Harvey used his lifelong interest in military aviation and technology to produce this history of the Vought F4U Corsair. A former transport pilot, he learned to fly at what was once called Bridgeport Airport, where the Corsair was designed, built and test flown. Since big changes in both the factory and the manufacturing process were necessary in order to mass-produce the Corsair, these often ignored topics became an important part of the research. Having personally known some of the Vought-Sikorsky engineers, production workers and F4U test pilots made the research and writing of this book especially rewarding. The author earned his Master of Science degree in manufacturing engineering from Worcester Polytechnic Institute and lives in Stratford, Connecticut, the birthplace of the gull-winged F4U Corsair.

Made in the USA
San Bernardino, CA
12 March 2014